Michelangelo (1475–1564) is universally recognized as being, within the field of the visual arts, a many-sided genius, with masterpieces of outstanding originality in sculpture, painting, drawing and architecture. What is less well known is that his creativity extended to the field of literature: he was the first artist in the western tradition to leave a substantial body of poetry (amounting to 302 pieces in the latest critical edition). This poetry is largely the work of Michelangelo's mature and late years. From a relatively early age, beginning around 1502, he produced the occasional poem; after 1520 his output achieved a modest rhythm of two to three poems per year. This somewhat dilettante interest (even here, Michelangelo could not be entirely casual) was transformed into a major concern in 1532 after the artist was captivated by the beauty of Tommaso Cavalieri, a young Roman nobleman. For the next decade-and-a-half, Michelangelo, in addition to producing such visual masterpieces as the *Last Judgement*, the *Conversion of St Paul* and a series of presentation drawings, devoted himself with flair, subtlety and rigour to finding words for the emotions and interests that gripped his soul: over two hundred poems poured from his pen in these years, exploring in a highly distinctive style the great themes of love, beauty, the transience of life and the yearning for salvation. In his final years his poetry returned to its original trickle, its character, however, strengthened and refined by the intervening years of dedication. Michelangelo's poetry has the sculptural quality that marks all his visual art, and a vitality that comes from an honest mind wrestling freshly and forcefully with language. As a means for understanding the man behind the myth that genius almost inevitably generates, it remains unsurpassed.

Christopher Ryan was educated at the Gregorian University, Rome, and the Universities of Glasgow and Cambridge. He has taught at the Pontifical Institute of Mediaeval Studies, Toronto, the University of Toronto, the Centre for Mediaeval and Renaissance Studies, Oxford, and the University of Cambridge. He is now Professor of Italian at the University of Sussex. His principal interest is in the interrelationship of poetry, culture and religion in late medieval and Renaissance Italy. He has edited a book on the mediaeval papacy, translated Dante's *Convivio*, and published numerous articles on Dante and his intellectual background. In editing and translating the poems of Michelangelo his aim has been to help others enjoy a body of poetry he has long believed unjustly neglected.

For
Francesca and Alexander

Michelangelo

THE POEMS

Edited and translated by
CHRISTOPHER RYAN
University of Sussex

J. M. Dent   London

A DENT PAPERBACK

Robin Kirkpatrick, University of Cambridge,
is consultant editor for this edition

First published in Great Britain in 1996 by J. M. Dent

First published in paperback by J. M. Dent,
a division of the Orion Publishing Group,
Orion House, 5 Upper St Martin's Lane,
London WC2H 9EA

A CIP catalogue record for this book is available from the
British Library.

ISBN 0 460 87878 6

Filmset by Selwood Systems, Midsomer Norton
Printed and bound in Great Britain by
Butler & Tanner Ltd, Frome and London

CONTENTS

CHRONOLOGY OF MICHELANGELO'S LIFE

Year Age Life

1475–96

1475   Michelangelo is born on 6 March at Caprese, near Arezzo, while his father holds a temporary political post there; the family home is in Florence

1481 6   Death of his mother

1487 12   Apprenticed in the painting studio of the brothers Ghirlandaio

1489 14   Begins training in sculpture in the Medici garden museum, under the patronage of Lorenzo the Magnificent

1492 17   Continues in the Casa de' Medici under Lorenzo's son Piero
Among major works of this period are the *Battle of the Centaurs* and the *Madonna of the Steps*

1496–1501

1496 21   Begins first period in Rome
His main works of this first Roman period are the *Bacchus* and the St Peter's *Pietà*

1501–5

1501 26   Returns to Florence; begins work on the *David*

1503 28   Begins writing poetry about this time

1504 29   Completes the *David*, which was erected in front of the Palazzo della Signoria
His other major works of his second Florentine period

CHRONOLOGY OF HIS TIMES

Year	Artistic Events	Historical Context
1478	Poliziano, *Stanze per la giostra*	
1481	Landino's edition of Dante's *Commedia*	
1483	Birth of Raphael	
1485	Birth of Titian	
1492	Death of Lorenzo de' Medici	Columbus's voyage to America Election of Pope Alexander VI
1494	Death of Poliziano	French invasion of Naples Expulsion of the Medici from Florence
1498		Execution of Savonarola
1499	Death of Ficino	Fall of Milan to the French
1500	Birth of Cellini	
1503		Election of Pope Julius II Spanish victory over French at Garigliano

include the *Doni Madonna*, the *Taddei Tondo*, the *Pitti Tondo*, the *Bruges Madonna* and the cartoon for *The Battle of Cascina* (now lost)

1505–17

1505 30   Begins his second period spent mainly in Rome, having been summoned there by Pope Julius II to build his tomb

1506 31   Difficulties over the Julius tomb lead to a two-year absence from Rome, in Florence (1506), in Bologna (1506–8) and Florence again (1508)

1508 33   Begins work on the ceiling of the Sistine Chapel

1512 37   Completes the ceiling of the Sistine Chapel

1513 38   Begins work on the Julius tomb
His major works of his second Roman period, in addition to the painting of the Sistine Ceiling, include the bronze statue of Julius II (done in Bologna, destroyed in 1512), two *Slaves* or *Prisoners* (now in the Louvre) and the *Moses*

1517–34

1517 42   Begins his third period spent mainly in Florence, having returned there at the request of Pope Leo X, to work on the façade of the church of San Lorenzo (a project never realized)

1519 44   Begins work on the Medici Chapel (= the New Sacristy) in San Lorenzo, while continuing work on the Julius tomb

1506		Laying of the foundation stone of the new St Peter's, Rome
1508		League of Cambrai against Venice
1510	Death of Botticelli Death of Giorgione	
1511	Erasmus, *In Praise of Folly*	Holy League against France
1512		Restoration of the Medici in Florence
1513	Machiavelli, *The Prince*	Election of Pope Leo X (Giovanni de' Medici)
1515		Accession of Francis I in France French conquest of Milan
1516	Castiglione, *Il libro del cortegiano* Ariosto, *Orlando furioso* More, *Utopia* Erasmus, edition of the Greek New Testament	
1517		Luther presents his 95 theses at Wittenburg
1518	Birth of Tintoretto	
1519	Death of Leonardo	Election of Emperor Charles V Magellan's voyage
1520	Death of Raphael	
1521		French defeated at Ravenna Luther excommunicated

1524 49   Begins work on the Laurentian Library

1527 52   Helps fortify Florence on behalf of the short-lived republic, during the years 1527–30
1528 53   Death of his favourite brother, Buonarroto

1532 57   Meets Tommaso Cavalieri during a visit to Rome; beginning of his greatest period of poetic creativity
His major artistic works of his third Florentine period include four *Slaves* or *Prisoners* (now in the Accademia in Florence), the *Victory, Leda and the Swan* (now lost), several presentation drawings, and, above all, the Medici chapel with its tombs and figures and the Laurentian Library

1534–64
1534 59   Begins his third period in Rome, where he lives until his death; commissioned by the new pope, Paul III, to continue with the plan of Pope Clement VII to fresco the east wall of the Sistine Chapel

1536 61   Starts work on the *Last Judgement* fresco; meets Vittoria Colonna
1541 66   Completes the *Last Judgement*
1542 67   Begins the frescos of the Pauline Chapel

1546 71   Death of Luigi del Riccio
1547 72   Death of Vittoria Colonna; death of Sebastiano del Piombo; end of his great period of poetic creativity; unveiling of the much-reduced Julius tomb in the church of S. Pietro ad Vincola, Rome

1555 80   Death of his brother Sigismondo, and of his loyal assistant and servant Urbino

1523		Death of Pope Leo X Election of Pope Clement VII (Giulio de' Medici)
1525	Bembo, *Prose della volgar lingua*	French defeated at Pavia Beginning of Spanish hegemony in Italy
1527		Sack of Rome Fall of the Medici in Florence
1528	Birth of Veronese	
1529		Crowning of Charles V at Bologna
1530		Restoration of the Medici in Florence
1534	Rabelais, *Gargantua*	England secedes from Roman jurisdiction Election of Paul III Cosimo de' Medici becomes Duke of Florence
1541		Diet of Ratisbon
1545		Opening of the Council of Trent
1550	Vasari, *Lives of the Artists*	Election of Pope Julius III
1553	Rabelais, *Quart Livre*	
1555		Election of Pope Paul IV Treaty of Augsburg

1563 88   Elected an academician of the Florentine *Accademia del Disegno*

1564 88   Dies 18 February

His other major works of this third Roman period include the *Brutus*, and the Florence *Pietà* and Rondanini *Pietà* of his final years; after 1549 he worked principally as an architect, his two main projects being the planning and redesigning of the Capitol and of St Peter's, the twin symbolic centres of secular and sacred Rome

1556	Abdication of Charles V
1559	Treaty of Câteau-Cambrésis
1563	Closure of the Council of Trent
1564	Birth of Galileo

INTRODUCTION

Many people, many even of those reasonably familiar with his art, are surprised to learn that Michelangelo was a poet at all, although in fact he left a significant body of poetry (amounting to 302 pieces in the latest critical edition), the first major artist in the western tradition to do so.

Such lack of awareness need not cause anyone to blush unduly, for Michelangelo's poetry has had to struggle against a number of obstacles before beginning to establish itself as a substantial, if highly idiosyncratic, achievement. Obstacles were there from the beginning. Although Michelangelo's poetry received some notice during his lifetime, with the unsolicited publication of several of his poems and the widespread circulation in manuscript of a much larger number, no edition was published until long after his death; the poet did indeed go some way towards preparing a large anthology for publication, but nothing materialized, probably because his main editor and poetic adviser, Luigi del Riccio, died before the project had reached a sufficiently advanced stage. Indeed Michelangelo himself on a number of occasions appeared to denigrate his own poetry,[1] although we may now regard these comments as humorous, if very real, expressions of diffidence about his own linguistic competence rather than a genuine denial that his poetry had any value.

When publication did come, it disguised as well as revealed Michelangelo's poetic gifts.[2] In 1623, almost sixty years after the artist's death, his great-nephew and namesake, Michelangelo the Younger, published over a hundred poems, but saw fit substantially to revise these. He did so partly to give them a linguistic garb more in accord with the mellifluous style dominant in the poetry of his day (as it had been in the time of his great-uncle), and partly, through changing the gender of the subjects and addressees of many of the poems from male to female, to suppress indications of Michelangelo's homosexuality and thus preclude the vehement criticism which, in the atmosphere of Counter-Reformation Italy, such evidence would certainly have drawn.

Even though Michelangelo's poetry, in its heavily truncated and revised form, attracted the often discriminating admiration of a small number of people, genuine and widespread appreciation of his full stature as a poet had to await the appearance of an accessible and accurate edition. This has been slow in coming. The edition of Cesare Guasti in 1863 was a major advance in terms of quantity, accuracy and elucidation (the last principally in its fine paraphrases), but it often lacked sufficient critical rigour, and, by presenting the poems in groups of genres, gave no sense of Michelangelo's evolution as a poet. Carl Frey's massively learned edition of 1897 did not lack rigour, but his dense presentation of the data supporting his readings made his work difficult to assimilate, and he, too, prevented the ready emergence of a true sense of the poetry's chronology, by opting to group in a separate sequence the poems evidently intended for publication by Michelangelo. It was not until relatively recently that Michelangelo's poetry found the editor it deserved: the critical edition by Enzo Noè Girardi, published in 1960, sets out the poetry in a single sequence as faithful to chronological order as the data will allow, and follows this with a paraphrase of each poem and an extensive, clearly articulated critical apparatus.

It would, however, be at best a half-truth to ascribe the lack of widespread appreciation of Michelangelo's poetry simply to the tardy appearance of an edition worthy of it. The obstacles have been not just external to the poetry but internal to it, and it may be helpful to address from the outset two of these latter in particular.

Compared to that of most poets, Michelangelo's work is fragmentary, in a double sense. Of the 302 poems which comprise Girardi's edition, around fifty are incomplete (although incomplete sonnets may constitute a special case: see p. xxvii). More to the point, only a dozen of the 302 poems are longer than twenty lines (and of these almost half are unfinished), while over a hundred are of less than ten lines, of which fully sixty are mere quatrains (though it must be granted that forty-eight of the quatrains form a series of epitaphs for one young man). This undoubtedly indicates a limitation: Michelangelo appears to have been poetically incapable of exploring themes at length in a single poem, except on occasion,[3] and frequently was either not able or not interested in doing more than sketch his poetic ideas. However, although this does indeed indicate a limitation, the seriousness of the criticism should not be exaggerated: we may regret that Michelangelo was neither a Dante nor a Petrarch, but to have produced more than 180 complete poems of roughly sonnet length or longer (provided, of course, that they are overall of some quality) is no mean achievement. Furthermore, many of Michelangelo's short poems will bear comparison with his working drawings:[4] sketches they may be, but not things of little worth.

A second obstacle is that Michelangelo's poems are in very many cases rough: they are sometimes grammatically imperfect, and much more frequently contorted in expression and harsh in sound. Although it seems fair to surmise that this feature of Michelangelo's poetry constitutes a greater aesthetic obstacle to native Italians, it must be admitted that for any unprejudiced reader the poetry's roughness appears occasionally indefensible and more than occasionally indicative simply of linguistic or conceptual limitation. Those for whom formal perfection is a necessary condition of poetry will find such roughness an insurmountable barrier. For many readers, though, this same feature will (extreme instances apart) be as much a strength as a weakness: the roughness, the jaggedness even, of Michelangelo's poetry will often seem no more than the inevitable counterpart of the poet's faithfulness both to the complexity of his own thought and, no less, to the harsh or at least severely testing nature of the fundamental issues of human life with which he customarily grapples.

This second obstacle may, especially for non-native Italian speakers, be phrased more broadly: Michelangelo's poetry is often extremely difficult to understand. This difficulty has two main sources (in addition to the more-than-occasional grammatical imperfection): the frequent use of ellipsis and of unusual word order. Michelangelo often leaves the reader to supply a word or phrase without which the words before him will not make sense; obviously, this does not make for easy reading. Likewise with the inversion of words: we are often obliged to unscramble the words from the order in which we find them and reconstruct them according to a more normal order before the poet's meaning and poetic intention become clear. Both points may be illustrated from a single example. In the course of a poem lamenting the death of his father, Michelangelo makes a general comment with regard to suffering, which begins: *Nostri intensi dolori e nostri guai / son come più e men ciascun gli sente* (86:25–6). For Michelangelo's meaning to become clear, we must transfer *intensi* to after *son* in the following line and add to it a qualifying *più e men* not present in the text, and reverse the order of *ciascun* and the *più e men* which is present, to give the reading (ignoring the demands of the poetic line): *Nostri dolori e nostri guai son [più e men] intensi come ciascun più e men gli [= li] sente.* It is no exaggeration to say that example could be multiplied hundreds of times.

If, then, Michelangelo's poetry often requires a considerable effort before it will yield its sense, why should one make that effort? Three reasons may briefly be suggested. It seems merely a matter of common sense to acknowledge that most of us come to Michelangelo's poetry in order to understand and appreciate better the outstanding artist with whose visual masterpieces we are already familiar. We shall not be disappointed, although our hopes may well be fulfilled in ways that we do not expect. There is no direct illumination of the art by the poet, in the sense that Michelangelo does not comment in the poetry on individual works of art (poem 5 is something of an exception).[5] Where light *is* thrown, and with intensity, is on the artist himself, in a whole variety of ways. Not infrequently we will, through the poetry, touch the source of the great impulses that animated Michelangelo in his artistic enterprises: his inspiration by beauty, principally human beauty; his aspiring through that finite beauty towards an infinite beauty and goodness which he saw as powerfully and exquisitely, but only very partially, reflected in this world; and his sense of life as a constant struggle against the ever-threatening ravages of physical death and moral failure. Perhaps surprisingly, if we identify Michelangelo totally with the towering genius who created monumental works in all three fields of sculpture, painting and architecture, we shall encounter a highly vulnerable personality: dependent for inspiration on, for example, Tommaso Cavalieri, a young man of outstanding physical and personal beauty by whom Michelangelo was captivated when he met him in 1532, as his own sixth decade was drawing to a close; dependent no less for religious support and companionship on the gifted if austere widow, Vittoria Colonna, whom he encountered four years later;[6] dependent above all (especially in his later years) on a sense of being saved by Christ from what he regarded as his own moral turpitude and from eternal damnation, although confident belief in such saving contact with Christ came to him only fitfully.

Perhaps more surprisingly still, in the man notorious for his *terribilità*, we shall discover a comic element, displayed not least in a vein of self-mockery that gleams throughout his poetic life, from his parodying of the awkward position he had to adopt to paint the Sistine Ceiling (poem 5) to the unflinching irony of his description of the ailments that afflicted him in old age (poem 267). The poetry is, in short, an invaluable way of coming to know the personality of Michelangelo, whose very stature as an artist has tended to obscure the complexity of his character. His artistic achievements were so awesome that even his contemporaries called him divine; the poetry can help us recover the man.

Whatever our original motivation in coming to Michelangelo's poetry, that poetry is also rewarding simply as poetry, and brings its own very particular poetic pleasure. The eminent critic A. J. Smith has written recently, apropos poem 174: 'there is a rhetoric at work ... A very little attention to the arrangement of clauses will show how carefully the syntax has been managed to catch not merely the balances and emphases but the cadences, nuances, pitch of the mood.' He adds immediately: 'Such writing does not come by chance, and there are like effects everywhere in this poet. They have evidently been worked at, hard and subtly.'[7] We are the beneficiaries of Michelangelo's hard and subtle work.

Sometimes, indeed quite frequently, Michelangelo's poetic artistry is readily appreciable, as in the opening lines of one of the most famous sonnets of his last years (poem 285):

> Giunto è già 'l corso della vita mia,
> con tempestoso mar, per fragil barca,
> al comun porto, ov'a render si varca
> conto e ragion d'ogni opra trista e pia.
> (My life's journey has finally arrived, after a stormy sea,
> in a fragile boat, at the common port, through which
> all must pass to render an account and explanation of
> their every act, evil and devout.)

Here it takes but 'a very little attention' to sense the firm, steady beat in the single movement of the opening line conveying the finality of arrival, and to feel the contrast with the broken rhythms of the next three half-line units which speak of the perilousness of the journey, while these rhythms in turn give way, in the following line-and-a-half, to the smoother description of the scene that will unfold once port has been reached. Individual words, too, are shaped to carry a particular force: the sense of finality is conveyed from the very outset in the heavy accent on the first word, *Giunto*, a finality emphatically applied to the poet himself in the first line's ending on *mia* (all the more noticeably placed for the adjective's having been drawn from its natural position before *vita*), while the emphasis on the poet as individual is set within the broad context of the destiny of the whole human race at lines 3–4, a change of perspective clearly signalled in the *al comun* that begins those lines.

Equally if not more often, though, appreciation of the poetic qualities of Michelangelo's work does not flow readily from the page, does not offer itself immediately. Here familiarity with Michelangelo's visual art can make us sensitive to the nature of his poetic achievement. Michelangelo regarded himself first and foremost as a sculptor, and few would wish to quarrel with that self-assessment: his painting and drawing often have a quality that can best be described as sculptural. The same holds true of his poetry. This derives from several features, not least from those already alluded to. The cumulative effect of ellipsis and inverted word order is that of density and volume: the words of Michelangelo's poetry often do not so much carry us along in their flow as stand firmly before us, waiting for our eyes to focus more finely so that the figure or figures may emerge gradually from the solid block. Or perhaps better, the apparently rough-hewn poetic object before us proves under closer scrutiny to be, certainly, unpolished, but not on that account unthoughtful, unsubtle, the work of a careless or incapable hand. Take, for instance, the culminating assurance of poem 34, a sonnet. Michelangelo is intent on conveying to his beloved that what he loves in him (or her – the gender is unspecified) is not the body but the person, and ultimately therein the beauty of the Creator. At lines 9–11 he seeks to summarize and clarify what he has declared in the octet:

> Come dal foco el caldo, esser diviso
> non può dal bell'etterno ogni mie stima,
> ch'exalta, ond'ella vien, chi più 'l somiglia.
> (My discerning power itself can no more be separated from the eternal beauty that can heat from fire; it exalts whoever most resembles him from whom it comes.)

To convey the inseparability of his discerning power or judgement (*stima*) from the eternal beauty, he begins not with the first but with the second term of a comparison, which refers to common phenomena that clearly are by their very nature indivisible (fire and heat). Then, to emphasize the point of the comparison, he anticipates its central term, *esser diviso*, even though this involves both an inversion of the normal word order (*esser diviso / non può* needs to be read grammatically as *non può esser diviso*) and the delaying of the subject (*ogni mie stima*) to the end of the sentence. And in the relative clause which follows at line 11, Michelangelo is so intent on relating the human to the divine that he introduces precipitately the phrase referring to the Creator (*ond'ella vien*) early in the line, rather than wait on mention of the pronoun (*'l*) on which grammatically that phrase depends.

What holds true of specific lines and details applies also to many poems in their entirety: they pulse with dense energy. Here again an analogy with Michelangelo's visual art may be illuminating. It has often been observed that many of the human figures in Michelangelo's sculpture, painting and drawing catch our eye because they manifest an extreme tension: between the apparently boundless energy and aspiration that animate the figures, and the physical limits of the human form. Our admiration is recurrently aroused by Michelangelo's ability to convey an infinity of spirit, as it were, energizing a finite human form without destroying or unacceptably distorting it: many of his figures are at once immensely powerful and believable. A comparable impression is created by many of his poems. There, too, he strains at the limits without finally breaking them.

As I hope will already be apparent, Michelangelo frequently sets himself the most profound and complex subjects: love, beauty, moral endeavour, the ravages of time and death. His language struggles and twists in its efforts to give, if not adequate, at least fresh and appropriate expression to such great themes. Yet the poetic boundaries which Michelangelo sets himself are extremely confining: as was noted above, very few of his poems are of more than twenty lines; the vast majority are quatrains, madrigals or sonnets.[8] It is a notable feature of Michelangelo's poetry that, with the exception of a relatively small number of occasions on which his technical ability failed him, he observes the poetic rules which in his time governed the overall form of the short genres in which he principally worked; indeed he often set himself more stringent rules than those which commonly applied. Thus, for instance, despite some latitude allowed by convention, all but one of the quatrains of the complete sonnets,[9] and all the independent quatrains, have the same rhyme-scheme ABBA,[10] while the sestets of the complete sonnets are almost all CDE×2, with the occasional CDC+DCD;[11] in his madrigals, a form which by convention was very loose indeed, Michelangelo chose never to allow himself three unrhymed line-endings, the conventionally permitted maximum, and rarely indeed allowed himself any unrhymed line-endings at all.[12] The poetic struggle internal to the lines, the tortuous attempt to express thought and exploit imagery fully yet economically, did not, then, lead Michelangelo to burst the constraining external limits set by the genres: it is as if he felt called to observe the confines of the short poetic forms in order to express the drama of human life, itself in absolute terms short and sharply bounded.

There is a third way, inextricably linked to the first two, in which Michelangelo's poetry rewards the effort spent on it: put simply, it makes one think. Francesco Berni, a young poetic icono-clast of Michelangelo's time, disparagingly addressing the majority of his fellow poets, who wrote in an ornate Petrarchan style which he abhorred, famously said of Michelangelo: *ei dice cose, e voi dite parole* ('he says things, while you speak words').[13] That critique has stood the test of time, provided that we understand *cose* in the broadest sense, to include things of the spirit (as we are meant to do). One 'thing' that Michelangelo would not have us forget, though most of us willingly do, is the brevity of life. From his earliest to his latest poetry Michelangelo recurrently brings before his and our mind the perspective of eternity and the fact that all human life is, in that perspective, short; as he put it in one simple juxtaposition: *Chiunche nasce a morte arriva* ('Whoever is born arrives at death', poem 21). Michelangelo is not, though, in his poetry as a whole (as he is not in his art as a whole), a jaundiced Jeremiah. The fleetingness of life strikes him forcibly because he so keenly appreciated life's beauties, above all human beauty, physical and personal. It is no accident that the poetic floodgates were opened for Michelangelo, transforming what was scarcely more than an occasional poetic impulse in his earlier years into a constant creative concern in his maturity, when he was captivated by the outstanding gifts of the young Cavalieri. The surge of poetry was intended to put into words an enthralment with one who by all accounts combined to an outstanding degree beauty of body and soul; to that combination we owe a series of gems, from the anxious *Se l'immortal desio, c'alza e corregge* ('If desire of the immortal, which raises and directs', poem 58), through the calmly laudatory *Veggio nel tuo bel viso, signor mio* ('I see in your beautiful face, my lord', poem 83) to the ecstatic love of *I' mi son caro assai più ch'i' non soglio* ('I am much dearer to myself than I ever used to be', poem 90).

Michelangelo's poetry also stimulates us to think by bringing home to us the intensity with which he shared some of the basic tenets of his time, a period very different from our own but intellectually among the most vigorous in the evolution of Western culture. Again the poetry does this in a whole variety of ways, of which one may be singled out as being perhaps as central to Michelangelo's time as it is alien to our own. Here poem 164 may be our guide. In that poem Michelangelo speaks with lucidity on what it is that inspires him in his artistic endeavours. The opening lines (1–4), where he intimates the strength of feeling with which he regarded himself as called to give expression to beauty in his art, are certainly interesting, but they are not surprising. As this short poem evolves, however, and Michelangelo elaborates on what beauty signifies for him, we enter a stranger world. Beauty alone carries the eye from this world 'to those heights' (*a quella altezza*) which he sets himself to paint and sculpt (lines 5–6); the poet goes on to make it clear that the phrase referring to heights is no lightly tossed off metaphor. He criticizes those who would drag down beauty and make it a thing of the senses (7–8), and contrasts this low view of beauty with what he simply states as being the truth (8–10), that *la beltà ... muove / e porta al cielo ogni intelletto sano* ('beauty ... moves and carries every healthy mind to heaven'), it inspires a movement *dal mortale al divin* ('from the mortal to the divine sphere'). As this poem briefly indicates, for Michelangelo (at least until his last years) art, and more generally the appreciation of beauty, was a religious task; by this he did not mean exclusively, nor even primarily, a church-related exercise, but a whole way of thinking about and looking at life, which affected the very texture of daily existence. For Michelangelo adhered passionately to the fundamentals of Neo-platonic philosophy,[14] such as the belief that this passing world is but the creation and reflection of a higher, immortal world, and that on this earth beauty is the supreme means of coming into contact with that divine world. The 'place' where the conjunction of physical and spiritual beauty is most evident is the human face, and particularly the eyes, which, in a person whose character matches the beauty of his (or her) face, have depths that are ultimately divine in the strictest sense. Michelangelo's almost exclusive concentration on the human being, in his poetry as in his art, reflects, then, his adherence, to an intense degree, to a philosophy shared by many in the educated circles of his time. We can only hope to understand Michelangelo (and one important strand in the culture of his period) with anything approaching adequacy if we remember that for him the artistic enterprise was an endeavour to make heaven more present on earth.

Readers approaching Michelangelo's poetry for the first time may find it helpful to have some of its broad 'physical' contours mapped out. Michelangelo's poetry is for the most part a product of his late maturity and old age. The artist began writing poetry at a fairly early age, around 1503–4, when he was approaching thirty, but in the following twenty years he showed an occasional interest rather than a serious concern, although that interest did undoubtedly deepen in the latter part of this period: a dozen poems were written between 1503/4 and 1518, and around forty over the following decade-and-a-half (poems 13–55 in Girardi's numbering). The turning point, as already noted, was Michelangelo's meeting with Tommaso Cavalieri in late 1532. In the following decade-and-a-half, Michelangelo's poetic output rose markedly in both quantity and quality (which is not to say that his earlier poetry lacked its outstanding moments): between the beginning of his friendship with Cavalieri and the death in 1547 of the other great friend of his later years, Vittoria Colonna, Michelangelo wrote, in the midst of a demanding and by any account extraordinarily fruitful artistic career, some two hundred poems (poems 56–266) which, although they undoubtedly contain much dross, often rise to considerable heights. Thereafter, in the thirteen or so years in which Michelangelo continued to write, the poetry in numerical terms reverted to its original trickle, but continued to display in many instances a quality made possible by the previous, intense dedication.

The two hundred poems of the great central block can be divided into four groups: two comprising those dedicated to Cavalieri and to Colonna; another made up of the love poems which have no apparent and possibly no real dedicatee, although most of them are traditionally referred to as poems to *la donna bella e crudele* ('the beautiful and cruel lady');[15] and a fourth containing the remaining miscellany. Michelangelo's poems may, then, be set out in the following broad chronological scheme:

1. Poetic apprenticeship, 1503/4–18 (poems 1–12)
2. The Florentine period, 1518–32 (poems 13–55)
3. The central years, 1532–47 (poems 56–266)
   a) Poems to Tommaso Cavalieri[16]
   b) Poems to Vittoria Colonna[17]
   c) Poems to 'the cruel and beautiful lady' and other love poems[18]
   d) Miscellaneous poems
4. The final years, 1547–60 (poems 267–302).

Thematically, Michelangelo's greatest concern by far is love, although a good number of his love poems, including many of his finest, are directed to claiming a close relationship between human love and divine love. A significant number of poems explore the transience of life, the pressing threat of death and eternal damnation, and Michelangelo's yearning for divine solace. In complete contrast is the vein of comic poems, thin in number but rich in vigour. Poems of social comment are few and far between, and there is likewise no more than a handful of letter poems, a form much in vogue in Michelangelo's time.

As regards genre, most of Michelangelo's poems, as noted above, are in three forms: the sonnet, the madrigal and the quatrain. The 302 poems comprise: 79 complete and 37 incomplete sonnets; 95 complete madrigals and four incomplete; 60 quatrains (48 of them constituting, together with a madrigal and a sonnet, a single sequence in memory of Cecchino Bracci[19]); and 25 poems of other genres.[20] Two short pieces included by Girardi in the poem sequence may be either free verse or rhythmic prose.[21] There are in addition 41 poetic fragments (given here in the Appendix).

CHRISTOPHER RYAN

References

1 The principal indication is the jocular or dismissive comments that Michelangelo appended to some thirty poems he sent to his friend Luigi del Riccio (quoted in the relevant Notes).

2 Publication details of all works mentioned in this Introduction may be found in the Bibliography of Works Cited.

3 Indeed only two of Michelangelo's longer poems (85 and 267), both comic, may be judged poetically successful.

4 We may recall that only a few of Michelangelo's drawings were finished, 'presentation' drawings.

5 The importance of Michelangelo's poetry for understanding his discourse on art has been examined in the magisterial study by Summers.

6 There are brief biographical sketches of Cavalieri and Colonna in the introductory notes to poems 56 and 111 respectively.

7 Smith (1986), p. 172.

8 See p. xxiv.

9 The exception is poem 43, which has the scheme ABAB common to the sonnet in earlier eras, and still found in the sixteenth century.

10 Only three of Michelangelo's incomplete sonnets (poems 18, 38 and 53) deviate from this scheme, and follow the older form ABAB: see last note.

11 There are nine instances of the latter (out of seventy-nine complete sonnets): poems 10, 25, 43, 47, 71, 98, 101, 248 and 299.

12 Of the ninety-five complete madrigals, two have two unrhymed line-endings (poems 11–12), and four have one (poems 7–8, 152 and 165).

13 See the introductory note to poem 85.

14 Although it is commonly accepted that (at least until his very late years) Michelangelo believed profoundly in the fundamental tenets of Neoplatonism, there is no agreement on how closely acquainted he was with the actual writings of Plato and those inspired by him.

15 See the introductory note to poem 112.

16 Poems 56–62, 72–84, 88–98, 101–8 and 259–60.

17 Poems 111, 113, 115–17, 120–22, 148–54, 156, 159–66, 229, 234–41, 254, 257–8 and 264–6.

18 These are respectively: poems 112, 114, 118–19, 123–31, 138–43, 145–7, 155, 157–8, 168–76, 230–33, 242; and 63–5, 69, 109, 134–7, 144, 167, 243–6, 253, 255–6, 261–3.

19 Poems 179–228.

20 These are made up of four complete *ottave* and two incomplete, three complete *capitoli* and three incomplete, two *canzoni*, two incomplete *sestine*, one *barzelletta* or *frottola*, a double sestet, three isolated tercets, and four unrhymed couplets.

21 Poems 13–14.

NOTE ON THE TEXT AND TRANSLATION

The present edition is based on the critical edition of E. N. Girardi: Michelangiolo Buonarroti, *Rime* (Bari: G. Laterza e Figli, 1960). I have introduced a small number of minor changes, to which attention is drawn in the Notes; these changes do not affect Girardi's numbering.[1] I have also indicated in the Notes where Girardi in his text (normally following Guasti) has deviated from the MSS readings to correct lines that are metrically faulty (or, very occasionally, faulty in rhyme), except in those cases where Girardi gives metrical indications in the text itself through the use of diaereses.[2] I have not thought it worthwhile to note the few instances in which I rectify what are undoubtedly typographical errors in Girardi's text, such as the omission of a period at the end of a poem.

It may be helpful to say a word on the translation. Its claims are few, and these depend completely on its single aim, that of facilitating direct appreciation of the original. There is a long tradition in English of partial translations of Michelangelo's poetry, the most notable being that of John Addington Symonds in the last century;[3] and the past thirty or so years have seen no less than four complete translations, two of them very recent.[4] Each has its merits, but all have been shaped, to a greater or lesser extent, by considerations intrinsic to the poetic genre which they adopt. It seems to me that there is a role for the modest enterprise of attempting to render Michelangelo's poetry in modern English prose. Although this cannot hope to convey, as poetic translation does at its best, the strictly poetic rhythms and force of the original, it may hope to avoid the expansion or contraction of the plain sense of the original to meet different poetic demands, and, perhaps more importantly, it may hope to avoid the danger of projecting onto the original a poetic voice which will inevitably be different and to some degree alien. The need for a translation that aims above all to be clear and simply faithful may be felt particularly in cases such as that of Michelangelo, where the poetry is frequently dense and tortuous – to the extent that even its basic meaning can be difficult to penetrate.

The use of prose does not, of course, eliminate the translator's own linguistic and intellectual deficiencies, nor spare him the agonies inherent in the interpretative task intrinsic to all translation, especially in the attempt to render words shaped by one historical matrix into those shaped by another. It may, though, by simplifying the translator's task, at least make possible a particular, pedestrian fidelity, whose very limitations can in a significant way allow the original to speak more fully and freely. That at least has been my hope.

There are two sets of notes. Immediately after the translation of each poem there is a basic annotation (in italics) stating genre, dedicatee where known or reasonably conjectured, and date; notes marked with an asterisk denote those poems which Michelangelo had intended to include in the publication which never came to fruition. Michelangelo left a considerable number of poems unfinished, and I normally designate these simply as incomplete. Incomplete sonnets are a case apart, however, since in some instances Michelangelo may have intended what is in terms of genre a part of a sonnet to be an independent, finished poem. I have, therefore, distinguished between partial and unfinished sonnets, the latter being those which are without doubt unfinished because they are grammatically incomplete. It cannot sufficiently be stressed that both the dedication and the dating of most of Michelangelo's poems can be only highly conjectural,[5] and in the case of dating also very approximate. At the end of the entire corpus are fuller notes on many of the poems. Line numbers refer to the Italian poems only.

References

1 See the notes to poems 5:11; 6:11; 14; 15; 18; 20:23; 68:15; 71:12; 86:31–32; 95:11; 102:6; 147:11–12; 151:10; 224:1; 245:13–15; 248:7; 259:10 and 267:15.

2 See the notes to poems 3:11; 10:11; 22:48; 46:3; 58:10; 59:12; 61:10; 67:109; 69:1; 98:7; 111:1; 147:9; 166:9 and 11; 184:4; 243:1; 257:10; 283:1; 289:13; 293:9 and 302:5.

3 Mention should be made also of Jennings' poetic rendering of the sonnets.

4 Those by Tusiani (1960), Gilbert (1st edn, 1963), Saslow (1991) and Alexander (1991).

5 As regards dedication, caution must be used when consulting Girardi's 1967 edition: the dedications there appear to have been set down rather haphazardly, with mysterious omissions (e.g., regarding poems 72–6), and puzzling confidence when tentativeness seems called for (e.g., regarding poems 95–6).

THE POEMS

1

Molti anni fassi qual felice, in una
brevissima ora si lamenta e dole;
o per famosa o per antica prole
altri s'inlustra, e 'n un momento imbruna.

Cosa mobil non è che sotto el sole   5
non vinca morte e cangi la fortuna.

2

Sol io ardendo all'ombra mi rimango,
quand'el sol de' suo razzi el mondo spoglia:
ogni altro per piacere, e io per doglia,
prostrato in terra, mi lamento e piango.

3

Grato e felice, a' tuo feroci mali
ostare e vincer mi fu già concesso;
or lasso, il petto vo bagnando spesso
contr'a mie voglia, e so quante tu vali.
E se i dannosi e preteriti strali   5
al segno del mie cor non fur ma' presso,
or puoi a colpi vendicar te stesso
di que' begli occhi, e fien tutti mortali.
Da quanti lacci ancor, da quante rete
vago uccelletto per maligna sorte   10
campa molt'anni per morir po' peggio,
tal di me, donne, Amor, come vedete,
per darmi in questa età più crudel morte,
campato m'ha gran tempo, come veggio.

4

Quanto si gode, lieta e ben contesta
di fior sopra ' crin d'or d'una, grillanda,
che l'altro inanzi l'uno all'altro manda,
come ch'il primo sia a baciar la testa!
Contenta è tutto il giorno quella vesta   5
che serra 'l petto e poi par che si spanda,
e quel c'oro filato si domanda
le guanci' e 'l collo di toccar non resta.

I

One person passes many years in happiness, and in a single fleeting hour is brought to misery and grief; another shines brightly because of famous or ancient lineage, and in a single moment loses all lustre.

Nothing mutable exists under the sun which death does not conquer and fortune change.

Partial sonnet, 1503–4.[1]

2

I alone remain burning in the shadows, when the sun strips the world of its rays: all others for pleasure, but I through suffering lie prostrate on the earth, lamenting and weeping.

Quatrain, 1503–4.

3

To me, grateful and happy, it was once given to resist and conquer your savage evils; now, alas, against my will I often bathe my breast with tears, and I know your true power.

And if previously your fatal arrows never came close to my heart, which was their target, now you can revenge yourself through those beautiful eyes, whose every blow is fatal.

Just as for many years a little, wandering bird may escape a host of snares and nets only to die a worse death later through evil fate,

so I, ladies, as you can see, have been allowed by Love to escape for a long time only for him to give me at this age a crueller death, as I can see.

Sonnet, after 1504.

4

The garland on her golden hair, cheerful and finely woven with flowers, is so joyful that each flower presses the one in front as if all are vying to be the first to kiss her head!

That dress which fits tightly round her breast, and then seems to flow down freely, is happy as the day is long, and that net made of what is called spun-gold never tires of touching her cheeks and neck.

---

[1] On the notes at the end of each translation, see above p. xxvii.

Ma più lieto quel nastro par che goda,
dorato in punta, con sì fatte tempre   10
che preme e tocca il petto ch'egli allaccia.
      E la schietta cintura che s'annoda
mi par dir seco: qui vo' stringer sempre.
Or che farebbon dunche le mie braccia?

5

      I' ho già fatto un gozzo in questo stento,
come fa l'acqua a' gatti in Lombardia
o ver d'altro paese che si sia,
c'a forza 'l ventre appicca sotto 'l mento.
      La barba al cielo, e la memoria sento   5
in sullo scrigno, e 'l petto fo d'arpia,
e 'l pennel sopra 'l viso tuttavia
mel fa, gocciando, un ricco pavimento.
      E' lombi entrati mi son nella peccia,
e fo del cul per contrapeso groppa,   10
e ' passi senza gli occhi muovo invano.
      Dinanzi mi s'allunga la corteccia,
e per piegarsi adietro si ragroppa,
e tendomi com'arco sorïano.
                  Però fallace e strano   15
surge il iudizio che la mente porta,
ché mal si tra' per cerbottana torta.
                  La mia pittura morta
difendi orma', Giovanni, e 'l mio onore,
non sendo in loco bon, né io pittore.   20

6

      Signor, se vero è alcun proverbio antico,
questo è ben quel, che chi può mai non vuole.
Tu hai creduto a favole e parole
e premiato chi è del ver nimico.
      I' sono e fui già tuo buon servo antico,   5
a te son dato come e' raggi al sole,
e del mie tempo non ti increse o dole,
e men ti piaccio se più m'affatico.
      Già sperai ascender per la tua altezza,
e 'l giusto peso e la potente spada   10
fussi al bisogno, e non la voce d'ecco.

But that happy ribbon of fine gold thread seems to rejoice more fully still, being so arranged that it presses and touches the bosom it encircles.

And the simple girdle that twines round her seems to be saying to itself: 'Here I wish to clasp forever.' So what then might my arms do?

Sonnet, c. 1507.

5

In this difficult position I've given myself a goitre – as does the water to the peasants of Lombardy, or anyway of some country or another – for it shoves my stomach up to hang beneath my chin.

My beard points to heaven, and I feel the nape of my neck on my hump; I bend my breast like a harpy's, and, with its non-stop dripping from above, my brush makes my face a richly decorated floor.

My loins have gone up into my belly, and I make my backside into a croup as a counterweight; and I cannot see where to put my feet.

In front my hide is stretched, and behind the curve makes it wrinkled, as I bend myself like a Syrian bow.

So the thoughts that arise in my mind are false and strange, for one shoots badly through a crooked barrel.

Defend my dead painting from now on, Giovanni, and my honour, for I am not well placed, nor indeed a painter.

Tailed sonnet, for Giovanni da Pistoia, 1509–10.

6

Lord, if any ancient proverb is true it is surely this: he who can never wants to. You have believed tales and talk, and rewarded those who are the enemies of truth.

I am and ever was your good and faithful servant, I have been as united to you as rays to the sun; and yet you do not feel concern or compassion for the time I've given, and I please you less the more hard work I do.

I once hoped to rise thanks to your high state, but what I needed was the just scales and the powerful sword, not to hear my own voice echo.

Ma 'l cielo è quel c'ogni virtù disprezza
locarla al mondo, se vuol c'altri vada
a prender frutto d'un arbor ch'è secco.

7

Chi è quel che per forza a te mi mena,
oilmè, oilmè, oilmè,
legato e stretto, e son libero e sciolto?
Se tu incateni altrui senza catena,
e senza mane o braccia m'hai raccolto,   5
chi mi difenderà dal tuo bel volto?

8

Come può esser ch'io non sia più mio?
O Dio, o Dio, o Dio,
chi m'ha tolto a me stesso,
c'a me fusse più presso
o più di me potessi che poss'io?   5
O Dio, o Dio, o Dio,
come mi passa el core
chi non par che mi tocchi?
Che cosa è questo, Amore,
c'al core entra per gli occhi,   10
per poco spazio dentro par che cresca?
E s'avvien che trabocchi?

9

Colui che 'l tutto fe', fece ogni parte
e poi del tutto la più bella scelse,
per mostrar quivi le suo cose eccelse,
com'ha fatto or colla sua divin'arte.

10

Qua si fa elmi di calici e spade
e 'l sangue di Cristo si vend'a giumelle,
e croce e spine son lance e rotelle,
e pur da Cristo pazïenzia cade.

But it is heaven itself that disdains to find a place on earth for any virtue, if it asks men to go and take fruit from a withered tree.

Sonnet, probably c. 1511.

7

Who is this who by force leads me to you, alas, alas, alas, bound and fettered, though by nature free and unconstrained? If you enchain people without a chain, and without moving arm or hand have gathered me in, who will defend me from your beautiful face?

Madrigal, c. 1511.

8

How can it be that I am no longer mine? Oh God, oh God, oh God, who has taken me from myself, that she might be closer to me or have more power over me than I myself? Oh God, oh God, oh God, how can someone penetrate my heart without seeming even to touch me? What is this, Love, that enters the heart through the eyes, and in the small space within seems to grow? And if it should happen to overflow?

Madrigal, c. 1511.

9

He who made all made every part and then from all chose the most beautiful, to show forth here his sublime qualities, as he has now done with his divine art.

Quatrain, c. 1511.

10

Here from chalices helmets and swords are made; the blood of Christ is sold by the bucketful; his cross and thorns are lances and shields – and still Christ shows patience.

Ma non ci arrivi più 'n queste contrade,   5
ché n'andre' 'l sangue suo 'nsin alle stelle,
poscia c'a Roma gli vendon la pelle,
e ècci d'ogni ben chiuso le strade.
   S'i' ebbi ma' voglia a perder tesauro,
per ciò che qua opra da me è partita,   10
può quel nel manto che Medusa in Mauro;
   ma se alto in cielo è povertà gradita,
qual fia di nostro stato il gran restauro,
s'un altro segno ammorza l'altra vita?

11

   Quanto sare' men doglia il morir presto
che provar mille morte ad ora ad ora,
da ch'in cambio d'amarla, vuol ch'io mora!
Ahi, che doglia 'nfinita
sente 'l mio cor, quando li torna a mente   5
che quella ch'io tant'amo amor non sente!
Come resterò 'n vita?
Anzi mi dice, per più doglia darmi,
che se stessa non ama: e vero parmi.
Come posso sperar di me le dolga,   10
se se stessa non ama? Ahi trista sorte!
Che fia pur ver, ch'io ne trarrò la morte?

12

   Com'arò dunche ardire
senza vo' ma', mio ben, tenermi 'n vita,
s'io non posso al partir chiedervi aita?
Que' singulti e que' pianti e que' sospiri
che 'l miser core voi accompagnorno,   5
madonna, duramente dimostrorno
la mia propinqua morte e ' miei martiri.
Ma se ver è che per assenzia mai
mia fedel servitù vadia in oblio,
il cor lasso con voi, che non è mio.   10

13

   La fama tiene gli epitaffi a giacere; non va né inanzi né
indietro, perché son morti, e el loro operare è fermo.

But let him not come to us again in these parts, for his blood would spurt right up to the stars, since in Rome his skin is sold, and here the way is barred to any good.

If I ever had a wish to lose treasure, now is the time, since here work has been taken from me, and he who wears the mantle can do what Medusa did in Mauritania;

but if high in heaven poverty is pleasing, who will bring about the great restoration of our state, if another standard kills that other life?

Sonnet, probably for Giovanni da Pistoia, probably 1512.

11

How much less painful it would be to die quickly than to experience a thousand deaths hour after hour, since in exchange for my loving her she wishes me to die! Oh, what infinite pain my heart feels, when it calls to mind that she whom I love so much feels no love for me! How can I go on living? Worse, to give me greater pain, she tells me that she does not love herself; and this seems to me true. How can I hope that she will take pity on me, if she does not love herself? Oh unhappy destiny! Might it be true after all, that from this I shall draw death?

Madrigal, probably 1513–18.

12

How, then, may I ever dare to keep hold on life without you, my good, if at our parting I cannot ask you for help? Those sobs, those tears, those sighs that accompanied my miserable heart to you, my lady, harshly heralded my approaching death and my torments. But since through my absence my faithful service may one day be forgotten, I leave with you my heart, which is no longer mine.

Madrigal, before 1518.

13

Fame holds epitaphs in low esteem: through them it neither increases nor decreases, because they are dead and their activity is over.

Prose draft for poem(?), c. 1520.

14

El Dì e la Notte parlano, e dicono: — Noi abbiàno col nostro veloce corso condotto alla morte el duca Giuliano; è ben giusto che e' ne facci vendetta come fa. E la vendetta è questa: che avendo noi morto lui, lui così morto ha tolta la luce a noi e cogli occhi chiusi ha serrato e' nostri, che non risplendon più sopra la terra. Che arrebbe di noi dunche fatto, mentre vivea? —

15

Di te me veggo e di lontan mi chiamo
per appressarm'al ciel dond'io derivo,
e per le spezie all'esca a te arrivo,
come pesce per fil tirato all'amo.

  E perc'un cor fra dua fa picciol segno   5
di vita, a te s'è dato ambo le parti;
ond'io resto, tu 'l sai, quant'io son, poco.

  E perc'un'alma infra duo va 'l più degno,
m'è forza, s'i' voglio esser, sempre amarti;
ch'i' son sol legno, e tu se' legno e foco.   10

16

D'un oggetto leggiadro e pellegrino,
d'un fonte di pietà nasce 'l mie male.

17

Crudele, acerbo e dispietato core,
vestito di dolcezza e d'amar pieno,
tuo fede al tempo nasce, e dura meno
c'al dolce verno non fa ciascun fiore.

  Muovesi 'l tempo, e compartisce l'ore   5
al viver nostr'un pessimo veneno;
lu' come falce e no' siàn come fieno,

. . . .

  La fede è corta e la beltà non dura,
ma di par seco par che si consumi,   10
come 'l peccato tuo vuol de' mie danni.

14

Day and Night speak, in these words: 'We with our swift course have led Duke Giuliano to death; it is only right that he should gain revenge on us, as he does. And his revenge is this: that since we have killed him, he being killed has deprived us of light, and by closing his eyes has shut ours, which no longer shed light on the earth. What, then, might he not have done for us if he had lived?'

Prose draft for poem(?), c. 1520.

15

I see that I am yours, and from afar I exhort myself to be so in order to come closer to heaven whence I derive; and drawn by the lure of your beauty I reach you, as a fish on the hook is pulled in by the line.

And since a heart split in two shows little sign of life, to you are given both parts; so I remain, as you know, just what I am, of small account.

And since a soul between two objects moves towards the more worthy, I am constrained, if I would live, to love you always: for I am wood only, but you are wood and fire.

Partial sonnet, c. 1520.

16

From something lovely yet fleeting, from a fountain of mercy my trouble is born.

Unrhymed couplet, c. 1520.

17

Cruel, harsh and pitiless heart, clothed in sweetness but filled with bitterness, your faithfulness is born in time's realm, and lasts less than a flower in the springtime.

Time passes, and the hours mark our life with a fateful poison; he is like the sickle and we the hay ....

Faithfulness is short, and beauty does not last but likewise seems to waste away, as you wrongly wish to happen to me through the harm you inflict.

· ·
· ·
sempre fra noi fare' con tutti gli anni.

18

Mille rimedi invan l'anima tenta:
poi ch'i' fu' preso alla prestina strada,
di ritornare endarno s'argomenta.
Il mare e 'l monte e 'l foco colla spada:
   in mezzo a questi tutti insieme vivo.   5
Al monte non mi lascia chi m'ha privo
dell'intelletto e tolto la ragione.

19

Natura ogni valore
di donna o di donzella
fatto ha per imparare, insino a quella
c'oggi in un punto m'arde e ghiaccia el core.
Dunche nel mie dolore   5
non fu tristo uom più mai;
l'angoscia e 'l pianto e ' guai,
a più forte cagion maggiore effetto.
Così po' nel diletto
non fu né fie di me nessun più lieto.   10

20

Tu ha' 'l viso più dolce che la sapa,
e passato vi par sù la lumaca,
tanto ben lustra, e più bel c'una rapa;
e' denti bianchi come pastinaca,
in modo tal che invaghiresti 'l papa;   5
e gli occhi del color dell'utriaca;
e' cape' bianchi e biondi più che porri:
ond'io morrò, se tu non mi soccorri.

. . . .

would always do among us through all the years.

Unfinished sonnet, c. 1521.

18

The soul in vain tries a thousand remedies; from the time I was taken from the ancient road, it has sought without success to find its way back there. The sea, the mountain and the fire with the sword:

I live in the very midst of all these. I am not allowed to climb the mountain by the one who has deprived me of intellect and taken away my reason.

Partial sonnet(?), c. 1522.

19

Nature created everything of worth in woman and maiden by way of experiment, until it made that one who today at one and the same time burns my heart and turns it to ice. And so when I suffer no one was ever sadder than I: the agony, lament and woes – from a greater cause comes a greater effect. But likewise when I experience delight, there never was nor will there ever be anyone happier than I.

Incomplete madrigal, c. 1522.

20

You have a face sweeter than must, and a snail seems to have passed across it, it shines so much, and it is more beautiful than a turnip; teeth white as parsnips, so that you would charm even the pope; and eyes the colour of theriac; and hair whiter and blonder than leeks: so I shall die if you do not come to my help.

La tua bellezza par molto più bella
che uomo che dipinto in chiesa sia: 10
la bocca tua mi par una scarsella
di fagiuo' piena, sì come'è la mia;
le ciglia paion tinte alla padella
e torte più c'un arco di Sorìa;
le gote ha' rosse e bianche, quando stacci,   15
come fra cacio fresco e' rosolacci.
    Quand'io ti veggo, in su ciascuna poppa
mi paion duo cocomer in un sacco,
ond'io m'accendo tutto come stoppa,
bench'io sia dalla zappa rotto e stracco.   20
Pensa: s'avessi ancor la bella coppa,
ti seguirrei fra l'altre me' c'un bracco:
dunche s'i massi aver fussi possibile,
io fare' oggi qui cose incredibile.

21

    Chiunche nasce a morte arriva
nel fuggir del tempo; e 'l sole
niuna cosa lascia viva.
Manca il dolce e quel che dole
e gl'ingegni e le parole;   5
e le nostre antiche prole
al sole ombre, al vento un fummo.
Come voi uomini fummo,
lieti e tristi, come siete;
e or siàn, come vedete,   10
terra al sol, di vita priva.
        Ogni cosa a morte arriva.
Già fur gli occhi nostri interi
con la luce in ogni speco;
or son voti, orrendi e neri,   15
e ciò porta il tempo seco.

22

    Che fie di me? che vo' tu far di nuovo
d'un arso legno e d'un afflitto core?
Dimmelo un poco, Amore,
acciò che io sappi in che stato io mi truovo.

Your beauty seems much more beautiful even than people painted in churches: your mouth seems to me a bag full of beans, as mine is; your eyebrows seem dyed by smoke from a frying pan and more bent than a Syrian bow; when you are sifting flour, your cheeks are white and red, like poppies among fresh cheese.

When I look at you, those breasts of yours seem to me like two watermelons in a sack, and so I am all on fire like tow, even though I'm broken and tired out by the hoe. Believe me: if I still had the cup of beauty, I'd follow you through the other women better than a hound; so if it were possible for me to have blocks of stone, I'd here today make incredible things.

Three octaves, 1518–24, possibly 1523.

21

Whoever is born arrives at death through time's swift passage; and the sun leaves nothing alive. They disappear – what is sweet and what brings pain, man's thoughts and words; and our ancient lineages are as shadows to the sun, smoke to the wind. Like you, we were men, happy and sad as you are; but now we are, as you see, dust in the sun, deprived of life.

Everything arrives at death. Once our eyes were fully formed, shining in both sockets; now these are empty, horrible and black: such is the work of time.

Barzelletta *or* frottola, *before 1524.*

22

What will become of me? What do you want to do afresh with a piece of burned-out wood and an afflicted heart? Tell me a little, Love, that I may know what my present situation is.

Gli anni del corso mio al segno sono,   5
come saetta c'al berzaglio è giunta,
onde si de' quetar l'ardente foco.
E' mie passati danni a te perdono,
cagion che 'l cor l'arme tu' spezza e spunta,
c'amor per pruova in me non ha più loco;   10
e s'e' tuo colpi fussin nuovo gioco
agli occhi mei, al cor timido e molle,
vorria quel che già volle?
Ond'or ti vince e sprezza, e tu tel sai,
sol per aver men forza oggi che mai.   15

Tu speri forse per nuova beltate
tornarmi 'ndietro al periglioso impaccio,
ove 'l più saggio assai men si difende:
più corto è 'l mal nella più lunga etate,
ond'io sarò come nel foco el ghiaccio,   20
che si distrugge e parte e non s'accende.
La morte in questa età sol ne difende
dal fiero braccio e da' pungenti strali,
cagion di tanti mali,
che non perdona a condizion nessuna,   25
né a loco, né tempo, né fortuna.

L'anima mia, che con la morte parla
e seco di se stessa si consiglia,
e di nuovi sospetti ognor s'attrista,
el corpo di dì in dì spera lasciarla: 30
onde l'immaginato cammin piglia,
di speranza e timor confusa e mista.
Ahi, Amor, come se' pronto in vista,
temerario, audace, armato e forte!
che e' pensier della morte   35
nel tempo suo di me discacci fori,
per trar d'un arbor secco fronde e fiori.

Che poss'io più? che debb'io? Nel tuo regno
non ha' tu tutto el tempo mio passato,
che de' mia anni un'ora non m'è tocca?   40
Qual inganno, qual forza o qual ingegno
tornar mi puote a te, signore ingrato,
c'al cuor la morte e pietà porti in bocca?
Ben sare' ingrata e sciocca
l'alma risuscitata, e senza stima,   45
tornare a quel che gli diè morte prima.

The years of my life's journey have reached their mark, like an arrow that has landed on its target, and so the burning fire ought to have died down. The ills done me in the past I pardon you, since thanks to them my heart snaps and blunts your weapons, for through experience love no longer has any place in me; and if your blows were a new game to my eyes, to my soft and timid heart, would it want what it once did? So now it conquers and despises you, as you well know, simply because it has less strength today than it once had.

You hope, perhaps, through some new beauty to turn me back to the dangerous trap, where the wiser one is the less one defends oneself: but the evil lasts a shorter time the longer one has lived, and so I shall be like ice in fire, which is destroyed and disappears and does not burst into flames. At this age, what defends one from the savage arm and the piercing arrows, cause of so many evils, is death alone, which does not spare any condition, or place, or time or fortune.

My soul, which speaks with death, and with it takes stock of its own situation, and is continually weighed down by new anxieties, hopes day after day to leave the body: so it sets out on the journey it has lived through in imagination, confused and unsettled between hope and fear. Alas, Love, how swift to act you are, reckless, bold, armed and strong! For you drive out of me the thoughts of death at the time when it is approaching, that you may draw from a withered tree flowers and foliage.

What more can I, ought I, to do? Have you not caused me to spend all my time until now in your kingdom, so that there is not one hour of all my years that I can count my own? What deception, what force or what strategem could hand me back to you, ungrateful lord, who bear death to the heart and pity on your lips? The soul restored to life would indeed be ungrateful and foolish, and unworthy of respect, were it to go back to him who before had brought it death.

Ogni nato la terra in breve aspetta;
d'ora in or manca ogni mortal bellezza:
chi ama, il vedo, e' non si può po' sciorre.
Col gran peccato la crudel vendetta   50
insieme vanno; e quel che men s'apprezza,
colui è sol c'a più suo mal più corre.
A che mi vuo' tu porre,
che 'l dì ultimo buon, che mi bisogna,
sie quel del danno e quel della vergogna?   55

23

I' fu', già son molt'anni, mille volte
ferito e morto, non che vinto e stanco
da te, mie colpa; e or col capo bianco
riprenderò le tuo promesse stolte?
Quante volte ha' legate e quante sciolte   5
le triste membra, e sì spronato il fianco,
c'appena posso ritornar meco, anco
bagnando il petto con lacrime molte!
Di te mi dolgo, Amor, con teco parlo,
sciolto da' tuo lusinghi: a che bisogna   10
prender l'arco crudel, tirare a voto?
Al legno incenerato sega o tarlo,
o dietro a un correndo, è gran vergogna
c'ha perso e ferma ogni destrezza e moto.

24

I' fe' degli occhi porta al mie veneno,
quand' el passo dier libero a' fier dardi;
nido e ricetto fe' de' dolci sguardi
della memoria che ma' verrà meno.
Ancudine fe' 'l cor, mantaco 'l seno   5
da fabricar sospir, con che tu m'ardi.

25

Quand'il servo il signor d'aspra catena
senz'altra speme in carcer tien legato,
volge in tal uso el suo misero stato,
che libertà domanderebbe appena.

The earth waits but a short time for all who are born; hour by hour all mortal beauty fades: I see now that whoever loves cannot then break free. Great sin and cruel revenge go hand in hand; and it is he alone who least esteems himself who most quickly hurries to his greatest ruin. To what do you wish to drive me: that my last day, which for me must be good, should be a day of harm and a day of shame?

Canzone of five stanzas, c. 1524.

23

A thousand times, many years ago now, I was not just overcome and exhausted but wounded and killed by you, through my own fault; shall I now, white-haired, take up again your foolish promises?

How many times have you bound and as often freed my sad limbs, and so spurred my flank that I can scarcely recover, even by bathing my breast with many tears!

I feel sorry for you, Love, and address you as one freed from your blandishments: what drives you to take up the cruel bow, and fire in vain?

As it is useless for saw or worm to apply themselves to wood burned to ashes, so there is great shame in running after one who has lost all agility and is halting in every movement.

Sonnet, c. 1524-8.

24

I made a doorway of my eyes for the poison in me, when they offered free passage to your savage darts; for the sweet glances, I made a nest and receptacle of my memory, which will never fade.

My heart I made an anvil, my breast a bellows to form sighs, with which you burn me.

Partial sonnet, c. 1524-8.

25

When a lord holds his servant bound in prison, with harsh chains and devoid of any hope, that servant becomes so accustomed to his wretched state that he would scarcely ask for freedom.

E el tigre e 'l serpe ancor l'uso raffrena,   5
e 'l fier leon ne' folti boschi nato;
e 'l nuovo artista, all'opre affaticato,
coll'uso del sudor doppia suo lena.
　　Ma 'l foco a tal figura non s'unisce;
ché se l'umor d'un verde legno estinge,   10
il freddo vecchio scalda e po' 'l nutrisce,
　　e tanto il torna in verde etate e spinge,
rinnuova e 'nfiamma, allegra e 'ngiovanisce,
c'amor col fiato l'alma e 'l cor gli cinge.
　　　　E se motteggia o finge,   15
chi dice in vecchia etate esser vergogna
amar cosa divina, è gran menzogna.
　　　　L'anima che non sogna,
non pecca amar le cose di natura,
usando peso, termine e misura.   20

26

　　Quand'avvien c'alcun legno non difenda
il propio umor fuor del terreste loco,
non può far c'al gran caldo assai o poco
non si secchi o non s'arda o non s'accenda.
　　Così 'l cor, tolto da chi mai mel renda,   5
vissuto in pianto e nutrito di foco,
or ch'è fuor del suo propio albergo e loco,
qual mal fie che per morte non l'offenda?

27

　　Fuggite, amanti, Amor, fuggite 'l foco;
l'incendio è aspro e la piaga è mortale,
c'oltr'a l'impeto primo più non vale
né forza né ragion né mutar loco.
　　Fuggite, or che l'esemplo non è poco   5
d'un fiero braccio e d'un acuto strale;
leggete in me, qual sarà 'l vostro male,
qual sarà l'impio e dispietato gioco.
　　Fuggite, e non tardate, al primo sguardo:
ch'i' pensa' d'ogni tempo avere accordo;   10
or sento, e voi vedete, com'io ardo.

And custom tames even the tiger and the serpent, and the fierce lion born in leafy wood; and the young artist, tired by work, on becoming accustomed to sweat redoubles his vigour.

But fire does not conform to such a pattern: for though it consumes the moisture of a green piece of wood, it heats the cold old one and then nourishes him,

and finally returns and propels him back to his green age, renews and inflames him, brings him joy and youthfulness, for with its breath love twines around his heart and soul.

And if anyone jeers or pretends otherwise, saying that in old age it is shameful to love something divine, this is a great lie.

The soul that does not dream commits no sin in loving the things of nature, if it does so with balance, restraint and measure.

Tailed sonnet, c. 1524–8.

26

Since it is the case that no piece of wood whatever can conserve its proper moisture when out of its place in the earth, if any such is touched even a little by a great heat it cannot avoid being dried up and bursting into flames and being burned.

So with my heart: taken by one who may never give it back, living in tears and nourished by fire, now that it is out of its proper dwelling-place, what injury will not be for it a fatal blow?

Partial sonnet, 1520s.

27

Flee Love, lovers, flee the fire; its burning is fierce and its wound is fatal, for after Love's first assault nothing can be of any help, neither strength nor reason nor change of place.

Flee, now that you have no small example of what his savage arm and sharp arrow can do; read in me what evil will be yours, what the cruel and pitiless game will be.

Flee, do not linger, at the first glance; for I thought that I could at any time come to terms with him; now I well know, and you can see, how I do burn.

Partial sonnet, c. 1524.

28

Perché pur d'ora in ora mi lusinga
la memoria degli occhi e la speranza,
per cui non sol son vivo, ma beato;
la forza e la ragion par che ne stringa,
Amor, natura e la mie 'ntica usanza,   5
mirarvi tutto il tempo che m'è dato.
E s'i' cangiassi stato,
vivendo in questo, in quell'altro morrei;
né pietà troverei
ove non fussin quegli.   10
O Dio, e' son pur begli!
Chi non ne vive non è nato ancora;
e se verrà dipoi,
a dirlo qui tra noi,
forz'è che, nato, di subito mora;   15
ché chi non s'innamora
de' begli occhi, non vive.

29

Ogn'ira, ogni miseria e ogni forza,
chi d'amor s'arma vince ogni fortuna.

30

Dagli occhi del mie ben si parte e vola
un raggio ardente e di sì chiara luce
che da' mie, chiusi ancor, trapassa 'l core.
Onde va zoppo Amore,
tant'è dispar la soma che conduce,   5
dando a me luce, e tenebre m'invola.

28

Since with every waking hour I am beguiled by the memory of her eyes and by the hope they give – from which I draw not only life but happiness – force and reason seem to drive me, Love, as do nature and my old habits, to gaze on them all the time that I am given. And if I were to change state, having lived in this one, in that other I should die; nor should I find pity where those eyes were not present. Oh God, how beautiful they are! Whoever does not live from them has not yet been born; and whoever will come later (I say this here between us) will, when born, instantly have to die; for he cannot live who does not love those beautiful eyes.

Incomplete madrigal, c. 1524–6.

29

All wrath, all misery, all force: he who arms himself with love can conquer all misfortune.

Unrhymed couplet, c. 1524–6.

30

From the eyes of the one who is my good there issues a swift, burning ray of light so bright that it passes to my heart through my eyes, even when closed. Thus Love limps along, so unequal is the burden he bears, bringing to me light, and taking from me darkness.

Madrigal, c. 1524–6.

31

Amor non già, ma gli occhi mei son quegli
che ne' tuo soli e begli
e vita e morte intera trovato hanno.
Tante meno m'offende e preme 'l danno,
più mi distrugge e cuoce;   5
dall'altra ancor mi nuoce
tante amor più quante più grazia truovo.
Mentre ch'io penso e pruovo
il male, el ben mi cresce in un momento.
O nuovo e stran tormento!   10
Però non mi sgomento:
s'aver miseria e stento
è dolce qua dove non è ma' bene,
vo cercando 'l dolor con maggior pene.

32

Vivo al peccato, a me morendo vivo;
vita già mia non son, ma del peccato:
mie ben dal ciel, mie mal da me m'è dato,
dal mie sciolto voler, di ch'io son privo.
    Serva mie libertà, mortal mie divo   5
a me s'è fatto. O infelice stato!
a che miseria, a che viver son nato!

33

Sie pur, fuor di mie propie, c'ogni altr'arme
difender par ogni mie cara cosa;
altra spada, altra lancia e altro scudo
fuor delle propie forze non son nulla,
tant'è la trista usanza, che m'ha tolta   5
la grazia che 'l ciel piove in ogni loco.
    Qual vecchio serpe per istretto loco
passar poss'io, lasciando le vecchie arme,
e dal costume rinnovata e tolta
sie l'alma in vita e d'ogni umana cosa,   10
coprendo sé con più sicuro scudo,
ché tutto el mondo a morte è men che nulla.

31

It is not simply love that my eyes have found in your unique and beautiful eyes, but life and death together. The less their harm hurts and oppresses me the more it destroys and burns me; on the other hand, love does me greater injury the greater grace I find. While I experience and think over the evil, the good in me suddenly increases. Oh new and strange torment! However, I am not daunted: if having misery and difficulty is sweet here where no good is ever found, I shall continue to seek suffering, though it bring greater pains.

Madrigal, c. 1525.

32

I live to sin, to kill myself I live; no longer is my life my own, but sin's; my good is given to me by heaven, my evil by myself, by my free will, of which I am deprived.

My freedom has made itself a slave, my mortal part has made itself a god for me. Oh unhappy state! to such misery, to such a life was I born!

Partial sonnet, c. 1525.

33

Although it seems that all other arms but my own can defend all that is dear to me, no sword, no lance, no shield other than my own powers are of any help, so strong is the evil habit that has taken from me the grace that heaven rains down on every place.

Like an old serpent through a narrow place may I pass, shedding my old protection, and may my soul be renewed in life and be rid of its old habits and of every human concern, guarding itself with a surer shield, for faced with death the whole world is less than nothing.

Amore, i' sento già di me far nulla;
natura del peccat' è 'n ogni loco.
Spoglia di me me stesso, e col tuo scudo,   15
colla pietra e tuo vere e dolci arme,
difendimi da me, c'ogni altra cosa
è come non istata, in brieve tolta.
   Mentre c'al corpo l'alma non è tolta,
Signor, che l'universo puo' far nulla,   20
fattor, governator, re d'ogni cosa,
poco ti fie aver dentr'a me loco;
. . . .
. . . .

. . . .   25
. . . .
che d'ogn' uomo veril son le vere arme,
senza le quali ogn' uom diventa nulla.

34

La vita del mie amor non è 'l cor mio,
c'amor di quel ch'i' t'amo è senza core;
dov'è cosa mortal, piena d'errore,
esser non può già ma', né pensier rio.
   Amor nel dipartir l'alma da Dio   5
me fe' san occhio e te luc' e splendore;
né può non rivederlo in quel che more
di te, per nostro mal, mie gran desio.
   Come dal foco el caldo, esser diviso
non può dal bell'etterno ogni mie stima,   10
ch'exalta, ond'ella vien, chi più 'l somiglia.
   Poi che negli occhi ha' tutto 'l paradiso,
per ritornar là dov'i' t'ama' prima,
ricorro ardendo sott'alle tuo ciglia.

35

El ciglio col color non fere el volto
col suo contrar, che l'occhio non ha pena
da l'uno all'altro stremo ov'egli è volto.
   L'occhio, che sotto intorno adagio mena,
picciola parte di gran palla scuopre,   5
che men rilieva suo vista serena,

Love, I already feel myself reduced to nothing; my nature has become sinful through and through. Strip me of myself, and with your shield, your rock and your true, sweet weapons, defend me from myself, for everything else is as if it had never been, quickly removed.

While the soul is not yet taken from the body, Lord who can reduce the universe to nothing, creator, ruler, king of all things, it would cost you little to make a place for yourself within me

. . . .

. . . .

. . . .

. . . .

which are the true weapons of every virile man, without which every man becomes nothing.

Incomplete sestina, 1524–8.

34

My love does not live in my heart, for the love with which I love you does not belong to the heart: such love can never be found where there is anything mortal and full of error, or evil thoughts.

In sending down our souls from God, Love gave me a clear eye and you light and splendour; and so my great desire cannot but see God again in that part of you which, to our misfortune, dies.

My discerning power itself can no more be separated from the eternal beauty than can heat from fire; it exalts whoever most resembles him from whom it comes.

Since in your eyes you have paradise entire, in order to return to where I first loved you, I hasten burning to find myself again under your eyes.

Sonnet, c. 1526.

35

When it contracts, the eyelid does not cover the entire sight in darkness, and so the eye has no difficulty in traversing its arc from one extreme to the other.

The eye, moving around slowly underneath, has only a small part of its great eyeball uncovered, and so enjoys less of its capacity for sight.

e manco sale e scende quand' el copre;
onde più corte son le suo palpebre,
che manco grinze fan quando l'aopre.

El bianco bianco, el ner più che funebre,   10
s'esser può, el giallo po' più leonino,
che scala fa dall'una all'altra vebre.

Pur tocchi sotto e sopra el suo confino,
e 'l giallo e 'l nero e 'l bianco non circundi.

36

Oltre qui fu, dove 'l mie amor mi tolse,
suo mercè, il core e vie più là la vita;
qui co' begli occhi mi promisse aita,
e co' medesmi qui tor me la volse.

Quinci oltre mi legò, quivi mi sciolse;   5
per me qui piansi, e con doglia infinita
da questo sasso vidi far partita
colui c'a me mi tolse e non mi volse.

37

In me la morte, in te la vita mia;
tu distingui e concedi e parti el tempo;
quante vuo', breve e lungo è 'l viver mio.
Felice son nella tuo cortesia.
Beata l'alma, ove non corre tempo,   5
per te s'è fatta a contemplare Dio.

38

Quanta dolcezza al cor per gli occhi porta
quel che 'n un punto el tempo e morte fura!
Che è questo però che mi conforta
e negli affanni cresce e sempre dura.
Amor, come virtù viva e accorta,   5
desta gli spirti ed è più degna cura.
Risponde a me: — Come persona morta
mena suo vita chi è da me sicura. —

and, thus covered, moves up and down less; so, too, the eyelids become shorter, and less wrinkled than when the eyes are fully functioning.

The white of the eye is truly white, its black darker than funereal, if that is possible; its yellow, which mounts from one fibre to the next, is a little more tawny than a lion.

No matter how much you examine above and below the edges of the eye, you will not fully appreciate its yellow, black, and white.

Incomplete capitolo, *c. 1526.*

36

Beyond here it was where my love in his goodness took away my heart, and a little way on there my life; here with his beautiful eyes he promised me help, and with the same here he wished to take it from me.

Further on from here he bound me, and there he set me free; here I wept for myself, and from this rock, with infinite suffering, I saw him depart who took me from myself and did not wish me with him.

Partial sonnet, 1524-34.

37

In me is death, in you my life; you determine, allot and parcel out time; as you wish, my life will be short or long.

I am happy according as you are kind. Blessed is the soul, where time does not run; through you it is formed to contemplate God.

Partial sonnet, 1520s.

38

What sweetness he brings to the heart through the eyes who in an instant bears off time and death! He it is, then, who comforts me, and in times of trial gains in strength and remains always with me.

Love, as a power that brings life and wisdom, awakens our spirits and is most worth our concern. He answers me: 'Whoever is immune to me leads his life like one who is dead.'

Amore è un concetto di bellezza
immaginata o vista dentro al core,   10
amica di virtute e gentilezza.

39

Del fiero colpo e del pungente strale
la medicina era passarmi 'l core;
ma questo è propio sol del mie signore,
crescer la vita dove cresce 'l male.
    E se 'l primo suo colpo fu mortale,   5
seco un messo di par venne d'Amore
che mi disse: — Ama, anz'ardi; ché chi muore
non ha da gire al ciel nel mondo altr'ale.
    I' son colui che ne' prim'anni tuoi
gli occhi tuo infermi volsi alla beltate   10
che dalla terra al ciel vivo conduce. —

40

Quand'Amor lieto al ciel levarmi è volto
cogli occhi di costei, anzi col sole,
con breve riso ciò che preme e dole
del cor mi caccia, e mettevi 'l suo volto;
    e s'i' durassi in tale stato molto,   5
l'alma, che sol di me lagnar si vole,
avendo seco là dove star suole,
. . . .

41

Spirto ben nato, in cu' si specchia e vede
nelle tuo belle membra oneste e care
quante natura e 'l ciel tra no' può fare,
quand'a null'altra suo bell'opra cede:
    spirto leggiadro, in cu' si spera e crede   5
dentro, come di fuor nel viso appare,
amor, pietà, mercè, cose sì rare,
che ma' furn'in beltà con tanta fede:
    l'amor mi prende e la beltà mi lega;
la pietà, la mercè con dolci sguardi   10
ferma speranz' al cor par che ne doni.

Love is a concept born of beauty that is imagined or seen in the heart, and that is a friend of virtue and graciousness.

Partial sonnet, 1520s.

39

The remedy for the savage blow from the piercing arrow would be for it to pass through my heart; but this power belongs to my lord alone, to increase life where hurt increases.

And if his first blow was fatal, with it came at the same time a messenger from Love who said to me: 'Love, indeed burn; for mortal beings have in this world no other wings with which to rise to heaven.

'I am he who in your early years turned your weak eyes to beauty, which leads those still alive from earth to heaven.'

Partial sonnet, 1520s.

40

When Love in happy mood is set on raising me to heaven through the eyes of that woman, or rather through the sun she is, he banishes from my heart with a quick smile what oppresses and pains it, and puts her face there;

and if I were to remain in such a state for long, my soul which, when alone, wants to groan against me, having with it where it is used to being, ...

Unfinished sonnet, 1520s.

41

Well-born spirit, in whose beautiful limbs, graceful and dear, one sees reflected how much nature and the heavens can achieve among us when they yield to no other beautiful work of theirs:

lovely spirit, within whom one confidently hopes to find what outwardly appears in your face – love, compassion, kindness, qualities so rare that they have never before been found so closely linked to beauty:

love takes me, and beauty binds me; compassion and kindness in sweet glances seem to give my heart firm hope.

Qual uso o qual governo al mondo niega,
qual crudeltà per tempo o qual più tardi,
c'a sì bell'opra morte non perdoni?

42

Dimmi di grazia, Amor, se gli occhi mei
veggono 'l ver della beltà c'aspiro,
o s'io l'ho dentro allor che, dov'io miro,
veggio scolpito el viso di costei.
Tu 'l de' saper, po' che tu vien con lei   5
a torm'ogni mie pace, ond'io m'adiro;
né vorre' manco un minimo sospiro,
né men ardente foco chiederei.
— La beltà che tu vedi è ben da quella,
ma cresce poi c'a miglior loco sale,   10
se per gli occhi mortali all'alma corre.
Quivi si fa divina, onesta e bella,
com'a sé simil vuol cosa immortale:
questa e non quella agli occhi tuo precorre. —

43

La ragion meco si lamenta e dole,
parte ch'i' spero amando esser felice;
con forti esempli e con vere parole
la mie vergogna mi rammenta e dice:
— Che ne riportera' dal vivo sole   5
altro che morte? e non come fenice. —
Ma poco giova, ché chi cader vuole,
non basta l'altru' man pront' e vittrice.
I' conosco e' mie danni, e 'l vero intendo;
dall'altra banda albergo un altro core,   10
che più m'uccide dove più m'arrendo.
In mezzo di duo mort' è 'l mie signore:
questa non voglio e questa non comprendo:
così sospeso, el corpo e l'alma muore.

What pattern or law on earth, what cruelty whether swift or slow, would prevent death from sparing a work so beautiful?

Sonnet, after 1528.

42

'Tell me in your kindness, Love, if my eyes do really see the beauty that I long for; or whether this is rather within me, since, wherever I gaze, I see as if sculpted that woman's face.

'You must know, because you come with her to take from me all my peace, which makes me angry; and yet I would not wish to lose the slightest sigh, nor would I ask for a fire that burned less fiercely.'

'The beauty that you see does indeed come from her, but it grows once it has risen to a better place, when through mortal eyes it speeds to the soul.

'There it becomes divine, virtuous and beautiful, since an immortal being wishes all else to be like itself: it is this beauty not that other which goes before your eyes.'

Sonnet, after 1528.

43

Reason laments and grieves over me, while I hope to find happiness in love; with powerful examples and truthful words it brings my shame before me, and says:

'What will you gain from the living sun, other than death? and not a death like that of the phoenix.' But little good it does me, for, if someone wishes to fall, another's hand is not enough, ready and victorious though it be.

I recognize the harm I do myself, and yearn for the true good; but elsewhere I harbour another heart, which kills me more the more I yield to it.

Between two deaths does my lord stand: the one I do not wish, the other I cannot grasp; suspended thus, both body and soul are dying.

Sonnet, after 1528.

44

Mentre c'alla beltà ch'i' vidi in prima
appresso l'alma, che per gli occhi vede,
l'immagin dentro cresce, e quella cede
quasi vilmente e senza alcuna stima.
    Amor, c'adopra ogni suo ingegno e lima,   5
perch'io non tronchi 'l fil ritorna e riede.

45

Ben doverrieno al sospirar mie tanto
esser secco oramai le fonti e ' fiumi,
s'i' non gli rinfrescassi col mie pianto.
    Così talvolta i nostri etterni lumi,
l'un caldo e l'altro freddo ne ristora,   5
acciò che 'l mondo più non si consumi.
    E similmente il cor che s'innamora,
quand'el superchio ardor troppo l'accende,
l'umor degli occhi il tempra, che non mora.
    La morte e 'l duol, ch'i' bramo e cerco, rende   10
un contento avenir, che non mi lassa
morir; ché chi diletta non offende.
    Onde la navicella mie non passa,
com'io vorrei, a vederti a quella riva
che 'l corpo per a tempo di qua lassa.   15
    Troppo dolor vuol pur ch'i' campi e viva,
qual più c'altri veloce andando vede,
che dopo gli altri al fin del giorno arriva.
    Crudel pietate e spietata mercede
me lasciò vivo, e te da me disciolse,   20
rompendo, e non mancando nostra fede,
    e la memoria a me non sol non tolse,
. . . .

46

Se 'l mie rozzo martello i duri sassi
forma d'uman aspetto or questo or quello,
dal ministro che 'l guida, iscorge e tiello,
prendendo il moto, va con gli altrui passi.

44

While I draw my soul, which sees through the eyes, close to the beauty that I first saw, the image within it grows, and my soul gives way like a coward lacking self-esteem.

Love, who employs and sharpens all his wits to prevent me from cutting the thread, returns again and again.

Partial sonnet, after 1528.

45

The springs and rivers would certainly by now be dry on account of my great sighing, if I did not replenish them with my tears.

In a similar way our eternal lights, one hot and other cold, alternately restore us, so that the world may not waste away.

And likewise with the heart in love: when excessive ardour causes it to burn too much, the moisture from the eyes cools it, that it may not die.

Death and sorrow, which I crave and seek, promise me a happy future, and it is this which will not let me die: for whatever brings delight causes no harm.

And so my little boat does not, as I should wish, cross over to see you on that bank which one reaches by leaving the body on this side for a certain time.

Too much sorrow means in fact that I shall survive and live, like someone who sees others going more speedily and arrives after the others at the day's end.

Cruel pity and pitiless mercy left me here alive, and separated you from me, interrupting though not destroying our faithful love,

and not only did they not take away from me the memory,
. . . .

Incomplete capitolo, *possibly on the death of Michelangelo's brother Buonarroto, c. 1528.*

46

If my rough hammer, in shaping the hard stones into the form of this or that human appearance, derives its motion from the master who guides, directs and sustains it, then it moves as another would have it do.

Ma quel divin che in cielo alberga e stassi,   5
altri, e sé più, col propio andar fa bello;
e se nessun martel senza martello
si può far, da quel vivo ogni altro fassi.

E perché 'l colpo è di valor più pieno
quant'alza più se stesso alla fucina,   10
sopra 'l mie questo al ciel n'è gito a volo.

Onde a me non finito verrà meno,
s'or non gli dà la fabbrica divina
aiuto a farlo, c'al mondo era solo.

47

Quand'el ministro de' sospir mie tanti
al mondo, agli occhi mei, a sé si tolse,
natura, che fra noi degnar lo volse,
restò in vergogna, e chi lo vide in pianti.

Ma non come degli altri oggi si vanti   5
del sol del sol, c'allor ci spense e tolse,
morte, c'amor ne vinse, e farlo il tolse
in terra vivo e 'n ciel fra gli altri santi.

Così credette morte iniqua e rea
finir il suon delle virtute sparte,   10
e l'alma, che men bella esser potea.

Contrari effetti alluminan le carte
di vita più che 'n vita non solea,
e morto ha 'l ciel, c'allor non avea parte.

48

Come fiamma più cresce più contesa
dal vento, ogni virtù che 'l cielo esalta
tanto più splende quant'è più offesa.

But that divine hammer, which lodges and abides in heaven, with its own movement makes others beautiful, and all the more itself; and if no hammer can be made without a hammer, then every other hammer is made from that living one.

And since every blow is of greater strength the higher the hammer is raised at the forge, this one has flown to heaven above mine.

So mine will remain unfinished for me, if the divine smith will not now give help to make it to him who was on earth my only help.

Sonnet: see poem 45.

47

When he who was the cause of my abundant sighs took himself from the world, from my eyes, and from himself, nature, which had favoured us with his presence, was left in shame, and all who had seen him were left in tears.

But today death may not boast, as it does over others, over the sun of suns whom it extinguished and took away, for love has conquered death, by taking him in order to make him live on earth and in heaven among the other saints.

Unjust and evil death believed that it would thus put an end to the widespread fame of his virtues, and of his soul, which it could make less beautiful.

The opposite has happened: his pages have been brought more brilliantly alive than during his life, and as dead he possesses heaven, of which he had then no part.

Sonnet, late 1520s or after.

48

As a flame grows stronger the more it is buffeted by the wind, every virtue that heaven exalts shines more brightly the more it is attacked.

Tercet, after c. 1528.

49

Amor, la tuo beltà non è mortale:
nessun volto fra noi è che pareggi
l'immagine del cor, che 'nfiammi e reggi
con altro foco e muovi con altr'ale.

50

Che fie doppo molt'anni di costei,
Amor, se 'l tempo ogni beltà distrugge?
Fama di lei; e anche questa fugge
e vola e manca più ch'i' non vorrei.
    Più e men   5

51

Oilmè, oilmè, ch'i' son tradito
da' giorni mie fugaci e dallo specchio
che 'l ver dice a ciascun che fiso 'l guarda!
Così n'avvien, chi troppo al fin ritarda,
com'ho fatt'io, che 'l tempo m'è fuggito: 5
si trova come me 'n un giorno vecchio.
Né mi posso pentir, né m'apparecchio,
né mi consiglio con la morte appresso.
Nemico di me stesso,
inutilmente i pianti e ' sospir verso,   10
ché non è danno pari al tempo perso.
    Oilmè, oilmè, pur riterando
vo 'l mio passato tempo e non ritruovo
in tutto un giorno che sie stato mio!
Le fallace speranze e 'l van desio,   15
piangendo, amando, ardendo e sospirando
(c'affetto alcun mortal non m'è più nuovo)
m'hanno tenuto, ond'il conosco e pruovo,
lontan certo dal vero.
Or con periglio pèro;   20
ché 'l breve tempo m'è venuto manco,
né sarie ancor, se s'allungassi, stanco.

49

Love, your beauty is not mortal: there is no face among us can match the image in the heart, which you inflame and rule with another fire, and move with other wings.

Quatrain, c. 1530.

50

What will remain of her after many years, Love, if time destroys all beauty? Her fame. Yet even this flees, flies away and disappears more quickly than I would wish.

More and less ....

Unfinished sonnet, c. 1528 or later.

51

Alas, alas, I have been betrayed by my fleeting days and by the mirror that tells the truth to everyone who looks steadily into it! This is what happens to anyone who too long puts off thinking about his end, as I have done, while time has slipped me by: like me, he suddenly finds himself old. And I cannot repent, nor do I prepare myself, nor reconsider my ways, even with death near. My own worst enemy, I uselessly pour out tears and sighs, for there is no harm to equal that of wasted time.

Alas, alas, though I keep going over my past life, I do not find a single day that has been my own! False hopes and vain desire have kept me weeping, loving, burning and sighing (for no mortal emotion is a stranger to me now), as I well know and daily prove again, far indeed from the true good. Now in danger I perish: time's short passage has run out for me, and even if it were to lengthen I should not tire of my ways.

I' vo lasso, oilmè, né so ben dove;
anzi temo, ch'il veggio, e 'l tempo andato
mel mostra, né mi val che gli occhi chiuda.   25
Or che 'l tempo la scorza cangia e muda,
la morte e l'alma insieme ognor fan pruove,
la prima e la seconda, del mie stato.
E s'io non sono errato
(che Dio 'l voglia ch'io sia),   30
l'etterna pena mia
nel mal libero inteso oprato vero
veggio, Signor, né so quel ch'io mi spero.

52

S'alcun se stesso al mondo ancider lice,
po' che per morte al ciel tornar si crede,
sarie ben giusto a chi con tanta fede
vive servendo miser e 'nfelice.
    Ma perché l'uom non è come fenice,   5
c'alla luce del sol resurge e riede,
la man fo pigra e muovo tardi el piede.

53

Chi di notte cavalca, el dì conviene
c'alcuna volta si riposi e dorma:
così sper'io, che dopo tante pene
ristori 'l mie signor mie vita e forma.
    Non dura 'l mal dove non dura 'l bene,   5
ma spesso l'un nell'altro si trasforma.

54

Io crederrei, se tu fussi di sasso,
amarti con tal fede, ch'i' potrei
farti meco venir più che di passo;
se fussi morto, parlar ti farei,
se fussi in ciel, ti tirerei a basso   5
co' pianti, co' sospir, co' prieghi miei.
Sendo vivo e di carne, e qui tra noi,
chi t'ama e serve che de' creder poi?

I go wearily on, alas, yet without really knowing where; or rather I fear I do, for I see where, and my past shows this to me, and it does me no good to close my eyes. Now that time is changing skin and moult, death and my soul are locked in battle every hour, one against the other, for my final state. And if I am not mistaken (God grant that I may be), I see the eternal punishment due for my having, in freedom, badly understood and acted on the truth, Lord; nor do I know what I may hope for.

Canzone of three stanzas, c. 1530.

52

If anyone were allowed in this world to kill himself, since he believed that through death one returned to heaven, this would surely be permitted for someone who with such faithfulness spends his life in miserable and unhappy service.

But since man is not like the phoenix, which rises again and returns to the sun's light, I keep my hand sluggish and am slow to move my feet.

Partial sonnet, c. 1531.

53

Whoever rides by night must by day sometime take rest and sleep; this gives me hope that after so much suffering my lord may give relief to my life and soul.

Evil does not last where good does not, but one is often transformed into the other.

Partial sonnet, c. 1531.

54

I do believe that if you were made of stone I should love you with such faithfulness that I should make you come to me at more than walking pace; if you were dead, I'd make you speak; if you were in heaven, I'd draw you down with my tears, my sighs, my prayers. Since in fact you are alive and in the flesh, and here among us, what then may I not hope for from loving and serving you?

I' non posso altro far che seguitarti,
e della grande impresa non mi pento.   10
Tu non se' fatta com'un uom da sarti,
che si muove di fuor, si muove drento;
e se dalla ragion tu non ti parti,
spero c'un dì tu mi fara' contento:
ché 'l morso il ben servir togli' a' serpenti,   15
come l'agresto quand'allega i denti.

   E' non è forza contr'a l'umiltate,
né crudeltà può star contr'a l'amore;
ogni durezza suol vincer pietate,
sì come l'allegrezza fa 'l dolore;   20
una nuova nel mondo alta beltate
come la tuo non ha 'ltrimenti il core;
c'una vagina, ch'è dritta a vedella,
non può dentro tener torte coltella.

   E non può esser pur che qualche poco   25
la mie gran servitù non ti sie cara;
pensa che non si truova in ogni loco
la fede negli amici, che è sì rara;
. . . .
. . . .   30
. . . .
. . . .

   Quando un dì sto che veder non ti posso,
non posso trovar pace in luogo ignuno;
se po' ti veggo, mi s'appicca addosso,   35
come suole il mangiar far al digiuno;
. . . .
. . . .
com'altri il ventre di votar si muore,
ch'è più 'l conforto, po' che pri' è 'l dolore.   40

   E non mi passa tra le mani un giorno
ch'i' non la vegga o senta con la mente;
né scaldar ma' si può fornace o forno
c'a' mie sospir non fussi più rovente;
e quando avvien ch'i' l'abbi un po' dintorno,   45
sfavillo come ferro in foco ardente;
e tanto vorre' dir, s'ella m'aspetta,
ch'i' dico men che quand'i' non ho fretta.

I can do nothing else but follow you, and I do not regret this great enterprise. You are not made like a tailor's dummy, whose every move, outside and in, is caused by others; and if you do not cast aside your gift of reason, I hope that one day you will make me happy, for faithful service causes the serpent to withhold its bite, and acts as vinegar does when it clamps the teeth together.

There is no power that can withstand being humbly honoured, nor can cruelty resist love; mercy overcomes all hardness, as happiness does sorrow; a beauty nobler than the world has ever seen, as yours is, must have a heart to match, for a sheath which outwardly is straight cannot contain a twisted knife within.

And it simply cannot be that my great service does not please you, at least a little; remember that faithfulness between friends is not found everywhere, indeed it is something rare;
. . . .
. . . .
. . . .
When I go a day without being able to see you, I cannot find peace anywhere; if I then see you, the desire for you assails me even more, as the sight of food affects a starving man
. . . .
like someone who was dying to empty his bowel, whose comfort is all the greater because previously he was in pain.

And not a single day slips through my fingers when I do not see or hear her in my mind; nor has there ever been a furnace or oven with a burning heat so great that my sighs would not have made it more scorching still; and when it happens that I have her somewhere near, I give off sparks like iron in a red-hot fire; and I want to say so much, when she waits on me to speak, that I say less than I would if I were not in such a hurry.

S'avvien che la mi rida pure un poco
o mi saluti in mezzo della via,   50
mi levo come polvere dal foco
o di bombarda o d'altra artiglieria;
se mi domanda, subito m'affioco,
perdo la voce e la risposta mia,
e subito s'arrende il gran desio,   55
e la speranza cede al poter mio.
    I' sento in me non so che grand'amore,
che quasi arrivere' 'nsino alle stelle;
e quando alcuna volta il vo trar fore,
non ho buco sì grande nella pelle   60
che nol faccia, a uscirne, assa' minore
parere, e le mie cose assai men belle:
c'amore o forza el dirne è grazia sola;
e men ne dice chi più alto vola.
    I' vo pensando al mie viver di prima,   65
inanzi ch'i' t'amassi, com'egli era:
di me non fu ma' chi facesse stima,
perdendo ogni dì il tempo insino a sera;
forse pensavo di cantare in rima
o di ritrarmi da ogni altra schiera?   70
Or si fa 'l nome, o per tristo o per buono,
e sassi pure almen che i' ci sono.
    Tu m'entrasti per gli occhi, ond'io mi spargo,
come grappol d'agresto in un'ampolla,
che doppo 'l collo cresce ov'è più largo;   75
così l'immagin tua, che fuor m'immolla,
dentro per gli occhi cresce, ond'io m'allargo
come pelle ove gonfia la midolla;
entrando in me per sì stretto vïaggio,
che tu mai n'esca ardir creder non aggio.   80
    Come quand'entra in una palla il vento,
che col medesmo fiato l'animella,
come l'apre di fuor, la serra drento,
così l'immagin del tuo volto bella
per gli occhi dentro all'alma venir sento;   85
e come gli apre, poi si serra in quella;
e come palla pugno al primo balzo,
percosso da' tu' occhi al ciel po' m'alzo.

If it happens that she smiles at me, even a little, or greets me in the middle of the street, I explode into the air like gunpowder touched by fire in a cannon or some other piece of artillery; if she asks me something, I immediately get hoarse and lose my voice and my reply, and immediately my great desire gives up, and my hope yields to my inability.

I feel in me a love too great for words, such as would make me ascend to the very stars; but when sometimes I wish to bring it out, I have no hole in my skin so great that, when something does come out, it can avoid making my love seem much smaller, and everything about me less beautiful: for love, or the power to express it, is a grace alone; and he says less who flies highest.

I think over my previous way of life, before I fell in love with you: no one thought highly of me, since I wasted time all day and every day; was I perhaps thinking of writing poetry or of withdrawing from the common crowd? Now, for better or for worse, my name is on people's lips, and they certainly know at least that I exist.

You entered me through my eyes (which make me dissolve in tears) as a bunch of unripe grapes goes into a bottle, spreading out below the neck where the phial is wider; your image (which outside makes me wet with tears) does likewise: after passing through my eyes it spreads out, so that I expand like skin that is swollen by fat; since you entered me by such a narrow passage, I cannot dare to believe that you will ever come out.

Just as air enters a ball in such a way that the same breath which opens the valve from outside closes it from within, so do I feel the image of your beautiful face come within my soul through my eyes: as it opens my eyes, so it shuts itself in my soul; and like a ball banged by a fist on its first bounce, when struck by your eyes I at once rise up to heaven.

Perché non basta a una donna bella
goder le lode d'un amante solo,   90
ché suo beltà potre' morir con ella;
dunche, s'i' t'amo, reverisco e colo,
al merito 'l poter poco favella;
c'un zoppo non pareggia un lento volo,
né gira 'l sol per un sol suo mercede,   95
ma per ogni occhio san c'al mondo vede.
  I' non posso pensar come 'l cor m'ardi,
passando a quel per gli occhi sempre molli,
che 'l foco spegnerien non ch'e' tuo sguardi.
Tutti e' ripari mie son corti e folli: 100
se l'acqua il foco accende, ogni altro è tardi
a camparmi dal mal ch'i' bramo e volli,
salvo il foco medesmo. O cosa strana,
se 'l mal del foco spesso il foco sana!

55

  I' t'ho comprato, ancor che molto caro,
un po' di non so che, che sa di buono,
perc'a l'odor la strada spesso imparo.
Ovunche tu ti sia, dovunch'i' sono,
senz'alcun dubbio ne son certo e chiaro.   5
Se da me ti nascondi, i' tel perdono:
portandol dove vai sempre con teco,
ti troverrei, quand'io fussi ben cieco.

56

  Vivo della mie morte e, se ben guardo,
felice vivo d'infelice sorte;
e chi viver non sa d'angoscia e morte,
nel foco venga, ov'io mi struggo e ardo.

57

  S'i' vivo più di chi più m'arde e cuoce,
quante più legne o vento il foco accende,
tanto più chi m'uccide mi difende,
e più mi giova dove più mi nuoce.

Since it is not enough for a beautiful woman to enjoy the praise of one lover only, because her beauty might die with such meagre nourishment, if I love, reverence and venerate you, my powers say little compared to your merits: for a lame walk does not match flight however slow, and the sun does not move round for the benefit of one person only, but for every eye in the world with healthy sight.

I cannot understand how you burn my heart, passing to it through eyes which are always so wet that they would extinguish not just your looks but a fire. All my defences are inadequate and vain: if fire sets water alight, everything else is insufficient to free me from the evil which I wish and long for, except fire itself. What a strange thing it is, that often the remedy for fire's evil is fire itself!

Incomplete series of thirteen octaves, c. 1531–2.

55

Dear though it is, I have bought you a little of I know not what; it has a fine smell, so that from its scent I often learn the way. Wherever I am, I shall without the slightest doubt be clear and certain about your whereabouts. If you hide from me, I shall forgive you: since you always carry it with you wherever you go, I should find you even if I were totally blind.

Octave, c. 1531–2.

56

I live from my death and, if I judge correctly, I happily live from an unhappy lot; and if anyone does not know what it is to live from anguish and death, let him come into the fire where I destroy myself and burn.

Quatrain, possibly for Tommaso Cavalieri, c. 1532.

57

Since I live from him who most burns and roasts me, the more wood or wind stirs up the fire the more he who kills me protects me, and helps me most where he most does me harm.

Quatrain, possibly for Tommaso Cavalieri, c. 1532.

58

Se l'immortal desio, c'alza e corregge
gli altrui pensier, traessi e' mie di fore,
forse c'ancor nella casa d'Amore
farie pietoso chi spietato regge.

Ma perché l'alma per divina legge   5
ha lunga vita, e 'l corpo in breve muore,
non può 'l senso suo lode o suo valore
appien descriver quel c'appien non legge.

Dunche, oilmè! come sarà udita
la casta voglia che 'l cor dentro incende   10
da chi sempre se stesso in altrui vede?

La mie cara giornata m'è impedita
col mie signor c'alle menzogne attende,
c'a dire il ver, bugiardo è chi nol crede.

59

S'un casto amor, s'una pietà superna,
s'una fortuna infra dua amanti equale,
s'un'aspra sorte all'un dell'altro cale,
s'un spirto, s'un voler duo cor governa;

s'un'anima in duo corpi è fatta etterna,   5
ambo levando al cielo e con pari ale;
s'Amor d'un colpo e d'un dorato strale
le viscer di duo petti arda e discerna;

s'amar l'un l'altro e nessun se medesmo,
d'un gusto e d'un diletto, a tal mercede   10
c'a un fin voglia l'uno e l'altro porre:

se mille e mille, non sarien centesmo
a tal nodo d'amore, a tanta fede;
e sol l'isdegno il può rompere e sciorre.

60

Tu sa' ch'i' so, signor mie, che tu sai
ch'i' vengo per goderti più da presso,
e sai ch'i' so che tu sa' ch'i' son desso:
a che più indugio a salutarci omai?

58

If desire of the immortal, which raises and directs men's thoughts aright, were to make mine show clearly, that would perhaps make merciful him who rules without mercy still in the realm of Love.

But since by divine law the soul has a long life, while the body after a short time dies, the senses cannot fully tell the soul's praise or worth, since this they cannot fully perceive.

Alas, then, how shall the chaste desire which sets aflame my heart within be heard by those who always see themselves in others?

I am shut off from the dear company of my lord who pays heed to falsehoods, while, if truth be told, he is a liar who does not believe it.

Sonnet, probably for Tommaso Cavalieri, late 1532 or after.

59

If one chaste love, if one sublime compassion, if one fortune affects two lovers equally, if one harsh fate matters as much to both, if one spirit, if one will rules two hearts;

if one soul in two bodies is made eternal, lifting both to heaven and with the same wings; if Love with one blow and with one golden arrow burns and tests the bowels in two bosoms;

if each loves the other, and neither himself, with one taste and with one delight, with this reward that both direct their will to the one end;

if these were multiplied a thousand times and more, they would not make a hundredth part of such a bond of love, and of such great faithfulness; and only disdain can break and dissolve it.

Sonnet, for Tommaso Cavalieri, late 1532 or after.

60

You know that I know, my lord, that you know that I come here to enjoy you nearer at hand, and you know that I know that you know who I really am: why then this hesitation to greet each other, even now?

Se vera è la speranza che mi dai,   5
se vero è 'l gran desio che m'è concesso,
rompasi il mur fra l'uno e l'altra messo,
ché doppia forza hann' i celati guai.
    S'i' amo sol di te, signor mie caro,
quel che di te più ami, non ti sdegni,   10
ché l'un dell'altro spirto s'innamora.
    Quel che nel tuo bel volto bramo e 'mparo,
e mal compres' è dagli umani ingegni,
chi 'l vuol saper convien che prima mora.

61

S'i' avessi creduto al primo sguardo
di quest'alma fenice al caldo sole
rinnovarmi per foco, come suole
nell'ultima vecchiezza, ond'io tutt'ardo,
    qual più veloce cervio o lince o pardo   5
segue 'l suo bene e fugge quel che dole,
agli atti, al riso, all'oneste parole
sarie cors'anzi, ond'or son presto e tardo.
    Ma perché più dolermi, po' ch'i' veggio
negli occhi di quest'angel lieto e solo   10
mie pace, mie riposo e mie salute?
    Forse che prima sarie stato il peggio
vederlo, udirlo, s'or di pari a volo
seco m'impenna a seguir suo virtute.

62

Sol pur col foco il fabbro il ferro stende
al concetto suo caro e bel lavoro,
né senza foco alcuno artista l'oro
al sommo grado suo raffina e rende;
    né l'unica fenice sé riprende   5
se non prim'arsa; ond'io, s'ardendo moro,
spero più chiar resurger tra coloro
che morte accresce e 'l tempo non offende.
    Del foco, di ch'i' parlo, ho gran ventura
c'ancor per rinnovarmi abbi in me loco,   10
sendo già quasi nel numer de' morti.

If the hope that you give me is true, if the great desire that has been granted me is true, let the wall raised up between these two be broken down, for hidden difficulties have a double force.

If in you, my dear lord, I love only what you most love in yourself, do not be disdainful, for it is simply one spirit loving the other.

What I long for and discover in your lovely face, and what is badly understood by human minds – whoever would know this must first die.

Sonnet, for Tommaso Cavalieri, late 1532 or after.

61

If I had believed that at the first sight of this dear phoenix in the hot sun I should renew myself through fire, as does that bird in its extreme old age, a fire in which my whole being burns,

then as the swiftest deer or lynx or leopard seeks its good and flees what does it harm, I should before this have run to his actions, smile and virtuous words, where now I am eager but slow.

But why go on lamenting, since I see in the eyes of this happy angel alone my peace, my rest and my salvation?

Perhaps it would have been for the worse to have seen and heard him before, if he now gives me wings like his to fly with him, following where his virtue leads.

Sonnet, for Tommaso Cavalieri, late 1532 or after.

62

It is only with fire that a smith can shape iron into a beautiful and cherished work in accordance with his concept, and without fire no craftsman can refine his gold and bring it to the highest quality;

nor can the unique phoenix recover life unless it first be burned; likewise, if I die by burning, I hope to rise again to a purer life among those whom death enriches and time no longer harms.

It is my good fortune that the fire of which I speak has even now taken hold in me to renew me, when I am already almost numbered among the dead.

O ver, s'al cielo ascende per natura,
al suo elemento, e ch'io converso in foco
sie, come fie che seco non mi porti?

63

Sì amico al freddo sasso è 'l foco interno
che, di quel tratto, se lo circumscrive,
che l'arda e spezzi, in qualche modo vive,
legando con sé gli altri in loco etterno.
    E se 'n fornace dura, istate e verno   5
vince, e 'n più pregio che prima s'ascrive,
come purgata infra l'altre alte e dive
alma nel ciel tornasse da l'inferno.
    Così tratto di me, se mi dissolve
il foco, che m'è dentro occulto gioco,   10
arso e po' spento aver più vita posso.
    Dunche, s'i' vivo, fatto fummo e polve,
etterno ben sarò, s'induro al foco;
da tale oro e non ferro son percosso.

64

Se 'l foco il sasso rompe e 'l ferro squaglia,
figlio del lor medesmo e duro interno,
che farà 'l più ardente dell'inferno
d'un nimico covon secco di paglia?

65

In quel medesmo tempo ch'io v'adoro,
la memoria del mie stato infelice
nel pensier mi ritorna, e piange e dice:
ben ama chi ben arde, ov'io dimoro.
    Però che scudo fo di tutti loro...   5

How can it be, then, if fire by nature ascends to the heavens, to its proper sphere, and I am turned to fire, that it does not carry me upwards along with it?

Sonnet, probably for Tommaso Cavalieri, late 1532 or after. *[1]

63

So friendly to the cold stone is the fire within it that if, when drawn forth from it, the fire so surrounds it that it burns and breaks it, the stone lives on in a certain way, binding with its substance other stones into an eternal place.

And if it survives in the furnace, it will defeat summer and winter, and become more highly prized than formerly, like a soul which after being purged takes its place among the other noble and divine souls, having returned to heaven from hell.

Likewise, if the fire that plays secretly within me when once drawn forth dissolves me, I then, though burned to the point of being spent, may have a fuller life.

So if, reduced to smoke and dust, I live after enduring in the fire, I shall indeed be eternal: it is by gold, then, not by iron that I am struck.

Sonnet, of uncertain date. *

64

If fire shatters stone and melts iron, though it be the child of those same hard substances, what will a fire hotter than hell's do to something quite the opposite, a dry sheaf of straw?

Quatrain, of uncertain date.

65

During the very time that I adore you, the memory of my unhappy state returns to my thoughts, and says tearfully: 'He truly loves who truly burns, which is the state I live in.'

Even though I make of them all a shield ....
....

Unfinished sonnet, c. 1532 or after.

---

[1] On the significance of the asterisk at the end of some of the notes, see above p. xxvii.

66

Forse perché d'altrui pietà mi vegna,
perché dell'altrui colpe più non rida,
nel mie propio valor, senz'altra guida,
caduta è l'alma che fu già sì degna.
Né so qual militar sott'altra insegna   5
non che da vincer, da campar più fida,
sie che 'l tumulto dell'avverse strida
non pèra, ove 'l poter tuo non sostegna.
O carne, o sangue, o legno, o doglia strema,
giusto per vo' si facci el mie peccato,   10
di ch'i' pur nacqui, e tal fu 'l padre mio.
Tu sol se' buon; la tuo pietà suprema
soccorra al mie preditto iniquo stato,
sì presso a morte e sì lontan da Dio.

67

Nuovo piacere e di maggiore stima
veder l'ardite capre sopr'un sasso
montar, pascendo or questa or quella cima,
e 'l mastro lor, con aspre note, al basso,
sfogare el cor colla suo rozza rima,   5
sonando or fermo, e or con lento passo,
e la suo vaga, che ha 'l cor di ferro,
star co' porci, in contegno, sott'un cerro;
quant'è veder 'n un eminente loco
e di pagli' e di terra el loro ospizio: 10
chi ingombra 'l desco e chi fa fora 'l foco,
sott'a quel faggio ch'è più lor propizio;
chi ingrassa e gratta 'l porco, e prende gioco,
chi doma 'l ciuco col basto primizio;
el vecchio gode e fa poche parole,   15
fuor dell'uscio a sedere, e stassi al sole.

66

Perhaps it is to make me have pity on others, to make me no longer laugh at others' faults, that, relying on my own strength, looking to no other guide, my soul has fallen that was once so worthy.

I know no other standard under which to fight that will give greater hope, not of victory but of escape, so that the tumult of the hostile shouts may not cause me to perish, where your power does not sustain me.

Oh flesh, oh blood, oh wood, oh utmost pain, may you atone for my sin, in which I was born, as was my father before me.

You alone are good; may your supreme mercy come to the help of this evil state of mine, so close to death and yet so far from God.

Sonnet, c. 1533.

67

It is a new pleasure, and a worthier one, to watch the bold goats clambering up the rocks, grazing first on one summit then on another, and to watch their shepherd down below: in a rough voice he pours out his heart in unpolished songs, sometimes standing still as he plays, sometimes walking slowly about, while the one for whom he yearns, who has a heart of iron, looks after the pigs, quite unconcerned, under an oak tree;

it is no less pleasing to see on high ground their dwelling place made of straw and earth: one person is setting the table, while another is lighting a fire outside, beneath that beech tree which best gives them shade; another again feeds up the pig, and scratches it and teases it, while someone else breaks in the donkey with its first pack-saddle; the old man enjoys himself and says little, as he sits outside the door taking the sun.

Di fuor dentro si vede quel che hanno:
pace sanza oro e sanza sete alcuna.
El giorno c'a solcare i colli vanno,
contar puo' lor ricchezze ad una ad una.   20
Non han serrami e non temon di danno;
lascion la casa aperta alla fortuna;
po', doppo l'opra, lieti el sonno tentano;
sazi di ghiande, in sul fien s'adormentano.

L'invidia non ha loco in questo stato;   25
la superbia se stessa si divora.
Avide son di qualche verde prato,
o di quell'erba che più bella infiora.
Il lor sommo tesoro è uno arato,
e 'l bomero è la gemma che gli onora;   30
un paio di ceste è la credenza loro,
e le pale e le zappe e' vasi d'oro.

O avarizia cieca, o bassi ingegni,
che disusate 'l ben della natura!
Cercando l'or, le terre e ' ricchi regni,   35
vostre imprese superbia ha forte e dura.
L'accidia, la lussuria par v'insegni;
l'invidia 'l mal d'altrui provvede e cura:
non vi scorgete, in insaziabil foco,
che 'l tempo è breve e 'l necessario è poco.   40

Color c'anticamente, al secol vecchio,
si trasser fame e sete d'acqua e ghiande
vi sieno esemplo, scorta, lume e specchio,
e freno alle delizie, alle vivande.
Porgete al mie parlare un po' l'orecchio: 45
colui che 'l mondo impera, e ch'è sì grande,
ancor disidra, e non ha pace poi;
e 'l villanel la gode co' suo buoi.

D'oro e di gemme, e spaventata in vista,
adorna, la Ricchezza va pensando;   50
ogni vento, ogni pioggia la contrista,
e gli agùri e ' prodigi va notando.
La lieta Povertà, fuggendo, acquista
ogni tesor, né pensa come o quando;
secur ne' boschi, in panni rozzi e bigi,   55
fuor d'obrighi, di cure e di letigi.

From what appears on the outside one sees what they have within: peace without gold and without any thirst for it. On the days that they go to plough the hills, you can count their riches one by one. They have no locks and fear no harm from this; they leave their houses open to fortune; once their work is done, they happily settle down to sleep; their hunger fully satisfied by acorns, they take their rest on hay.

Envy has no place in this condition, pride there is self consuming. They set their hearts on some green meadow, or on that grass which is most lovely with flower. Their highest treasure is a plough, its blade the gem that brings them honour; a pair of baskets is their sideboard, shovels and hoes their vessels of gold.

Oh blind avarice, oh low minds who make ill use of the goods given by nature! As you seek gold, lands and rich kingdoms, hard, stiff pride governs your actions. Sloth and luxury seem to be your teachers; envy plots and plans the downfall of others; it passes you by, in your insatiable burning, that time is short and little is necessary.

Those who in ancient times, in centuries long past, satisfied their hunger with acorns and their thirst with water, should be for you example, guide, light and mirror, and a curb on your pleasures and your feastings. Give ear a little to what I have to say: he who rules the world, despite being so great, still desires more and thus lacks peace, while the peasant with his oxen enjoys it.

Adorned with gold and gems, but with fear written on her face, Wealth is always preoccupied: every wind, every shower troubles her, and she is always taking account of signs and portents. Happy Poverty in fleeing from all treasure finds it, and does not think on how or when, safe in the woods, in plain, rough clothes, free of obligations, care and quarrels.

L'avere e 'l dar, l'usanze streme e strane,
el meglio e 'l peggio, e le cime dell'arte
al villanel son tutte cose piane,
e l'erba e l'acqua e 'l latte è la sua parte;   60
e 'l cantar rozzo, e ' calli delle mane,
è 'l dieci e 'l cento e ' conti e le suo carte
dell'usura che 'n terra surger vede;
e senza affanno alla fortuna cede.
    Onora e ama e teme e prega Dio   65
pe' pascol, per l'armento e pel lavoro,
con fede, con ispeme e con desio,
per la gravida vacca e pel bel toro.
El Dubbio, el Forse, el Come, el Perché rio
no 'l può ma' far, ché non istà fra loro: 70
se con semplice fede adora e prega
Iddio e 'l ciel, l'un lega e l'altro piega.
    El Dubbio armato e zoppo si figura,
e va saltando come la locuste,
tremando d'ogni tempo per natura,   75
qual suole al vento far canna paluste.
El Perché è magro, e 'ntorn'alla cintura
ha molte chiave, e non son tanto giuste,
c'agugina gl'ingegni della porta,
e va di notte, e 'l buio è la suo scorta.   80
    El Come e 'l Forse son parenti stretti,
e son giganti di sì grande altezza,
c'al sol andar ciascun par si diletti,
e ciechi fur per mirar suo chiarezza;
e quello alle città co' fieri petti   85
tengon, per tutto adombran lor bellezza;
e van per vie fra sassi erte e distorte,
tentando colle man qual istà forte.
    Povero e nudo e sol se ne va 'l Vero,
che fra la gente umìle ha gran valore: 90
un occhio ha sol, qual è lucente e mero,
e 'l corpo ha d'oro, e d'adamante 'l core;
e negli affanni cresce e fassi altero,
e 'n mille luoghi nasce, se 'n un muore;
di fuor verdeggia sì come smeraldo,   95
e sta co' suo fedel costante e saldo.

Having and giving, strained and strange behaviour, better and worse, the heights of art – all these to the peasant are matters of indifference; his concern is with grass, water and milk; rough song and callouses on his hand have for him the importance that tens and hundreds, accounts and registers, have for usurers, who are seen springing up everywhere; and he bends without struggle to fortune.

He honours, loves and fears God, and prays to him for his pastures, for his herd, for his work; with faith, hope and desire he prays for his pregnant cow and for his beautiful bull. Evil Doubt, Perhaps, How and Why can do him no harm, because he never keeps their company; when with simple faith he adores and prays to God and heaven, he binds the latter and bends the former to him.

Doubt is depicted as armed and lame, and moves around by jumping like a locust, trembling all the time by his very nature, like a marshy reed in the wind. Why is thin, and has many keys hanging from his belt: these do not fit very well, so he must force the locks of the doors; he goes about at night, with darkness as his escort.

How and Perhaps are close relatives; they are giants so tall that they both seem to take delight in reaching up to the sun, though gazing into its brightness has made them blind; and with their fierce chests they keep the sun hidden from the cities, everywhere casting a shadow over the beauty of these; and they move along steep and twisting paths among rocks, testing with their hands which will hold.

Truth goes about poor, naked and alone, being held in great esteem among humble people; he has only one eye, though this is bright and clear, and a body made of gold, a heart of diamond; when troubles come he grows in strength and dignity, and if he dies in one place he is born in a thousand others; he is green in appearance, like an emerald, and with those who are faithful to him he is staunch and strong.

Cogli occhi onesti e bassi in ver' la terra,
vestito d'oro e di vari ricami,
il Falso va, c'a' iusti sol fa guerra;
ipocrito, di fuor par c'ognuno ami;   100
perch'è di ghiaccio, al sol si cuopre e serra;
sempre sta 'n corte, e par che l'ombra brami;
e ha per suo sostegno e compagnia
la Fraude, la Discordia e la Bugia.

L'Adulazion v'è poi, ch'è pien d'affanni,   105
giovane destra e di bella persona;
di più color coperta di più panni,
che 'l cielo a primavera a' fior non dona:
ottien ciò che la vuol con dolci inganni,
e sol di quel che piace altrui ragiona;   110
ha 'l pianto e 'l riso in una voglia sola;
cogli occhi adora, e con le mani invola.

Non è sol madre in corte all'opre orrende,
ma è lor balia ancora, e col suo latte
le cresce, l'aümenta e le difende.   115

68

Un gigante v'è ancor, d'altezza tanta
che da' sua occhi noi qua giù non vede,
e molte volte ha ricoperta e franta
una città colla pianta del piede;
al sole aspira e l'alte torre pianta   5
per aggiunger al cielo, e non lo vede,
chè 'l corpo suo, così robusto e magno,
un occhio ha solo e quell'ha 'n un calcagno.

Vede per terra le cose passate,
e 'l capo ha fermo e prossim'a le stelle;   10
di qua giù se ne vede dua giornate
delle gran gambe, e irsut' ha la pelle;
da indi in su non ha verno né state,
ché la stagion gli sono equali e belle;
e come 'l ciel fa pari alla suo fronte,   15
in terra al pian col piè fa ogni monte.

With eyes modestly cast down, clothed in robes of gold richly embroidered, Falsehood goes about, waging war only on the just; hypocrite that he is, he seems on the outside to love everyone; being made of ice, he hides and shuts himself off from the sun; he is always to be found in courts, and seems to yearn for shade; he turns for support and companionship to Fraud, Discord and Lying.

Then there is Flattery, who is full of troubles, a nimble young woman of beautiful appearance; the various clothes she wears have more colours than the heavens give to flowers in springtime: she gets what she wants with sweet deceits, and will say only what others want to hear; she will as easily put on tears as laughter; she adores with her eyes, while stealing with her hands.

In courts she is not only mother to horrible deeds but their wet-nurse too, and with her milk nourishes them, builds them up, and protects them.

Incomplete series of fourteen octaves, before 1534.

68

Then there is a giant, so tall that his eyes cannot see down to us here below, and he has many times covered and smashed a whole city with the sole of his foot; he aspires to be as tall as the sun and sets up high towers to reach to heaven, but he does not see it, for his body, despite being so robust and large, has only one eye and that is set in one of his heels.

He sees near to the ground only what lies behind, and he holds his head firm and close to the stars; from here below one can see that his legs are two days' journey in length, and their skin is hairy; from there on up he feels neither hot nor cold, for the seasons to him are all equally beautiful; and just as he has brought his forehead to the same height as heaven, so on earth he makes every mountain level with his step.

Com'a noi è 'l minuzzol dell'arena,
sotto la pianta a lui son le montagne;
fra ' folti pel delle suo gambe mena
diverse forme mostruose e magne: 20
per mosca vi sarebbe una balena;
e sol si turba e sol s'attrista e piagne
quando in quell'occhio il vento seco tira
fummo o festuca o polvere che gira.
    Una gran vecchia pigra e lenta ha seco,   25
che latta e mamma l'orribil figura,
e 'l suo arrogante, temerario e cieco
ardir conforta e sempre rassicura.
Fuor di lui stassi in un serrato speco,
nelle gran rocche e dentro all'alte mura;   30
quand'è lui in ozio, e le' in tenebre vive,
e sol inopia nel popol prescrive.
    Palida e gialla, e nel suo grave seno
il segno porta sol del suo signore:
cresce del mal d'altrui, del ben vien meno,   35
né s'empie per cibarsi a tutte l'ore;
il corso suo non ha termin né freno,
e odia altrui e sé non porta amore;
di pietra ha 'l core e di ferro le braccia,
e nel suo ventre il mare e ' monti caccia.   40
    Sette lor nati van sopra la terra,
che cercan tutto l'uno e l'altro polo,
e solo a' iusti fanno insidie e guerra,
e mille capi ha ciascun per sé solo.
L'etterno abisso per lor s'apre e serra,   45
tal preda fan nell'universo stuolo;
e lor membra ci prendon passo passo,
come edera fa el mur fra sasso e sasso.

69

Ben provvide natura, né conviene
a tanta crudeltà minor bellezza,
ché l'un contrario l'altro ha temperato.
    Così può 'l viso vostro le mie pene
tante temprar con piccola dolcezza,   5
e lieve fare quelle e me beato.

As tiny grains of sand are to us so to him are the mountains under his tread; in among the hairy skin of his legs he carries various large and monstrous forms; a whale there would be like a fly; he is only troubled, only saddened and tearful, when the wind carries into that eye smoke or bits of straw or dust blowing about.

He has with him a large, old lady, lazy and slow, who suckles and nourishes the horrible figure and always supports and encourages his arrogant, rash and blind boldness. When not with him, she lives in a closed-off cave, in the great rocks and behind high walls; while he is at rest, she lives in darkness, concerned only with condemning people to misery.

Pale and yellow, she bears only in her heavy bosom the sign of her lord; she gains strength from others' ills, and wastes away at their good, and is never full even though she eats all the time; her headlong course knows no limit or restraint, she hates everyone and has no love for herself; her heart is made of stone, her arms of iron, and she thrusts the sea and the mountains into her stomach.

Their seven offspring wander the earth, searching everywhere from one pole to the other; it is only for the just that they lay traps, only on them do they wage war; and each and every one has a thousand heads. They prey so heavily on the whole human crowd that the eternal abyss is always opening and closing for them; and their limbs take us in their grasp little by little, as ivy does a wall, stone by stone.

Series of six octaves, before 1534.

69

Nature provided wisely, since no less beauty should have been joined to such great cruelty, for one contrary has tempered the other.

So your face can temper my immense sufferings with a little sweetness, and make them light and me happy.

Partial sonnet, before 1534.

70

Crudele stella, anzi crudele arbitrio
che 'l potere e 'l voler mi stringe e lega;
né si travaglia chiara stella in cielo
dal giorno [in qua?] che mie vela disciolse,
ond'io errando e vagabondo andai,   5
qual vano legno gira a tutti e' venti.
    Or son qui, lasso, e all'incesi venti
convien varar mie legno, e senza arbitrio
solcar l'alte onde ove mai sempre andai.
Così quagiù si prende, preme e lega   10
quel che lassù già 'll'alber si disciolse,
ond'a me tolsi la dote del cielo.
    Qui non mi regge e non mi spinge il cielo,
ma potenti e terrestri e duri venti,
ché sopra me non so qual si disciolse   15
per [darli mano?] e tormi del mio arbitrio.
Così fuor di mie rete altri mi lega.
Mie colpa è, ch'ignorando a quello andai?
    Maladetto [sie] 'l dì che ïo andai
col segno che correva su nel cielo!   20
Se non ch'i' so che 'l giorno el cor non lega,
né sforza l'alma, ne' contrari venti,
contra al nostro largito e sciolto arbitrio,
perché [...] e pruove ci disciolse.
    Dunche, se mai dolor del cor disciolse   25
sospiri ardenti, o se orando andai
fra caldi venti a quel ch'è fuor d'arbitrio,
[...], pietoso de' mie caldi venti,
vede, ode e sente e non m'è contra 'l cielo;
ché scior non si può chi se stesso lega.   30
    Così l'atti suo perde chi si lega,
e salvo sé nessun ma' si disciolse.
E come arbor va retto verso il cielo,
ti prego, Signor mio, se mai andai,
ritorni, come quel che non ha venti,   35
sotto el tüo grande el mïo arbitrio.
    Colui che sciolse e lega 'l mio arbitrio,
ov'io andai agl'importuni venti,
fa' mie vendetta, s' tu mel desti, o cielo.

70

Cruel star, indeed cruel tyranny, that constrains my powers and binds my will, no friendly star in heaven has taken me under its care from the day that my sails were unfurled; and so I have wandered aimlessly, like an empty ship carried this way and that by every wind.

Here I am now, weary, and must launch my boat into the burning winds, and without any choice plough the high waves where I have ever journeyed. This is what happens when one takes that which up there was once taken from the tree (and it then crushes and binds), so that I deprived myself of the gift of heaven.

Here it is not heaven that governs and drives me, but powerful and harsh earthly winds, for some unknown person above me has been unleashed to put me in their hands and deprive me of my free will. So someone else holds me bound, with nets that are not mine. Is it my fault, then, if it was in ignorance that I went towards him?

Cursed be the day that I set out under the sign through which the heavens were then passing! And yet I know the day of birth does not bind the heart, nor force the soul, through hostile winds, to act contrary to the free will bestowed on us, because [...] and sets us free from ordeals.

And so if ever suffering loosed ardent sighs from the heart, or if as I went buffeted by hot winds I prayed to him who is above free will [...], taking pity on my hot winds heaven sees, hears and heeds, and is not ranged against me, for whoever binds himself cannot set himself free.

In fact whoever binds himself loses power over his actions, and no one ever on his own set himself free. But if I ever acted as a tree does in growing straight towards heaven, I beg you, my Lord, to put once more under your great will my will, as one no longer borne about by the winds.

On him towards whom I went, driven by the importunate winds, who once loosed and now binds my will, take revenge for me, oh heaven, for you set him on me.

Incomplete sestina, before 1534.

71

I' l'ho, vostra mercè, per ricevuto
e hollo letto delle volte venti.
Tal pro vi facci alla natura i denti,
co' 'l cibo al corpo quand'egli è pasciuto.
    I' ho pur, poi ch'i' vi lasciai, saputo   5
che Cain fu de' vostri anticedenti,
né voi da quel tralignate altrimenti;
ché, s'altri ha ben, vel pare aver perduto.
    Invidiosi, superbi, al ciel nimici,
la carità del prossimo v'è a noia,   10
e sol del vostro danno siete amici.
    Se ben dice il Poeta, di Pistoia,
istieti a mente, e basta; e se tu dici
ben di Fiorenza, tu mi dai la soia.
        Qual prezïosa gioia   15
è certo ma per te già non si intende,
perché poca virtù non la comprende.

72

Se nel volto per gli occhi il cor si vede,
altro segno non ho più manifesto
della mie fiamma; addunche basti or questo,
signor mie caro, a domandar mercede.
    Forse lo spirto tuo, con maggior fede   5
ch'i' non credo, che sguarda il foco onesto
che m'arde, fie di me pietoso e presto,
come grazia c'abbonda a chi ben chiede.
    O felice quel dì, se questo è certo!
Fermisi in un momento il tempo e l'ore,   10
il giorno e 'l sol nella su' antica traccia;
    acciò ch'i' abbi, e non già per mie merto,
il desïato mie dolce signore
per sempre nell'indegne e pronte braccia.

73

Mentre del foco son scacciata e priva,
morir m'è forza, ove si vive e campa;
e 'l mie cibo è sol quel c'arde e avvampa,
e di quel c'altri muor, convien ch'i' viva.

71

I have received what you sent, thank you, and read it a good twenty times. May your teeth be as much good to you as food to the body when it has been fed.

Since I left you I have come to realize that Cain was among your ancestors, and you are in no way a deviant offspring of his, for if someone else possesses some good you feel you have lost it.

Envious, proud, enemies of heaven, charity shown by others is irksome to you, and you are keen only on what is harmful to you.

If the Poet is right in what he says about Pistoia, keep that in mind, and it will be enough; and if you speak well of Florence, you are trying to make a fool of me.

Florence is indeed a precious jewel, but is certainly not appreciated by you, because a small mind cannot grasp its worth.

Tailed sonnet, possibly for Giovanni da Pistoia, before 1534.

72

Since a person's heart is seen in his face through his eyes, I have no other sign that more clearly shows the flame within me; so now let this be enough, my sweet lord, to ask for mercy.

Perhaps your spirit, responding more warmly than I dare believe, when it sees the virtuous fire that burns me, will take pity on me and draw near, just as grace abounds for those who truly ask for it.

Happy will that day be when it comes, as it surely must! May time and the passing hours stop at that very moment, and the day, and the sun in its ancient course,

so that I may have, though not through any merit of mine, my sweet, longed-for lord forever in my unworthy and yet ready arms.

Sonnet, for Tommaso Cavalieri, probably early 1533.

73

When I am driven from the fire and deprived of it, this can only bring me death, while to others it means life and safety; for my food is only what burns and scorches, and in what brings others death I must find life.

Quatrain, probably for Tommaso Cavalieri, probably 1533.

74

I' piango, i' ardo, i' mi consumo, e 'l core
di questo si nutrisce. O dolce sorte!
chi è che viva sol della suo morte,
come fo io d'affanni e di dolore?
　　Ahi! crudele arcier, tu sai ben l'ore   5
da far tranquille l'angosciose e corte
miserie nostre con la tuo man forte;
ché chi vive di morte mai non muore.

75

Egli è pur troppo a rimirarsi intorno
chi con la vista ancide i circustanti
sol per mostrarsi andar diporto attorno.
　　Egli è pur troppo a chi fa notte il giorno,
scurando il sol co' vaghi e be' sembianti,   5
aprirgli spesso, e chi con risi e canti
ammuta altrui non esser meno adorno.

76

Non so se s'è la desïata luce
del suo primo fattor, che l'alma sente,
o se dalla memoria della gente
alcun'altra beltà nel cor traluce;
　　o se fama o se sogno alcun produce   5
agli occhi manifesto, al cor presente,
di sé lasciando un non so che cocente
ch'è forse or quel c'a pianger mi conduce.
　　Quel ch'i' sento e ch'i' cerco e chi mi guidi
meco non è; né so ben veder dove   10
trovar mel possa, e par c'altri mel mostri.
　　Questo, signor, m'avvien, po' ch'i' vi vidi,
c'un dolce amaro, un sì e no mi muove:
certo saranno stati gli occhi vostri.

74

I weep, I burn, I waste away, and on this the heart nourishes itself. Oh sweet destiny! Who else is there who lives only on what brings death, as I do on troubles and sorrow?

Alas, cruel archer, you know just when to bring rest to our anguished and brief miseries with your strong arm; for whoever lives on death will never die.

Partial sonnet, probably for Tommaso Cavalieri, probably 1533.

75

It really is too much that he who with a look kills those standing by should gaze around only to show that he goes about for his own amusement.

It really is too much that he who makes day night, darkening the sun with his bright and beautiful eyes, should often open them, and that he who with smiles and songs strikes others dumb should not be less bountifully blessed.

Partial sonnet, probably for Tommaso Cavalieri, c. 1533.

76

I do not know if it is the very longed-for light of the one who first made it that my soul feels; or if some other beauty lodged in my memory of people shines in my heart;

or if fame or dreaming brings someone before my eyes, or makes him present in my heart, leaving behind a burning trace I cannot describe – perhaps it is this which draws my heart to tears.

What I feel and what I seek, and who may guide me to it, lie beyond my power; and I cannot clearly see where I may find it, though it seems that someone may show me.

This, lord, is what has happened to me from the time I saw you: something bitter and sweet, a yes and no move me: it is certainly your eyes that have brought this about.

Sonnet, probably for Tommaso Cavalieri in its final version, 1533–42/6.

77

Se 'l foco fusse alla bellezza equale
degli occhi vostri, che da que' si parte,
non avrie 'l mondo sì gelata parte
che non ardessi com'acceso strale.
　Ma 'l ciel, pietoso d'ogni nostro male,　　　　　　5
a noi d'ogni beltà, che 'n voi comparte,
la visiva virtù toglie e diparte
per tranquillar la vita aspr'e mortale.
　Non è par dunche il foco alla beltate,
ché sol di quel s'infiamma e s'innamora　　　　　　10
altri del bel del ciel, ch'è da lui inteso.
　Così n'avvien, signore, in questa etate:
se non vi par per voi ch'i' arda e mora,
poca capacità m'ha poco acceso.

78

Dal dolce pianto al doloroso riso,
da una etterna a una corta pace
caduto son: là dove 'l ver si tace,
soprasta 'l senso a quel da lui diviso.
　Né so se dal mie core o dal tuo viso　　　　　　5
la colpa vien del mal, che men dispiace
quante più cresce, o dall'ardente face
de gli occhi tuo rubati al paradiso.
　La tuo beltà non è cosa mortale,
ma fatta su dal ciel fra noi divina;　　　　　　10
ond'io perdendo ardendo mi conforto,
　c'appresso a te non esser posso tale.
Se l'arme il ciel del mie morir destina,
chi può, s'i' muoio, dir c'abbiate il torto?

79

Felice spirto, che con zelo ardente,
vecchio alla morte, in vita il mio cor tieni,
e fra mill'altri tuo diletti e beni
me sol saluti fra più nobil gente;

77

If the fire that springs from your eyes were equal to their beauty, the world would have no part so frozen that it would not burn like a flaming arrow.

But heaven, merciful towards our every ill, blocks and distances our power to see from the entire beauty that is has lavished on you, to make peaceful our harsh and mortal life.

My fire is not, then, equal to that beauty, for men are inflamed by and fall in love with only that part of heaven's beauty which they can understand.

This is what happens to me, lord, at this age: if it does not seem to you that for you I burn and die, my slight ability is the cause of my weak flame.

Sonnet, very probably for Tommaso Cavalieri, probably mid 1533.

78

From sweet lament to suffering smile, from an eternal to a passing peace have I fallen: for when the truth keeps silent in someone, the senses, cut off from the truth, dominate in him.

And I do not know what is to be blamed for the evil which displeases less the more it grows: whether my heart, or your face, or the burning light of your eyes stolen from paradise.

Your beauty is no mortal thing, but something divine among us made in heaven above; so when the burning overwhelms me I comfort myself

that near you I could not be otherwise. If heaven destines the weapons to bring about my death, who could say, if I should die, that the fault were yours?

Sonnet, probably for Tommaso Cavalieri, c. 1533.

79

Happy spirit, who, with eager burning, keep alive my heart which old age turns towards death, and, among the thousand other delights and blessings you bring, greet me alone among more noble people;

come mi fusti agli occhi, or alla mente,　　　　5
per l'altru' fiate a consolar mi vieni,
onde la speme il duol par che raffreni,
che non men che 'l disio l'anima sente.

Dunche, trovando in te chi per me parla
grazia di te per me fra tante cure,　　　　10
tal grazia ne ringrazia chi ti scrive.

Che sconcia e grande usur saria a farla,
donandoti turpissime pitture
per rïaver persone belle e vive.

80

I' mi credetti, il primo giorno ch'io
mira' tante bellezze uniche e sole,
fermar gli occhi com'aquila nel sole
nella minor di tante ch'i' desio.

Po' conosciut'ho il fallo e l'erro mio:　　　　5
ché chi senz'ale un angel seguir vole,
il seme a' sassi, al vento le parole
indarno isparge, e l'intelletto a Dio.

Dunche, s'appresso il cor non mi sopporta
l'infinita beltà che gli occhi abbaglia,　　　　10
né di lontan par m'assicuri o fidi,

che fie di me? qual guida o qual scorta
fie che con teco ma' mi giovi o vaglia,
s'appresso m'ardi e nel partir m'uccidi?

81

Ogni cosa ch'i' veggio mi consiglia
e priega e forza ch'i' vi segua e ami;
ché quel che non è voi non è 'l mie bene.
Amor, che sprezza ogni altra maraviglia,
per mie salute vuol ch'i' cerchi e brami　　　　5
voi, sole, solo; e così l'alma tiene
d'ogni alta spene e d'ogni valor priva;
e vuol ch'i' arda e viva
non sol di voi, ma chi di voi somiglia
degli occhi e delle ciglia alcuna parte.　　　　10
E chi da voi si parte,
occhi, mie vita, non ha luce poi;
ché 'l ciel non è dove non siate voi.

as once to my eyes so now to my mind you come to give a consolation others cannot offer; and so hope seems to curb the suffering which my soul feels no less than desire.

Since, then, he who speaks for me finds in you a graciousness towards me among your many concerns, he who writes to you thanks you for such graciousness.

For it would be vile usury on a grand scale were I to give you pictures of the basest kind, and in return receive most beautiful and living people.

Sonnet, for Tommaso Cavalieri, c. 1533.

80

On the day that I first gazed on so many unique, singular beauties, I thought I should be able to fix my eyes, like the eagle on the sun, on the least of the many I desire.

Then I recognized my fault and error: for if someone who lacked wings wished to pursue an angel, this would be as useless as throwing seeds on stones, words on the wind, and the intellect on God.

If, then, when near, the infinite beauty that dazzles my eyes does not allow my heart to bear up, and from afar seems not to reassure me or give me confidence,

what will become of me? What guide or escort can there be who in regard of you will ever give me help or strength, if you, when near, burn me, and, by parting, kill me?

Sonnet, very probably for Tommaso Cavalieri, c. 1533.

81

Everything I see advises, begs and forces me to follow you and love you; for whatever is not you is not my good. Love, who despises everything else however wonderful, for my welfare wishes me to seek and crave for you alone, my sun; and so it keeps my soul deprived of all high hopes and of all strength; and wishes me to burn and live not from you alone but from all whose eyes or brows in any way resemble yours. And anyone who parts from you, oh eyes, my life, loses all light: for heaven is not present where you are not.

Madrigal, probably for Tommaso Cavalieri in its final version, 1526–33/4, revised in 1546. *

82

Non posso altra figura immaginarmi
o di nud'ombra o di terrestre spoglia,
col più alto pensier, tal che mie voglia
contra la tuo beltà di quella s'armi.

Ché da te mosso, tanto scender parmi,   5
c'Amor d'ogni valor mi priva e spoglia,
ond'a pensar di minuir mie doglia
duplicando, la morte viene a darmi.

Però non val che più sproni mie fuga,
doppiando 'l corso alla beltà nemica,   10
ché 'l men dal più veloce non si scosta.

Amor con le sue man gli occhi m'asciuga,
promettendomi cara ogni fatica;
ché vile esser non può chi tanto costa.

83

Veggio nel tuo bel viso, signor mio,
quel che narrar mal puossi in questa vita;
l'anima, della carne ancor vestita,
con esso è già più volte ascesa a Dio.

E se 'l vulgo malvagio, isciocco e rio,   5
di quel che sente, altrui segna e addita,
non è l'intensa voglia men gradita,
l'amor, la fede e l'onesto desio.

A quel pietoso fonte, onde siàn tutti,
s'assembra ogni beltà che qua si vede   10
più c'altra cosa alle persone accorte;

né altro saggio abbiàn né altri frutti
del cielo in terra; e chi v'ama con fede
trascende a Dio e fa dolce la morte.

84

Sì come nella penna e nell'inchiostro
è l'alto e 'l basso e 'l medïocre stile,
e ne' marmi l'immagin ricca e vile,
secondo che 'l sa trar l'ingegno nostro;

82

Not even by raising my thoughts as high as possible can I imagine another figure, whether of pure spirit or of earthly flesh, with which my will may arm itself against your beauty.

For, separated from you, I seem to sink so low that Love deprives and strips me of all strength; so when I think of lessening my sufferings he, doubling them, threatens me with death.

It is useless, then, for me to spur on my flight, doubling the pace at which I fly from hostile beauty, for the less speedy never gains distance on one who moves more swiftly.

Love with his own hands dries my eyes, promising that I shall hold all effort dear: for he who costs so much cannot himself be base.

Sonnet, for Tommaso Cavalieri, c. 1534.

83

I see in your beautiful face, my lord, what in this life words cannot well describe; with it my soul, still clothed in flesh, has already often risen to God.

And if the common people, evil, stupid and base as they are, attribute and assign to others only what they themselves can feel, my intense longing is no less cherished for that, nor my love, faithfulness and virtuous desire.

To those who are wise, nothing more resembles that merciful spring whence all derive than every beauty to be found here;

nor have we any other sign or other fruits of heaven on earth; and he who loves you faithfully rises to God above and holds death sweet.

Sonnet, for Tommaso Cavalieri, c. 1534.

84

Just as in pen and ink there lie all styles from high to low, and, in marble, images rich and feeble, according as our mind knows how to bring each forth;

così, signor mie car, nel petto vostro,   5
quante l'orgoglio è forse ogni atto umile;
ma io sol quel c'a me propio è e simile
ne traggo, come fuor nel viso mostro.

Chi semina sospir, lacrime e doglie,
(l'umor dal ciel terreste, schietto e solo,   10
a vari semi vario si converte),

però pianto e dolor ne miete e coglie;
chi mira alta beltà con sì gran duolo,
ne ritra' doglie e pene acerbe e certe.

85

Com'io ebbi la vostra, signor mio,
cercand'andai fra tutti e' cardinali
e diss'a tre da vostra part' addio.

Al Medico maggior de' nostri mali
mostrai la detta, onde ne rise tanto   5
che 'l naso fe' dua parti dell'occhiali.

Il servito da voi pregiat' e santo
costà e qua, sì come voi scrivete,
n'ebbe piacer, che ne ris'altro tanto.

A quel che tien le cose più secrete   10
del Medico minor non l'ho ancor visto;
farebbes'anche a lui, se fusse prete.

Ècci molt'altri che rinegon Cristo
che voi non siate qua; né dà lor noia,
ché chi non crede si tien manco tristo.   15

Di voi a tutti caverò la foia
di questa vostra; e chi non si contenta
affogar possa per le man del boia.

La Carne, che nel sal si purg' e stenta,
che saria buon per carbonat' ancora,   20
di voi più che di sé par si rammenta.

Il nostro Buonarroto, che v'adora,
visto la vostra, se ben veggio, parmi
c'al ciel si lievi mille volte ogn'ora;

e dice che la vita de' sua marmi   25
non basta a far il vostro nom' eterno,
come lui fanno i divin vostri carmi.

so, my dear lord, in your breast there perhaps may lie as much as pride an attitude of complete humility; but from it I bring forth only what characterizes and resembles me, as my face shows clearly.

The moisture which from the heavens descends to earth, though in itself unmixed and of a single kind, is differently transformed by different seeds; so, too, whoever sows sighs, tears and suffering

reaps and gathers from them lament and pain; and whoever gazes on high beauty with so much pain draws forth from it ·suffering and sorrow sharp and sure.

Sonnet, for Tommaso Cavalieri, c. 1534.

85

When I received your letter, my lord, I went searching among all the cardinals and gave greetings on your behalf to the three.

To the greatest Doctor of our ills I showed what you had written, and he laughed at it so much that his nose split his glasses in two.

He who, as you say, is served by you both there and here, a man greatly esteemed and saintly, was so pleased by it that he laughed just as much.

I have not yet shown it to him who holds the closest secrets of the lesser Doctor; what you say would apply to him, if he were a priest.

There are many others who would deny Christ to have you here; this would not do them any harm, for whoever does not believe is regarded as less of a rogue.

Through this letter I'll take away from everyone the passion to see you, and if anyone is not content with that he can be drowned at the hands of the executioner.

The Meat, which is purged and hardened in salt, and which would also be tasty if done over coals, seems to have you more in mind than himself.

Our Buonarroti, who adores you, having seen your letter, seems to me, if my eyesight isn't faulty, to be raised to heaven a thousand times every hour;

and he says that the life he gives to his marbles would not be enough to make your name eternal, as your divine songs do his.

Ai qual non nuoce né state né verno,
dal temp' esenti e da morte crudele,
che fama di virtù non ha in governo.   30
  E come vostro amico e mio fedele
disse: — Ai dipinti, visti i versi belli,
s'appiccon voti e s'accendon candele.
  Dunque i' son pur nel numero di quelli,
da un goffo pittor senza valore   35
cavato a' pennell' e alberelli.
  Il Bernia ringraziate per mio amore,
che fra tanti lui sol conosc' il vero
di me; ché chi mi stim' è 'n grand'errore.
  Ma la sua disciplin' el lum' intero   40
mi può ben dar, e gran miracol fia,
a far un uom dipint' un uom da vero. —
  Così mi disse; e io per cortesia
vel raccomando quanto so e posso,
che fia l'apportator di questa mia.   45
  Mentre la scrivo a vers'a verso, rosso
diveng'assai, pensando a chi la mando,
send' il mio non professo, goffo e grosso.
  Pur nondimen così mi raccomando
anch'io a voi, e altro non accade;   50
d'ogni tempo son vostro e d'ogni quando.
  A voi nel numer delle cose rade
tutto mi v'offerisco, e non pensate
ch'i' manchi, se 'l cappuccio non mi cade.
  Così vi dico e giuro, e certo siate,   55
ch'i' non farei per me quel che per voi:
e non m'abbiat'a schifo come frate.
  Comandatemi, e fate poi da voi.

86

Ancor che 'l cor già mi premesse tanto,
per mie scampo credendo il gran dolore
n'uscissi con le lacrime e col pianto,
  fortuna al fonte di cotale umore
le radice e le vene ingrassa e 'mpingua   5
per morte, e non per pena o duol minore,
  col tuo partire; onde convien destingua
dal figlio prima e tu morto dipoi,
del quale or parlo, pianto, penna e lingua.

These will be harmed neither by summer nor by winter, being exempt from time and cruel death, which has no power over fame based on virtue.

And as your faithful friend and mine, he said, after seeing your beautiful lines: 'Votive offerings are hung in front of painted figures and candles are lit there.

'So I am certainly among such figures, but one of no value, brought forth by a clumsy painter from his brushes and pots.

'Thank Berni with my love, for he alone among so many knows what I am really like, for anyone who has a high opinion of me is badly mistaken.

'But his teaching can certainly bring me to the true light; and it will be a great miracle to make a painted man a real one.'

This is what he said to me; and I beg leave to commend him to you as much as I possibly can; he will be the bearer of this letter.

As I write it line by line I become quite red, thinking of the one I'm sending it to, for my poetry is rough and clumsy, not that of a professional.

None the less, I commend myself likewise to you; there is nothing else of note; I am always and ever yours.

To you who are numbered among life's special gifts I offer myself wholly; and do not think that I would ever fail you, even if I were to lose my cowl.

So I say and swear to you, and you may rest assured, that I would not do for myself what I would do for you: and do not despise me because I am a friar.

Command me, and then do as you wish.

Capitolo, *for Francesco Berni, late 1533 or early 1534.*

86

Although my heart was already grievously weighed down, I was coming to think that I should find release through my great suffering's being washed away with my tears and crying,

when fortune enlarged and expanded the roots and channels of such water at its source through death, and not through some lesser burden or pain,

with your departure; so I must distinguish when I weep, write or speak between your son who died first and you who died later, of whom I am now speaking.

L'un m'era frate, e tu padre di noi;   10
l'amore a quello, a te l'obrigo strigne:
non so qual pena più mi stringa o nòi.

La memoria 'l fratel pur mi dipigne,
e te sculpisce vivo in mezzo il core,
che 'l core e 'l volto più m'affligge e tigne.   15

Pur mi quieta che il debito, c'all'ore
pagò 'l mio frate acerbo, e tu maturo;
ché manco duole altrui chi vecchio muore.

Tanto all'increscitor men aspro e duro
esser diè 'l caso quant'è più necesse,   20
là dove 'l ver dal senso è più sicuro.

Ma chi è quel che morto non piangesse
suo caro padre, c'ha veder non mai
quel che vedea infinite volte o spesse?

Nostri intensi dolori e nostri guai   25
son come più e men ciascun gli sente:
quant'in me posson tu, Signor, tel sai.

E se ben l'alma alla ragion consente,
tien tanto in collo, che vie più abbondo
po' doppo quella in esser più dolente.   30

E se 'l pensier, nel quale i' mi profondo,
non fussi che 'l ben morto in ciel si ridi
del timor della morte in questo mondo,

crescere' 'l duol; ma ' dolorosi stridi
temprati son d'una credenza ferma   35
che 'l ben vissuto a morte me' s'annidi.

Nostro intelletto dalla carne inferma
è tanto oppresso, che 'l morir più spiace
quanto più 'l falso persuaso afferma.

Novanta volte el sol suo chiara face   40
prim'ha nell'oceàn bagnata e molle,
che tu sie giunto alla divina pace.

Or che nostra miseria el ciel ti tolle,
increscati di me, che morto vivo,
come tuo mezzo qui nascer mi volle.   45

Tu se' del morir morto e fatto divo,
né tem'or più cangiar vita né voglia,
che quasi senza invidia non lo scrivo.

Fortuna e 'l tempo dentro a vostra soglia
non tenta trapassar, per cui s'adduce   50
fra no' dubbia letizia e certa doglia.

One was my brother, and you the father of us both; to him I am bound by love, to you by obligation; I do not know which affliction crushes or torments me more.

My memory indeed paints my brother, but you it sculpts alive within my heart – this more afflicts my heart and stains my face.

Yet it comforts me that, while my brother paid time's debt when he was unripe, you paid it when mature, for if someone dies when he is old this brings us less pain.

To the one who suffers, the loss should be less keen and hard the more it is seen as necessary by that place where truth is safest from the senses.

But who is there who would not weep at the death of his dear father? For he will never again be able to see him whom he has seen over and over again, times without number.

The intensity of our sufferings and our misfortunes depends on how much or little each person feels them: how powerfully they affect me you, Lord, know.

And although my soul does indeed pay heed to reason, it costs it such an effort that afterwards I collapse again into greater suffering.

And if there were not the thought, on which I ponder deeply, that in heaven whoever dies well laughs at the fear of death experienced in this world,

my sorrow would be greater, but sorrowful cries are tempered by a firm belief that anyone who has lived well finds in death a better place to nestle.

Our mind is so weighed down by our weak flesh that dying is seen as more displeasing the more this persuader of falsehoods gains mastery over us.

Ninety times did the sun bathe and soak its bright torch in the ocean before you attained to the divine peace.

Now that heaven has taken you from our misery, have pity on me, who live as one dead, here where by means of you heaven wished me to be born.

You have died to death and become divine, and no longer fear that you will change either life or will – something I cannot write without feeling envy.

Fortune and time do not try to penetrate within your threshold, while among us they bring doubtful happiness and certain pain.

Nube non è che scuri vostra luce,
l'ore distinte a voi non fanno forza,
caso o necessità non vi conduce.

    Vostro splendor per notte non s'ammorza,   55
né cresce ma' per giorno, benché chiaro,
sie quand'el sol fra no' il caldo rinforza.

    Nel tuo morire el mie morire imparo,
padre mie caro, e nel pensier ti veggio
dove 'l mondo passar ne fa di raro.   60

    Non è, com'alcun crede, morte il peggio
a chi l'ultimo dì trascende al primo,
per grazia, etterno appresso al divin seggio

    dove, Die grazia, ti prosumo e stimo
e spero di veder, se 'l freddo core   65
mie ragion tragge dal terrestre limo.

    E se tra l' padre e 'l figlio ottimo amore
cresce nel ciel, crescendo ogni virtute,

．．．．．．．．．．．．．．．．．．．．．．．．．．．．．．．

87

Vorrei voler, Signor, quel ch'io non voglio:
tra 'l foco e 'l cor di ghiaccia un vel s'asconde
che 'l foco ammorza, onde non corrisponde
la penna all'opre, e fa bugiardo 'l foglio.

    I' t'amo con la lingua, e poi mi doglio   5
c'amor non giunge al cor; né so ben onde
apra l'uscio alla grazia che s'infonde
nel cor, che scacci ogni spietato orgoglio.

    Squarcia 'l vel tu, Signor, rompi quel muro
che con la suo durezza ne ritarda   10
il sol della tuo luce, al mondo spenta!

    Manda 'l preditto lume a noi venturo,
alla tuo bella sposa, acciò ch'io arda
il cor senz'alcun dubbio, e te sol senta.

88

Sento d'un foco un freddo aspetto acceso
che lontan m'arde e sé con seco agghiaccia;
pruovo una forza in due leggiadre braccia
che muove senza moto ogni altro peso.

No cloud can obscure your light, you are not harried by the passage of each hour; chance or necessity has no power over you.

Your splendour is not dimmed by night, nor is it ever increased by day, however bright, as when here the summer sun most fiercely burns.

In your death I learn how I should die, my beloved father, and in my thoughts I see you where the world rarely lets us pass.

Though some think death the greatest evil, this is not so for those who move beyond their last to their first and, through grace, eternal day, near to the divine throne,

where, through the grace of God, I presume and believe you are, and where I hope to see you, if my mind will but draw my cold heart out of the earthly slime.

And if the finest love between father and son grows in heaven, where every virtue grows, ...

Incomplete capitolo, *on the death of Michelangelo's father, 1531/4.*

87

I should like to will, Lord, what I do not will: between the fire and my heart lies hidden a veil of ice that quenches the fire, and so my pen does not correspond to my actions, and the paper is made a liar.

I love you with my tongue, and then I grieve that love does not reach my heart; and yet I am completely at a loss to know how I may open the door to grace, that it may pour into my heart and drive out all unfeeling pride.

Tear you, Lord, the veil, break down that wall which with its hardness keeps from us the light of your sun, now quenched in the world!

Send that light, promised to come to us one day, to your lovely spouse, so that my heart may burn free from all doubt, and feel you alone.

Sonnet, probably c. 1534.

88

I feel a cold face lit by a fire that burns me from afar, yet in itself is freezing; I sense in two lovely arms a power that itself unmoved moves every other weight.

Unico spirto e da me solo inteso,　　　　　　　　　5
che non ha morte e morte altrui procaccia,
veggio e truovo chi, sciolto, 'l cor m'allaccia,
e da chi giova sol mi sento offeso.
　　Com'esser può, signor, che d'un bel volto
ne porti 'l mio così contrari effetti,　　　　　　10
se mal può chi non gli ha donar altrui?
　　Onde al mio viver lieto, che m'ha tolto,
fa forse come 'l sol, se nol permetti,
che scalda 'l mondo e non è caldo lui.

89

Veggio co' be' vostr'occhi un dolce lume
che co' mie ciechi già veder non posso;
porto co' vostri piedi un pondo addosso,
che de' mie zoppi non è già costume.
　　Volo con le vostr'ale senza piume;　　　　　　5
col vostro ingegno al ciel sempre son mosso;
dal vostro arbitrio son pallido e rosso,
freddo al sol, caldo alle più fredde brume.
　　Nel voler vostro è sol la voglia mia,
i miei pensier nel vostro cor si fanno,　　　　　10
nel vostro fiato son le mie parole.
　　Come luna da sé sol par ch'io sia,
ché gli occhi nostri in ciel veder non sanno
se non quel tanto che n'accende il sole.

90

I' mi son caro assai più ch'i' non soglio;
poi ch'i' t'ebbi nel cor più di me vaglio,
come pietra c'aggiuntovi l'intaglio
è di più pregio che 'l suo primo scoglio.
　　O come scritta o pinta carta o foglio　　　　5
più si riguarda d'ogni straccio o taglio,
tal di me fo, da po' ch'i' fu' berzaglio
segnato dal tuo viso, e non mi doglio.
　　Sicur con tale stampa in ogni loco
vo, come quel c'ha incanti o arme seco,　　　　10
c'ogni periglio gli fan venir meno.

I see a unique spirit understood by me alone, who is himself untouched by death yet causes death in others, and find one who, himself free, holds my heart bound; and by one who offers only help, I feel myself harmed.

How can it be, lord, if one can scarcely give to others what one does not oneself possess, that from a beautiful face mine should draw such opposite effects?

So as regards my joy in life, which it has taken from me, your face perhaps acts (unless you prevent it) as does the sun, which heats the world yet is not hot itself.

*Sonnet, for Tommaso Cavalieri, c. 1532–4.**

89

With your beautiful eyes I see a sweet light which with my blind eyes I certainly cannot see; with your feet I carry on my back a weight which my lame feet certainly could not bear.

Though lacking feathers I fly with your wings; with your mind I am always carried to heaven; on your decision turns whether I am pale or red, cold in the sun, warm in the coldest mists.

In your will alone does my will consist, my thoughts spring from your heart, with your breath are my words formed.

On my own I seem like the moon left to itself, for our eyes can see nothing whatever in the heavens except what is lit up by the sun.

*Sonnet, for Tommaso Cavalieri, c. 1534.**

90

I am much dearer to myself than I ever used to be; since I have had you in my heart I value myself more, as a stone once worked on is more highly prized than it was as a raw block.

Or as a page once written on or a sheet when painted is considered of greater worth than any crumpled or torn-off piece, so I consider myself since I became a target marked by your face; and I have no regrets.

Nowhere do I fear to go bearing such an image, like one possessing charms or arms, that make every danger fade before him.

I' vaglio contr'a l'acqua e contr'al foco,
col segno tuo rallumino ogni cieco,
e col mie sputo sano ogni veleno.

91

Perc'all'estremo ardore
che toglie e rende poi
il chiuder e l'aprir degli occhi tuoi
duri più la mie vita,
fatti son calamita   5
di me, de l'alma e d'ogni mie valore;
tal c'anciderm' Amore,
forse perch'è pur cieco,
indugia, triema e teme.
C'a passarmi nel core,   10
sendo nel tuo con teco,
pungere' prima le tuo parte streme;
e perché meco insieme
non mora, non m'ancide. O gran martire,
c'una doglia mortal, senza morire,   15
raddoppia quel languire
del qual, s'i' fussi meco, sare' fora.
Deh rendim' a me stesso, acciò ch'i' mora.

I am proof against water and against fire, with your mark I restore light to all the blind, and with my spittle I cure every poison.

Sonnet, probably for Tommaso Cavalieri, probably c. 1534. *

91

That my life may better sustain the extreme heat which your eyes by closing take away and by opening bring back, these have been made a magnet for me, for my soul and for all my powers; so Love, perhaps because he is indeed blind, hesitates, trembles and is afraid to kill me. For since my heart lies in yours with you, to penetrate it he would first have to pierce your outward parts; and that you may not die along with me, he does not kill me. Oh what great torment: that a fatal agony, without bringing death, should redouble the slow suffering of which, were I mine alone, I should be free. Ah restore me to myself, that I may die.

Madrigal, probably for Tommaso Cavalieri, possibly 1534–6, revised 1542–6. *

92

Quantunche 'l tempo ne costringa e sproni
ognor con maggior guerra
a rendere alla terra
le membra afflitte, stanche e pellegrine,
non ha però 'ncor fine   5
chi l'alma attrista e me fa così lieto.
Né par che men perdoni
a chi 'l cor m'apre e serra,
nell'ore più vicine
e più dubiose d'altro viver quieto;   10
ché l'error consueto,
com più m'attempo, ognor più si fa forte.
O dura mia più c'altra crudel sorte!
Tardi orama' puo' tormi tanti affanni;
c'un cor che arde e arso è già molt'anni   15
torna, se ben l'ammorza la ragione,
non più già cor, ma cenere e carbone.

93

Spargendo il senso il troppo ardor cocente
fuor del tuo bello, in alcun altro volto,
men forza ha, signor, molto
qual per più rami alpestro e fier torrente.
Il cor, che del più ardente   5
foco più vive, mal s'accorda allora
co' rari pianti e men caldi sospiri.
L'alma all'error presente
gode c'un di lor mora
per gire al ciel, là dove par c'aspiri.   10
La ragione i martiri
fra lor comparte; e fra più salde tempre
s'accordan tutt'a quattro amarti sempre.

94

D'altrui pietoso e sol di sé spietato
nasce un vil bruto, che con pena e doglia
l'altrui man veste e la suo scorza spoglia
e sol per morte si può dir ben nato.

92

Although time forces us and spurs us, every hour waging war more fiercely, to give back to the earth our afflicted, tired and pilgrim limbs, his work is not yet finished who saddens my soul and makes me so happy. Nor does it seem right to him who opens and closes my heart to spare me more in the hours nearer to, but less certain of, that other, peaceful life, for as I grow older my habitual error gains greater strength with each passing hour. Oh what a harsh fate is mine, crueller than any other! It is by now too late for you to take such torments from me; for a heart that burns and has burned for many years, even if reason should at last put out its fire, does not become a heart once more but ashes and charred wood.

Madrigal, probably for Tommaso Cavalieri, probably 1534–6, revised 1546. *

93

When the senses spread their excessive, searing heat by going beyond your beautiful face to others', its force is greatly lessened, like a wild mountain torrent when it spreads into several branches. The heart, which draws most life from the most fiercely burning fire, then feels ill at ease with the rare laments and the cooler sighs. The soul, conscious of the error, rejoices that one of them dies down, thus allowing the soul to go to heaven, to where it seems to aspire. Reason divides the torments equally among them; and with each in a steadier state, all four agree among themselves to love you always.

Madrigal, probably for Tommaso Cavalieri, probably 1534–6, revised 1546. *

94

A lowly worm is born considerate of others and inconsiderate only of itself: with pain and suffering it sheds its own covering and clothes another's hand, and may really be said to be born only in order to die.

Così volesse al mie signor mie fato   5
vestir suo viva di mie morta spoglia,
che, come serpe al sasso si discoglia,
pur per morte potria cangiar mie stato.
     O fussi sol la mie l'irsuta pelle
che, del suo pel contesta, fa tal gonna   10
che con ventura stringe sì bel seno,
     ch'i' l'are' pure il giorno; o le pianelle
che fanno a quel di lor basa e colonna,
ch'i' pur ne porterei duo nevi almeno.

95

Rendete agli occhi mei, o fonte o fiume,
l'onde della non vostra e salda vena,
che più v'innalza e cresce, e con più lena
che non è 'l vostro natural costume.
     E tu, folt'aïr, che 'l celeste lume   5
tempri a' trist'occhi, de' sospir mie piena,
rendigli al cor mie lasso e rasserena
tua scura faccia al mie visivo acume.
     Renda la terra i passi alle mie piante,
c'ancor l'erba germugli che gli è tolta,   10
e 'l suono Ecco, già sorda a' mie lamenti;
     gli sguardi agli occhi mie tuo luce sante,
ch'i' possa altra bellezza un'altra volta
amar, po' che di me non ti contenti.

96

Sì come secco legno in foco ardente
arder poss'io, s'i' non t'amo di core,
e l'alma perder, se null'altro sente.
     E se d'altra beltà spirto d'amore
fuor de' tu' occhi è che m'infiammi o scaldi,   5
tolti sien quegli a chi sanz'essi muore.
     S'io non t'amo e ador, ch'e' mie più baldi
pensier sien con la speme tanto tristi
quanto nel tuo amor son fermi e saldi.

Would that my destiny wished the same for me as regards my lord: that I might clothe his living skin with my dead skin, so that, as a serpent sloughs on a stone, I might through death change my condition.

Oh might my skin alone be the hairy skin that, woven from its own skin, makes the gown whose good fortune it is to bind so lovely a breast,

so that I should have it at least in daytime; or might I be the slippers which make themselves a base and support for him, that I might at the very least carry him for two winters.

Sonnet, probably for Tommaso Cavalieri, c. 1535.

95

Give back to my eyes, oh fountain, oh stream, the waves of a perpetual spring not yours, which causes you to rise and swell, and flow with a vigour greater than is natural to you.

And you, dense air, who shade the heavenly light from my sad eyes, and are full of my sighs, give these back to my weary heart, and make your dark face clear for my power of sight.

May the earth give back to my feet their footsteps, so that the grass taken from it may sprout again, and Echo, now deaf to my laments, may restore their sound;

may your holy lights give back to my eyes my longing looks, that I may another time love another beauty, since you take no pleasure in me.

Sonnet, possibly for Tommaso Cavalieri, 1534–8 or later. *

96

May I burn like dry wood in a burning fire, if I do not love you from my heart, and lose my soul, if it feels for any other.

And if it is a spirit of love from a beauty other than your eyes that inflames and scorches me, may those eyes be taken from one who without them dies.

If I do not love and adore you, may my most daring thoughts, and the hopes that go with them, become as sad as they are now firm and steadfast in love of you.

Capitolo, possibly for Tommaso Cavalieri, 1534–8 or later.

97

Al cor di zolfo, a la carne di stoppa,
a l'ossa che di secco legno sièno;
a l'alma senza guida e senza freno
al desir pronto, a la vaghezza troppa;
    a la cieca ragion debile e zoppa   5
al vischio, a' lacci di che 'l mondo è pieno;
non è gran maraviglia, in un baleno
arder nel primo foco che s'intoppa.
    A la bell'arte che, se dal ciel seco
ciascun la porta, vince la natura,   10
quantunche sé ben prema in ogni loco;
    s'i' nacqui a quella né sordo né cieco,
proporzionato a chi 'l cor m'arde e fura,
colpa è di chi m'ha destinato al foco.

98

A che più debb'i' omai l'intensa voglia
sfogar con pianti o con parole meste,
se di tal sorte 'l ciel, che l'alma veste,
tard' o per tempo alcun mai non ne spoglia?
    A che 'l cor lass' a più languir m'invoglia,   5
s'altri pur dee morir? Dunche per queste
luci l'ore del fin fian men moleste;
c'ogni altro ben val men c'ogni mia doglia.
    Però se 'l colpo ch'io ne rub' e 'nvolo
schifar non posso, almen, s'è destinato,   10
chi entrerà 'nfra la dolcezza e 'l duolo?
    Se vint' e preso i' debb'esser beato,
maraviglia non è se nudo e solo
resto prigion d'un cavalier armato.

99

Ben mi dove' con sì felice sorte,
mentre che Febo il poggio tutto ardea,
levar da terra, allor quand'io potea,
con le suo penne, e far dolce la morte.

97

If one's heart is made of sulphur, one's skin of tow, one's bones of dry wood; if one's soul is without guide and without rein for its ready desire and its excessive attraction;

if one's reason is blind, weak and lamed by the birdlime and the snares of which the world is full; it is little wonder that one should in a flash be burned up by the first fire one comes across.

If to the art of beauty which conquers nature, if anyone brings it with him from heaven, even though nature strives well everywhere,

if to that art I was born neither deaf nor blind, responsive then to whoever burns and steals my heart, this is the fault of the one who has destined me to the fire.

Sonnet, for Tommaso Cavalieri, 1534–8 or later. *

98

What point is there in my still giving vent to my intense emotion in weeping or sad words, if heaven, which clothes the soul, neither late nor early rescues one from such a fate?

What point is there in my tired heart's driving me more and more to pine away, if all must surely die? The final hours will be less troubling to my eyes, knowing that no good whatever is worth all my suffering.

So if I cannot avoid the blow which I steal and rob from him, since it is in fact destined, who will enter there where sweetness wars with pain?

If it is only by being overcome and taken that I may be happy, then it is not to be wondered at if defenceless and alone I remain the prisoner of an armed cavalier.

Sonnet, for Tommaso Cavalieri, of uncertain date, but probably 1534–8
or later.

99

While to my good fortune Phoebus was setting the whole hill aflame, I ought certainly then, when I was able, to have lifted myself from earth with his feathers, and happily faced death.

Or m'è sparito; e se 'l fuggir men forte   5
de' giorni lieti invan mi promettea,
ragione è ben c'all'alma ingrata e rea
pietà le mani e 'l ciel chiugga le porte.

Le penne mi furn'ale e 'l poggio scale,
Febo lucerna a' piè; né m'era allora   10
men salute il morir che maraviglia.

Morendo or senza, al ciel l'alma non sale,
né di lor la memoria il cor ristora:
ché tardi e doppo il danno, chi consiglia?

100

Ben fu, temprando il ciel tuo vivo raggio,
solo a du' occhi, a me di pietà vòto,
allor che con veloce etterno moto
a noi dette la luce, a te 'l vïaggio.

Felice uccello, che con tal vantaggio   5
da noi, t'è Febo e 'l suo bel volto noto,
e più c'al gran veder t'è ancora arroto
volare al poggio, ond'io rovino e caggio.

101

Perché Febo non torce e non distende
d'intorn' a questo globo freddo e molle
le braccia sua lucenti, el vulgo volle
notte chiamar quel sol che non comprende.

E tant'è debol, che s'alcun accende   5
un picciol torchio, in quella parte tolle
la vita dalla notte, e tant'è folle
che l'esca col fucil la squarcia e fende.

E s'egli è pur che qualche cosa sia,
cert'è figlia del sol e della terra;   10
ché l'un tien l'ombra, e l'altro sol la cria.

Ma sia che vuol, che pur chi la loda erra,
vedova, scura, in tanta gelosia,
c'una lucciola sol gli può far guerra.

Now he has vanished from me; and if his promise proved empty, that joyful days would speed by less quickly, it is quite right that to an ungrateful and guilty soul pity should close its hands and heaven its doors.

For me the feathers were wings, the hill a ladder, Phoebus a lamp for my footsteps; and to die would then have meant for me salvation no less than joy.

Dying now without these, my soul cannot rise to heaven, nor does the memory of them revive my heart: for now that it is late and the harm done, who can offer guidance?

Sonnet, possibly on the death of Febo di Poggio, probably 1535.

100

When heaven strengthened your living ray it was indeed merciful only to your eyes, but to me was devoid of pity, when with its swift, eternal movement it gave us your light and you the journey back.

Happy bird, with this advantage over us, that to you Phoebus and his beautiful face are known; and, better even than this great sight, it is also given to you to fly to that height from which I fall to my ruin.

Partial sonnet: see poem 99.

101

Because Phoebus does not bend and wrap his shining arms around this cold, damp globe, the common people wish to call night only what he does not embrace.

And night is so weak that anyone who lights a little torch takes life from it at that spot; and it is so feeble that flint on tinder tears and rends it.

Yet if one grants that night really is something, then certainly it is the daughter of the sun and of the earth; for the latter bears its darkness, the former alone creates it.

But however that may be, he surely errs who praises night, desolate, dark and so fragile that a mere firefly can wage war on it.

Sonnet, possibly for Tommaso Cavalieri, 1535–46, possibly 1545.

102

O notte, o dolce tempo, benché nero,
con pace ogn' opra sempr' al fin assalta;
ben vede e ben intende chi t'esalta,
e chi t'onor' ha l'intelletto intero.

    Tu mozzi e tronchi ogni stanco pensiero   5
ché l'umid' ombra ogni quiet' appalta,
e dall'infima parte alla più alta
in sogno spesso porti, ov'ire spero.

    O ombra del morir, per cui si ferma
ogni miseria a l'alma, al cor nemica,   10
ultimo delli afflitti e buon rimedio;

    tu rendi sana nostra carn' inferma,
rasciughi i pianti e posi ogni fatica,
e furi a chi ben vive ogn'ira e tedio.

103

Ogni van chiuso, ogni coperto loco,
quantunche ogni materia circumscrive,
serba la notte, quando il giorno vive,
contro al solar suo luminoso gioco.

    E s'ella è vinta pur da fiamma o foco,   5
da lei dal sol son discacciate e prive
con più vil cosa ancor sue specie dive,
tal c'ogni verme assai ne rompe o poco.

    Quel che resta scoperto al sol, che ferve
per mille vari semi e mille piante,   10
il fier bifolco con l'aratro assale;

    ma l'ombra sol a piantar l'uomo serve.
Dunche, le notti più ch'e' dì son sante,
quanto l'uom più d'ogni altro frutto vale.

104

Colui che fece, e non di cosa alcuna,
il tempo, che non era anzi a nessuno,
ne fe' d'un due e diè 'l sol alto all'uno,
all'altro assai più presso diè la luna.

102

Oh night, oh sweet time, although black, all work finally struggles to an end and reaches peace; whoever exalts you sees clearly and clearly understands, and whoever honours you is of sound mind.

You break and cut off all tired thoughts, for your soft shadow offers complete rest, and in dreams you often carry one from the lowest to the highest sphere, where I hope to go.

Oh shadow of death, through which is ended every misery hostile to man's soul and heart, last of man's afflictions and their true remedy:

you restore health to our sick flesh, dry away our tears and bring all toil to rest; and you banish from those who live rightly all anger and frustration.

Sonnet, possibly for Tommaso Cavalieri, 1535–46, possibly 1545.

103

Every empty space closed over, every covered place, everywhere that matter encompasses, preserves the night even when day reigns, keeping out day's playful, sunny light.

And since night is overcome merely by flame or fire, its divine qualities are driven away and nullified even by what is lowlier than the sun, so that every firefly breaks them much or little.

What remains open to the sun, and teems with a thousand diverse seeds and a thousand plants, is assaulted by the fierce peasant with his plough;

but only the dark serves to plant man. Nights are more sacred, then, than days, as man is more worthy than any other fruit.

Sonnet, possibly for Tommaso Cavalieri, c. 1535–46, possibly 1545. *

104

He who, from nothing whatever, made time, which did not exist before all else, divided it in two: to one part he gave the high sun, to the other the moon, which is much nearer.

Onde 'l caso, la sorte e la fortuna   5
in un momento nacquer di ciascuno;
e a me consegnaro il tempo bruno,
come a simil nel parto e nella cuna.

E come quel che contrafà se stesso,
quando è ben notte, più buio esser suole,   10
ond'io di far ben mal m'affliggo e lagno.

Pur mi consola assai l'esser concesso
far giorno chiar mia oscura notte al sole
che a voi fu dato al nascer per compagno.

105

Non vider gli occhi miei cosa mortale
allor che ne' bei vostri intera pace
trovai, ma dentro, ov'ogni mal dispiace,
chi d'amor l'alma a sé simil m'assale;

e se creata a Dio non fusse equale,   5
altro che 'l bel di fuor, c'agli occhi piace,
più non vorria; ma perch'è si fallace,
trascende nella forma universale.

Io dico c'a chi vive quel che muore
quetar non può disir; né par s'aspetti   10
l'eterno al tempo, ove altri cangia il pelo.

Voglia sfrenata el senso è, non amore,
che l'alma uccide; e 'l nostro fa perfetti
gli amici qui, ma più per morte in cielo.

106

Per ritornar là donde venne fora,
l'immortal forma al tuo carcer terreno
venne com'angel di pietà sì pieno,
che sana ogn'intelletto e 'l mondo onora.

Questo sol m'arde e questo m'innamora,   5
non pur di fuora il tuo volto sereno:
c'amor non già di cosa che vien meno
tien ferma speme, in cui virtù dimora.

Né altro avvien di cose altere e nuove
in cui si preme la natura, e 'l cielo   10
è c'a' lor parti largo s'apparecchia;

From these were born the chance, condition and fortune of every individual; to me they assigned the dark time, as being similar to me at birth and in the cradle.

Just as night as it advances grows ever darker, so I grow more like myself in being ever more evil, which troubles me and grieves me.

Yet it consoles me greatly that to change my dark night into bright day has been granted to the sun which was given to you at birth as your companion.

*Sonnet, probably for Tommaso Cavalieri, c. 1535–46, possibly 1545.**

105

It was not something mortal my eyes saw when in your beautiful eyes I found complete peace; rather, they saw within, where all evil displeases, him who assails my soul, similar to himself, with love;

if my soul had not been created by God equal to himself, then indeed it would wish for nothing more than external beauty, which pleases the eyes; but because this is so deceptive, the soul rises above to beauty's universal form.

I declare that what dies cannot satisfy the desire of one who lives; nor likewise should one look for the eternal in time, where man's body grows old.

To the senses belongs not love but unbridled desire, which kills the soul; but our love makes our friendships perfect here, and even more beyond death in paradise.

Sonnet, probably for Tommaso Cavalieri, c. 1535–46.

106

In order to return to the place from which it came, the immortal form came to your earthly prison like an angel so full of mercy that it heals every intellect and brings honour to the world.

This alone inflames me and calls forth my love, not something merely external, your bright face: love in which virtue dwells certainly does not place firm hope in what passes away.

This is what happens to all excellent and rare beings which nature labours to produce, and which heaven generously endows at their birth;

né Dio, suo grazia, mi si mostra altrove
più che 'n alcun leggiadro e mortal velo;
e quel sol amo perch'in lui si specchia.

107

Gli occhi mie vaghi delle cose belle
e l'alma insieme della suo salute
non hanno altra virtute
c'ascenda al ciel, che mirar tutte quelle.
Dalle più alte stelle   5
discende uno splendore
che 'l desir tira a quelle,
e qui si chiama amore.
Né altro ha il gentil core
che l'innamori e arda, e che 'l consigli,   10
c'un volto che negli occhi lor somigli.

108

Indarno spera, come 'l vulgo dice,
chi fa quel che non de' grazia o mercede.
Non fu', com'io credetti, in vo' felice,
privandomi di me per troppa fede,
né spero com'al sol nuova fenice   5
ritornar più; ché 'l tempo nol concede.
Pur godo il mie gran danno sol perch'io
son più mie vostro, che s'i' fussi mio.

but God, in his graciousness, does not show himself more fully to me elsewhere than in some lovely, mortal veil; and I love that solely because in it He is reflected.

Sonnet, for Tommaso Cavalieri, 1536–42, revised 1546. *

107

My eyes, eager for beautiful things, and my soul no less for its salvation, have no other means by which they may ascend to heaven than to gaze on all such things. From the highest stars descends a shining light which draws our desire to them: this we here call love. The noble heart has nothing else that can make it love and burn, nothing else to guide it, than a face which in its eyes acts as those stars do.

Madrigal, possibly for Tommaso Cavalieri, 1534–46. *

108

As the common saying has it, he hopes in vain for favour or for kindness who does what he should not do. I did not, as I once believed I would, find happiness in you, for I deprived me of myself by too much trust; nor do I hope to return again, as does the phoenix renewed by the sun, for time does not permit this. Yet I rejoice in the great harm done me, for this reason only, that I am more mine being yours, than were I mine.

Octave, possibly for Tommaso Cavalieri, 1534–46. *

109

Non sempre a tutti è sì pregiato e caro
quel che 'l senso contenta,
c'un sol non sia che 'l senta,
se ben par dolce, pessimo e amaro.
Il buon gusto è sì raro   5
c'al vulgo errante cede
in vista, allor che dentro di sé gode.
Così, perdendo, imparo
quel che di fuor non vede
chi l'alma ha trista, e ' suo sospir non ode.   10
El mondo è cieco e di suo gradi o lode
più giova a chi più scarso esser ne vuole,
come sferza che 'nsegna e parte duole.

110

Io dico a voi c'al mondo avete dato
l'anima e 'l corpo e lo spirto 'nsïeme:
in questa cassa oscura è 'l vostro lato.

111

S'egli è, donna, che puoi
come cosa mortal, benché sia diva
di beltà, c'ancor viva
e mangi e dorma e parli qui fra noi,
a non seguirti poi,   5
cessato il dubbio, tuo grazia e mercede,
qual pena a tal peccato degna fora?
Ché alcun ne' pensier suoi,
co' l'occhio che non vede,
per virtù propia tardi s'innamora.   10
Disegna in me di fuora,
com'io fo in pietra od in candido foglio,
che nulla ha dentro, e èvvi ciò ch'io voglio.

109

What satisfies the senses is not so prized and dear to all that there is no one who does not regard this as most harmful and bitter, although it seems indeed to be sweet. So rare is good taste that it gives the appearance of yielding to the erring crowd, while inwardly rejoicing in itself. Thus, in losing, I learn what is not seen on the outside by those whose soul is evil, and who fail to hear its sighing. The world is blind, and with its rewards and praise most benefits him whom it least wishes to favour with them, like a whip that teaches even as it hurts.

Madrigal, 1536–44.*

110

I say to you who have given to the world your whole selves – body, soul and spirit: you will end up in this dark coffin.

Tercet, 1534–5 or later.

111

If it is true, lady, that though divine in beauty you can act like any mortal being, who still lives and eats and sleeps and speaks here among us, then not to follow you when, thanks to your grace and mercy, all doubt on this has ceased – what punishment would be sufficient for such a sin? For anyone who relies on his own thoughts, using the eye that does not see, is slow to love through his own power. Form in me a shape from outside, as I do in stone or on a blank sheet, which in itself contains nothing, and then has there what I wish.

Madrigal, for Vittoria Colonna, c. 1536.

112

Il mio refugio e 'l mio ultimo scampo
qual più sicuro è, che non sia men forte
che 'l pianger e 'l pregar? e non m'aita.
Amore e crudeltà m'han posto il campo:
l'un s'arma di pietà, l'altro di morte;   5
questa n'ancide, e l'altra tien in vita.
Così l'alma impedita
del mio morir, che sol poria giovarne,
più volte per andarne
s'è mossa là dov'esser sempre spera,   10
dov'è beltà sol fuor di donna altiera;
ma l'imagine vera,
della qual vivo, allor risorge al core,
perché da morte non sia vinto amore.

113

Esser non può già ma' che gli occhi santi
prendin de' mie, com'io di lor, diletto,
rendendo al divo aspetto,
per dolci risi, amari e tristi pianti.
O fallace speranza degli amanti!   5
Com'esser può dissimile e dispari
l'infinita beltà, 'l superchio lume
da ogni mie costume,
che meco ardendo, non ardin del pari?
Fra duo volti diversi e sì contrari   10
s'adira e parte da l'un zoppo Amore;
né può far forza che di me gl'incresca,
quand'in un gentil core
entra di foco, e d'acqua par che n'esca.

112

What refuge or final escape could offer me greater security, and not be less strong than tears or prayer? But these, too, are of no help. Love and cruelty have laid siege to me: one arms itself with pity, the other with death; of these the latter kills me, the former keeps me alive. So my soul, prevented from dying, which alone could bring it benefit, has often tried to go to where it wishes to be forever, where beauty exists alone, not linked to a proud woman; but then there rises again in my heart the true image, from which I live, so that love may not be overcome by death.

Madrigal, for 'the beautiful and cruel lady', 1536–46. *

113

It cannot ever be that her holy eyes should draw delight from mine, as I do from them, since to her divine countenance I offer, in return for sweet smiles, sad and bitter tears. Oh vain hope of lovers! How can that infinite beauty and overpowering light be so unlike, so far surpass, my whole way of being, that while I am made to burn by them they do not likewise burn? Between two faces so different and even contrary, Love becomes angry and from one limps lamely off, and he cannot fail to feel sorry for me, when into a noble heart he enters as fire, and seems to leave as water.

Madrigal, probably for Vittoria Colonna, probably c. 1536. *

114

Ben vinci ogni durezza
cogli occhi tuo, com'ogni luce ancora;
ché, s'alcun d'allegrezza avvien che mora,
allor sarebbe l'ora
che gran pietà comanda a gran bellezza.   5
E se nel foco avvezza
non fusse l'alma, già morto sarei
alle promesse de' tuo primi sguardi,
ove non fur ma' tardi
gl'ingordi mie nimici, anz'occhi mei;   10
né doler mi potrei
di questo non poter, che non è teco.
Bellezza e grazia equalmente infinita,
dove più porgi aita,
men puoi non tor la vita,   15
né puoi non far chiunche tu miri cieco.

115

Lezi, vezzi, carezze, or, feste e perle,
chi potria ma' vederle
cogli atti suo divin l'uman lavoro,
ove l'argento e l'oro
da le' riceve o duplica suo luce?   5
Ogni gemma più luce
dagli occhi suo che da propia virtute.

114

With your eyes you surpass completely every hardness, as you indeed do every other light; so if it is true that someone may die of happiness, now would be that time, when great mercy rules over great beauty. And if my soul had not been accustomed to the fire, I should have died at once on receiving the promises held out by your first glances, on which my greedy enemies, I should say my eyes, were never slow to feed; nor ought I to complain about this inability, for it is no fault of yours. Beauty and grace equally infinite, where you most offer help there you can least avoid taking life away, nor can you not make blind all on whom you gaze.

Madrigal, possibly for 'the beautiful and cruel lady', 1536-46. *

115

Wiles, charms, caresses, gold, feasts and pearls: who could distinguish what comes from human effort in her divine actions, since even the silver and gold she wears receive their light from her, or double it? The light that shines in every gem owes more to her eyes than to its own power.

Incomplete madrigal, possibly for Vittoria Colonna, probably 1536-42.

116

Non mi posso tener né voglio, Amore,
crescendo al tuo furore,
ch'i' nol te dica e giuri:
quante più inaspri e 'nduri,
a più virtù l'alma consigli e sproni;   5
e se talor perdoni
a la mie morte, agli angosciosi pianti,
com'a colui che muore,
dentro mi sento il core
mancar, mancando i mie tormenti tanti.   10
Occhi lucenti e santi,
mie poca grazia m'è ben dolce e cara,
c'assai acquista chi perdendo impara.

117

S'egli è che 'l buon desio
porti dal mondo a Dio
alcuna cosa bella,
sol la mie donna è quella,
a chi ha gli occhi fatti com'ho io.   5
Ogni altra cosa oblio
e sol di tant'ho cura.
Non è gran maraviglia,
s'io l'amo e bramo e chiamo a tutte l'ore;
né propio valor mio,   10
se l'alma per natura
s'appoggia a chi somiglia
ne gli occhi gli occhi, ond'ella scende fore.
Se sente il primo amore
come suo fin, per quel qua questa onora: 15
c'amar diè 'l servo chi 'l signore adora.

116

As your fury against me grows, Love, I am not able, nor do I wish, to restrain myself from saying to you and swearing: the more you become harsh and indifferent the more you guide and spur my soul to virtue; and if sometimes you show pity towards my death, towards my anguished laments as of one who is dying, I feel my heart weaken within me as my great torments grow weaker. Bright and holy eyes, the meagre grace I have received is indeed sweet and dear to me, for he gains much who by losing learns.

Madrigal, probably for Vittoria Colonna, probably c. 1536. *

117

If it is true that something beautiful may carry good desire from the world to God, that can be only my lady, for one whose eyes have been fashioned as have mine. I forget all else, and care for her alone. It is no great wonder if I love and long for her, and call to her all the time; nor is mine the merit if my soul by its very nature rests on her who resembles in her eyes those eyes from which it first came forth. And if my soul feels the first love as its end, it is for that end's sake that it honours her here: for whoever adores the lord must love his servant.

Madrigal, possibly for Vittoria Colonna, 1536–46. *

118

Ancor che 'l cor già molte volte sia
d'amore acceso e da troppi anni spento,
l'ultimo mie tormento
sarie mortal senza la morte mia.
Onde l'alma desia   5
de' giorni mie, mentre c'amor m'avvampa,
l'ultimo, primo in più tranquilla corte.
Altro refugio o via
mie vita non iscampa
dal suo morir, c'un aspra e crudel morte;   10
né contr'a morte è forte
altro che morte, sì c'ogn'altra aita
è doppia morte a chi per morte ha vita.

119

Dal primo pianto all'ultimo sospiro,
al qual son già vicino,
chi contrasse già mai sì fier destino
com'io da sì lucente e fera stella?
Non dico iniqua o fella,   5
che 'l me' saria di fore,
s'aver disdegno ne troncasse amore;
ma più, se più la miro,
promette al mio martiro
dolce pietà, con dispietato core.   10
O desïato ardore!
ogni uom vil sol potria vincer con teco,
ond'io, s'io non fui cieco,
ne ringrazio le prime e l'ultime ore
ch'io la vidi; e l'errore   15
vincami; e d'ogni tempo sia con meco,
se sol forza e virtù perde con seco.

118

Although my heart has many times before been set alight by love, and is now extinguished by excessive years, this last torment of mine will be death-dealing unless death intervenes. So while love is scorching me, my soul desires the day that will be my last, and first in a more peaceful court. My life has no other refuge, it has no other means of escape from dying than a harsh and cruel death; nor is anything strong against death other than death, so that every other help would be a double death to him who through death gains life.

Madrigal, possibly for 'the beautiful and cruel lady', 1536–46. *

119

From the first cry until the final breath, to which I am already near, who has ever been assigned such a harsh destiny as I have from a star so bright and fierce? I do not call her evil or destructive, although it would be better if she showed herself to be so, that her disdain might put an end to my love; but the more I look on her the more she promises my torment sweet mercy, with a merciless heart. Oh longed-for burning! only base men can conquer you, so for not having been blind I give thanks to the first and last hours I saw her. May error conquer me, and be with me for all time, if to lose against her shows only strength and virtue.

Madrigal, for 'the beautiful and cruel lady', 1536–46. *

120

Ben tempo saria omai
ritrarsi dal martire,
ché l'età col desir non ben s'accorda;
ma l'alma, cieca e sorda,
Amor, come tu sai,   5
del tempo e del morire
che, contro a morte ancor, me la ricorda;
e se l'arco e la corda
avvien che tronchi o spezzi
in mille e mille pezzi,   10
prega te sol non manchi un de' suoi guai:
ché mai non muor chi non guarisce mai.

121

Come non puoi non esser cosa bella,
esser non puoi che pietosa non sia;
sendo po' tutta mia,
non puo' poter non mi distrugga e stempre.
Così durando sempre   5
mie pietà pari a tua beltà qui molto,
la fin del tuo bel volto
in un tempo con ella
fie del mie ardente core.
Ma poi che 'l spirto sciolto   10
ritorna alla suo stella,
a fruir quel signore
ch'e' corpi a chiunche muore
eterni rende o per quiete o per lutto;
priego 'l mie, benché brutto,   15
com'è qui teco, il voglia in paradiso:
c'un cor pietoso val quant'un bel viso.

120

Now should certainly be the time to withdraw from torment, for desire is certainly not appropriate to my age; but, as you well know, Love, my soul, blind and deaf to time's passing and to dying, calls her to mind, even as I face death; and it begs only this of you, that, even if you have to break and shatter your bow and string into many thousands of pieces, you do not spare it one of its misfortunes: for he never dies who never ceases suffering.

Madrigal, possibly for Vittoria Colonna, possibly late 1530s. *

121

Just as you cannot but be beautiful, so you cannot but be merciful; however, being entirely mine, you cannot help but destroy and consume me. Since, then, your mercy towards me will always endure here as long as your great beauty, the end of your beautiful face along with your mercy will mean the end of my burning heart. But since the spirit when freed returns to its star, to delight in that lord who restores their bodies to all who die, to be eternal whether in peace or torment, I pray that just as you wished my body, ugly as it is, to be with you here, you may do the same in paradise: for a devoted heart is as worthy as a beautiful face.

Madrigal, possibly for Vittoria Colonna, possibly late 1530s. *

122

Se 'l foco al tutto nuoce,
e me arde e non cuoce,
non è mia molta né sua men virtute,
ch'io sol trovi salute
qual salamandra, là dove altri muore.   5
Né so chi in pace a tal martir m'ha volto:
da te medesma il volto,
da me medesmo il core
fatto non fu, né sciolto
da noi fia mai il mio amore;   10
più alto è quel signore
che ne' tu' occhi la mia vita ha posta.
S'io t'amo, e non ti costa,
perdona a me, come io a tanta noia,
che fuor di chi m'uccide vuol ch'i' muoia.   15

123

Quante più par che 'l mie mal maggior senta,
se col viso vel mostro,
più par s'aggiunga al vostro
bellezza, tal che 'l duol dolce diventa.
Ben fa chi mi tormenta,   5
se parte vi fa bella
della mie pena ria:
se 'l mie mal vi contenta,
mie cruda e fera stella,
che farie dunche con la morte mia?   10
Ma s'è pur ver che sia
vostra beltà dall'aspro mie martire,
e quel manchi al morire,
morend'io, morrà vostra leggiadria.
Però fate ch'i' stia   15
col mie duol vivo, per men vostro danno;
e se più bella al mie mal maggior siete,
l'alma n'ha ben più quiete:
c'un gran piacer sopporta un grande affanno.

122

If fire harms everything but burns me without consuming me, it is not a sign of great power in me or lesser power in it that I alone, like a salamander, find safety where others die. Nor do I know who brought me from a state of peace to such a torment: it was not you yourself who made your face, nor I myself who made my heart, nor shall we ourselves ever undo the bonds of my love – a higher power than we is that lord who has placed my life in your eyes. If I love you, and this does not trouble you, forgive me, as I do the great suffering that aims at bringing about my death, though this is not the will of the one who kills me.

Madrigal, possibly for Vittoria Colonna, possibly late 1530s. *

123

It seems that the more deeply I feel the hurt done me, and show this to you in my face, the more the beauty in yours seems to grow, so that my suffering becomes sweet. He who torments me does well, if he makes you beautiful partly through my cruel pain; but if the harm done me makes you happy, my harsh and fierce star, what would you do if I were to die? For if it really is true that your beauty depends on my bitter torment, and that this torment will disappear with my death, when I die your loveliness will die too. So keep me alive with my suffering, that less harm may come to you; and if through my being hurt more deeply you become more beautiful, my soul gains more peace from that: for great pleasure makes great suffering bearable.

Madrigal, for 'the beautiful and cruel lady', 1536–46. *

124

Questa mie donna è sì pronta e ardita,
c'allor che la m'ancide ogni mie bene
cogli occhi mi promette, e parte tiene
il crudel ferro dentro a la ferita.
E così morte e vita,   5
contrarie, insieme in un picciol momento
dentro a l'anima sento;
ma la grazia il tormento
de ma discaccia per più lunga pruova:
c'assai più nuoce il mal che 'l ben non giova.   10

125

Tanto di sé promette
donna pietosa e bella,
c'ancor mirando quella
sarie qual fu' per tempo, or vecchio e tardi.
Ma perc'ognor si mette   5
morte invidiosa e fella
fra ' mie dolenti e ' suo pietosi sguardi,
solo convien ch'i' ardi
quel picciol tempo che 'l suo volto oblio.
Ma poi che 'l pensier rio   10
pur la ritorna al consueto loco,
dal suo fier ghiaccio è spento il dolce foco.

126

Se l'alma è ver, dal suo corpo disciolta,
che 'n alcun altro torni
a' corti e brevi giorni,
per vivere e morire un'altra volta,
la donna mie, di molta   5
bellezza agli occhi miei,
fie allor com'or nel suo tornar sì cruda?
Se mie ragion s'ascolta,
attender la dovrei
di grazia piena e di durezza nuda.   10
Credo, s'avvien che chiuda
gli occhi suo begli, arà, come rinnuova,
pietà del mie morir, se morte pruova.

124

This lady of mine is so bold and daring that even as she kills me she promises me every possible good with her eyes, while at the same time keeping the cruel steel within the wound. And so death and life, contraries, I feel together in a single instant within my soul; but her graciousness banishes the torment from me only to make it last longer: for the harm done by her evil is far greater than the benefit brought by her good.

Madrigal, for 'the beautiful and cruel lady', 1536–46. *

125

The merciful and beautiful lady promises to favour me so much that while I gaze on her I could be as I once was, though now old and slow. But since envious, destructive death constantly inserts itself between my sorrowing and her merciful looks, I am able to burn only for that little time that I forget its face. But as soon as my wretched thoughts make it reappear in its accustomed place, the sweet fire is extinguished by its cruel ice.

Madrigal, for 'the beautiful and cruel lady', 1536–46. *

126

If it is true that the soul, freed from its body, returns in another body to these brief and fleeting days to live and die another time, will my lady, so beautiful in my eyes, then be on her return as cruel as she now is? If my reason is to be heeded, I ought to expect her to be full of grace and free of harshness. I believe that were it to happen that she should close her beautiful eyes, she would, when renewed, take pity on my dying, having herself experienced death.

Madrigal, for 'the beautiful and cruel lady', 1536–46. *

127

Non pur la morte, ma 'l timor di quella
da donna iniqua e bella,
c'ognor m'ancide, mi difende e scampa;
e se talor m'avvampa
più che l'usato il foco in ch'io son corso,   5
non trovo altro soccorso
che l'immagin sua ferma in mezzo il core:
ché dove è morte non s'appressa Amore.

128

Se 'l timor della morte
chi 'l fugge e scaccia sempre
lasciar là lo potessi onde ei si muove,
Amor crudele e forte
con più tenaci tempre   5
d'un cor gentil faria spietate pruove.
Ma perché l'alma altrove
per morte e grazia al fin gioire spera,
chi non può non morir gli è 'l timor caro
al qual ogni altro cede.   10
Né contro all'alte e nuove
bellezze in donna altera
ha forza altro riparo
che schivi suo disdegno o suo mercede.
Io giuro a chi nol crede,   15
che da costei, che del mio pianger ride,
sol mi difende e scampa chi m'uccide.

127

Not just death itself but the very fear of it defends and rescues me from an evil but beautiful woman, who at every moment kills me; and if sometimes the fire into which I have fallen burns me with a more searing heat than usual, I find no other help than death's firm image deep in my heart: for where death is there Love will not approach.

*Madrigal, for 'the beautiful and cruel lady', 1536–46.**

128

If he who always flees and drives from himself the fear of death could let it remain in the place whence it comes, Love, cruel and strong, would put to pitiless test with even steelier grip the noble heart. But since through death and grace the soul hopes finally to rejoice elsewhere, to him who cannot but die that fear is dear to which every other yields. And against the high, strange beauties of a proud woman there is no other defence that may protect one from her disdain and from her pity. I swear to all who do not believe this, that from her who laughs at my tears he alone defends and rescues me who kills me.

*Madrigal, for 'the beautiful and cruel lady', 1536–46.**

129

Da maggior luce e da più chiara stella
la notte il ciel le sue da lunge accende:
te sol presso a te rende
ognor più bella ogni cosa men bella.
Qual cor più questa o quella   5
a pietà muove o sprona,
c'ognor chi arde almen non s'agghiacc'egli?
Chi, senza aver, ti dona
vaga e gentil persona
e 'l volto e gli occhi e ' biondi e be' capegli.   10
Dunche, contr'a te quegli
ben fuggi e me con essi,
se 'l bello infra ' non begli
beltà cresce a se stessi.
Donna, ma s' tu rendessi   15
quel che t'ha dato il ciel, c'a noi l'ha tolto,
sarie più 'l nostro, e men bello il tuo volto.

130

Non è senza periglio
il tuo volto divino
dell'alma a chi è vicino
com'io a morte, che la sento ognora;
ond'io m'armo e consiglio   5
per far da quel difesa anzi ch'i' mora.
Ma tuo mercede, ancora
che 'l mie fin sie da presso,
non mi rende a me stesso;
né danno alcun da tal pietà mi scioglie: 10
ché l'uso di molt'anni un dì non toglie.

129

From a greater light and from a more brilliant star far off, the heavens at night light up their stars; you alone at every hour are given more beauty by everything less beautiful near to you. Which of these two reasons may more move or spur your heart to pity, so that he who burns continually may at least not be frozen? All they must move you who, though not being such themselves, making winning and attractive your person, face and eyes, your blonde and beautiful hair. And so you harm yourself in fleeing them, and me among them, if for one who is beautiful to be in the midst of those without beauty increases her very beauty. But if, lady, you were to give back what heaven has given you and withheld from us, our faces would gain in beauty, but yours would lose.

*Madrigal, for 'the beautiful and cruel lady', 1536–46.**

130

Your divine face is not without danger to the soul of one who is near to death, as I am, who feel death ever present; so I arm myself and take counsel how to defend myself against your face before I die. But though my end be near, your mercy cannot restore me to myself; nor does any threat of harm free me from such pity: for one day cannot take away the habit of many years.

*Madrigal, for 'the beautiful and cruel lady', 1536–46.**

131

Sotto duo belle ciglia
le forze Amor ripiglia
nella stagion che sprezza l'arco e l'ale.
Gli occhi mie, ghiotti d'ogni maraviglia
c'a questa s'assomiglia,   5
di lor fan pruova a più d'un fero strale.
E parte pur m'assale,
appresso al dolce, un pensier aspro e forte
di vergogna e di morte;
né perde Amor per maggior tema o danni: 10
c'un'or non vince l'uso di molt'anni.

132

Mentre che 'l mie passato m'è presente,
sì come ognor mi viene,
o mondo falso, allor conosco bene
l'errore e 'l danno dell'umana gente:
quel cor, c'alfin consente   5
a' tuo lusinghi e a' tuo van diletti,
procaccia all'alma dolorosi guai.
Ben lo sa chi lo sente,
come spesso prometti
altrui la pace e 'l ben che tu non hai   10
né debbi aver già mai.
Dunche ha men grazia chi più qua soggiorna:
ché chi men vive più lieve al ciel torna.

131

Under two beautiful eyebrows, Love gathers it forces again when I am at the time of life which scorns its bow and wings. My eyes, greedy for every marvel that resembles the one found there, make themselves the target of more than one fierce arrow. And yet soon after the sweet thought of her, another, harsh and strong, of shame and death, assails me; but Love does not lose strength before greater fear or perils: for one hour cannot conquer a habit of many years.

Madrigal, for 'the beautiful and cruel lady', 1536–46. *

132

While my past is present to me, as continually happens, I then, oh false world, recognize full well the error of the human race and the harm this causes: the heart which finally gives in to your enticements and to your empty pleasures brings to the soul painful troubles. He knows this well who experiences it: how you often promise men the peace and the good that you do not have, nor ever ought to have. So he has the lesser grace whose stay is longer here: for whoever lives less long returns to heaven more lightly.

Madrigal, 1536–46. *

133

Condotto da molt'anni all'ultim'ore,
tardi conosco, o mondo, i tuo diletti:
la pace che non hai altrui prometti
e quel riposo c'anzi al nascer muore.
La vergogna e 'l timore   5
degli anni, c'or prescrive
il ciel, non mi rinnuova
che 'l vecchio e dolce errore,
nel qual chi troppo vive
l'anima 'ncide e nulla al corpo giova.   10
Il dico e so per pruova
di me, che 'n ciel quel sol ha miglior sorte
ch'ebbe al suo parto più presso la morte.

134

— Beati voi che su nel ciel godete
le lacrime che 'l mondo non ristora,
favvi amor forza ancora,
o pur per morte liberi ne siete?
— La nostra etterna quiete,   5
fuor d'ogni tempo, è priva
d'invidia, amando, e d'angosciosi pianti.
— Dunche a mal pro' ch'i' viva
convien, come vedete,
per amare e servire in dolor tanti.   10
Se 'l cielo è degli amanti
amico, e 'l mondo ingrato,
amando, a che son nato?
A viver molto? E questo mi spaventa:
ché 'l poco è troppo a chi ben serve e stenta.   15

133

Brought by many years to my last hours, too late, oh world, I recognize your delights for what they are: you promise men a peace which you do not have and that repose which dies before it is born. The shame and fear that come with old age, which heaven now ordains for me, serve only to renew in me the old, sweet error, by which he who lives too long kills the soul and brings no benefit to the body. This I declare, and know the truth of it from what I have undergone, that in heaven only he has the happier state who at his birth had death closer to him.

Madrigal, 1536-46.

134

'Oh happy you who in heaven above enjoy the reward of tears to which this world pays no heed, does love still have power over you, or are you instead freed from it by death?'

'Our eternal rest, entirely beyond time, is, though we love, unmarked by envy or by anguished tears.'

'It is my misfortune, then, that, as you can see, I must live to love and serve with such great sufferings. If to lovers heaven is friendly and the world uncaring, why, since I love, was I born? To live long? But it is this which terrifies me: for even a short life is too much for anyone who serves well and goes unrewarded.'

Madrigal, 1536-46.

135

Mentre c'al tempo la mie vita fugge,
amor più mi distrugge,
né mi perdona un'ora,
com'i' credetti già dopo molt'anni.
L'alma, che trema e rugge,   5
com'uom c'a torto mora,
di me si duol, de' sua etterni danni.
Fra 'l timore e gl'inganni
d'amore e morte, allor tal dubbio sento,
ch'i' cerco in un momento   10
del me' di loro e di poi il peggio piglio;
sì dal mal uso è vinto il buon consiglio.

136

L'alma, che sparge e versa
di fuor l'acque di drento,
il fa sol perché spento
non sie da loro il foco in ch'è conversa.
Ogni altra aita persa   5
saria, se 'l pianger sempre
mi resurge al tuo foco, vecchio e tardi.
Mie dura sorte e mie fortuna avversa
non ha sì dure tempre,
che non m'affligghin men, dove più m'ardi;   10
tal ch' e' tuo accesi sguardi,
di fuor piangendo, dentro circumscrivo,
e di quel c'altri muor sol godo e vivo.

137

Se per gioir pur brami affanni e pianti,
più crudo, Amor, m'è più caro ogni strale,
che fra la morte e 'l male
non dona tempo alcun, né brieve spazio:
tal c'a 'ncider gli amanti   5
i pianti perdi, e 'l nostro è meno strazio.
Ond'io sol ti ringrazio
della mie morte e non delle mie doglie,
c'ogni mal sana chi la vita toglie.

135

While my life flees away with time's passing, love destroys me more and more, and does not leave me free one hour, as I had hoped it would now after many years. My soul which trembles and cries out, like a man condemned to die unjustly, grieves over me and its eternal damnation. Between the fear of death and the deceits of love I now live in this uncertain state, that one moment I seek the better of the two, but then grasp the worse: thus good resolve is conquered by bad habit.

Madrigal, 1536–46. *

136

The soul which scatters and pours out the waters that are within does so only that the fire into which it has been transformed may not be extinguished by them. All other help would be in vain, for it is weeping that always renews my life in your fire, old and slow though I am. My hard lot and my hostile fortune are not of a temper so hard that they do not afflict me less the more you burn me. And so when outside I weep because of your burning looks, I cherish them within, and from what makes others die I alone draw life and joy.

Madrigal, 1536–46. *

137

If you find joy only by yearning for troubles and tears, Love, each arrow of yours is dearer to me the crueller it is, such as to leave no time, not the shortest space, between the evil inflicted and death, for by thus killing lovers you lose their tears, and our agony is lessened. So I thank you only for my death, not for my sufferings, for he heals every ill who takes one's life away.

Madrigal, 1536–46. *

138

Porgo umilmente all'aspro giogo il collo,
il volto lieto a la fortuna ria,
e alla donna mia
nemica il cor di fede e foco pieno;
né dal martir mi crollo,   5
anz'ogni or temo non venga meno.
Ché se 'l volto sereno
cibo e vita mi fa d'un gran martire,
qual crudel doglia mi può far morire?

139

In più leggiadra e men pietosa spoglia
altr'anima non tiene
che la tuo, donna, il moto e 'l dolce anelo;
tal c'alla ingrata voglia
al don di tuo beltà perpetue pene   5
più si convien c'al mie soffrire 'l cielo.
I' nol dico e nol celo
s'i' bramo o no come 'l tuo 'l mie peccato,
ché, se non vivo, morto ove te sia,
o, te pietosa, che dove beato   10
mi fa 'l martir, si' etterna pace mia.
Se dolce mi saria
l'inferno teco, in ciel dunche che fora?
Beato a doppio allora
sare' a godere i' sol nel divin coro   15
quel Dio che 'n cielo e quel che 'n terra adoro.

138

I offer my neck humbly to the harsh yoke, my face happily to evil fortune, and to my hostile lady my heart full of faithfulness and fire; and I do not flinch from the torment, indeed I am constantly in fear that it may lessen. For if her serene face makes of a great torment food and life for me, what cruel suffering could make me die?

Madrigal, for 'the beautiful and cruel lady', 1536–46. *

139

No soul, lady, moves and sweetly breathes in a covering more beautiful and less merciful than yours, and so your ungrateful attitude to the gift of your beauty deserves eternal pains more than my suffering does heaven. I neither declare nor deny whether I desire to be a sinner like you, so that if not when alive then when dead I may be with you; or whether, if you become merciful, you may be my eternal peace where my martyrdom will make me blessed. If with you hell would be sweet for me, what then might my state be in heaven? I should then be doubly blessed, for I alone in the divine choir would enjoy both that God in heaven and that god on earth whom I adore.

Madrigal, for 'the beautiful and cruel lady', 1536–46. *

140

    Se l'alma al fin ritorna
nella suo dolce e desïata spoglia,
o danni o salvi il ciel, come si crede,
ne l'inferno men doglia,
se tuo beltà l'adorna,   5
fie, parte c'altri ti contempla e vede.
S'al cielo ascende e riede,
com'io seco desio
e con tal cura e con sì caldo affetto,
fie men fruire Dio,   10
s'ogni altro piacer cede,
come di qua, al tuo divo e dolce aspetto.
Che me' d'amarti aspetto,
se più giova men doglia a chi è dannato,
che 'n ciel non nuoce l'esser men beato.   15

141

    Perc'all'alta mie speme è breve e corta,
donna, tuo fé, se con san occhio il veggio,
goderò per non peggio
quante di fuor con gli occhi ne prometti;
ché dove è pietà morta,   5
non è che gran bellezza non diletti.
E se contrari effetti
agli occhi di mercé dentro a te sento,
la certezza non tento,
ma prego, ove 'l gioire è men che 'ntero,   10
sie dolce il dubbio a chi nuocer può 'l vero.

142

    Credo, perc'ancor forse
non sia la fiamma spenta
nel freddo tempo dell'età men verde,
l'arco subito torse
Amor, che si rammenta   5
che 'n gentil cor ma' suo colpo non perde;
e la stagion rinverde
per un bel volto; e peggio è al sezzo strale
mie ricaduta che 'l mio primo male.

140

If, as we believe, the soul finally returns to its sweet and longed-for covering, whether heaven damns or saves, there will in hell be less suffering if your beauty adorns it, provided that one can there see and contemplate you. If that beauty ascends and returns to heaven, as with keenest care and warmest affection I desire to do along with it, there will be less delight taken in God, if, as here, every other pleasure gives way to that taken in your divine, sweet countenance. So I look forward to loving you better where the lessening of pain in the damned will bring more benefit than will the harm done by being less blessed in heaven.

Madrigal, for 'the beautiful and cruel lady', 1536–46. *

141

Since compared to my high hopes, lady, your faithfulness is short and fleeting, if my eyes do not mislead me, I shall, for lack of better, rejoice in what your eyes make outward show of promising, for even where pity is dead great beauty cannot but bring delight. And since I sense within you feelings opposite to the mercy in your eyes, I do not seek for certainty, but pray that, where joy is less than complete, doubt may be sweet for one whom the truth could hurt.

Madrigal, for 'the beautiful and cruel lady', 1536–46. *

142

I believe that it was perhaps so that the flame might not be extinguished in the cold time of the less green age that Love suddenly seized his bow, remembering that his blow never fell vainly on a noble heart; and he makes the season green again through a beautiful face; and my falling again to this last arrow is worse than the evil I first suffered.

Madrigal, for 'the beautiful and cruel lady', 1536–46. *

143

Quant'ognor fugge il giorno che mi resta
del viver corto e poco,
tanto più serra il foco
in picciol tempo a mie più danno e strazio:
c'aita il ciel non presta   5
contr'al vecchio uso in così breve spazio.
Pur poi che non se' sazio
del foco circumscritto,
in cui pietra non serva suo natura
non c'un cor, ti ringrazio,   10
Amor, se 'l manco invitto
in chiuso foco alcun tempo non dura.
Mie peggio è mie ventura,
perché la vita all'arme che tu porti
cara non m'è, s'almen perdoni a' morti.   15

144

Passo inanzi a me stesso
con alto e buon concetto,
e 'l tempo gli prometto
c'aver non deggio. O pensier vano e stolto!
Ché con la morte appresso   5
perdo 'l presente, e l'avvenir m'è tolto;
e d'un leggiadro volto
ardo e spero sanar, che morto viva
negli anni ove la vita non arriva.

143

The faster the daytime left to me in this short and meagre life flees unceasingly, the tighter does the fire enclose me in the little time remaining, to my greater harm and anguish, for heaven cannot offer help against old habits in so brief a space. Since, however, you are not satisfied with the fire that hems me in, in which not even a stone would preserve its nature, never mind a heart, I thank you, for of these the less resistant, enclosed in fire, can last no time at all. The worst that can befall me would be for me good fortune, since life exposed to the arms you bear is no longer dear to me, while you at least spare the dead.

Madrigal, for 'the beautiful and cruel lady', 1536–46, possibly 1544. *

144

I run ahead of myself with fine and lofty thoughts, promising them fulfilment in a time to which I have no claim. Oh empty, stupid thoughts! For with death near I lose the present, and the future is taken from me; and I burn because of a lovely face, yet hope to be cured so that, though dead, I may live in those years that my life will not reach.

Madrigal, 1536–46. *

145

Se costei gode e tu solo, Amor, vivi
de' nostri pianti, e s'io, come te, soglio
di lacrime e cordoglio
e d'un ghiaccio nutrir la vita mia;
dunche, di vita privi   5
saremo da mercé di donna pia.
Meglio il peggio saria:
contrari cibi han sì contrari effetti
c'a lei il godere, a noi torrien la vita;
tal che 'nsieme prometti   10
più morte, là dove più porgi aita.
A l'alma sbigottita
viver molto più val con dura sorte
che grazia c'abbi a sé presso la morte.

146

Gli sguardi che tu strazi
a me tutti gli togli;
né furto è già quel che del tuo non doni;
ma se 'l vulgo ne sazi
e ' bruti, e me ne spogli,   5
omicidio è, c'a morte ognor mi sproni.
Amor, perché perdoni
tuo somma cortesia
sie di beltà qui tolta
a chi gusta e desia,   10
e data a gente stolta?
Deh, falla un'altra volta
pietosa dentro e sì brutta di fuori,
c'a me dispiaccia, e di me s'innamori.

145

If she rejoices in our weeping and you, Love, live from that alone, and if I, like you, am used to nourishing my life on tears and grief and iciness, then we should be deprived of life were she to show the compassion of a merciful lady. The better would turn out the worse: opposite foods have such opposite effects that they would take joy from her and life from us; so that at one and the same time you most offer help where you most threaten death. To the frightened soul, a long life marked by a difficult fate is worth more than a graciousness that brings death with it.

Madrigal, for 'the beautiful and cruel lady', 1536-46. *

146

The looks that you squander on others you take from me; it is not robbing, I agree, if you do not give what belongs to you; but if you sate the common people and the beasts with them, yet deny them to me, this is murder, for you drive me hour by hour to death. Love, why do you allow your highest favour, beauty, to be taken from him who appreciates and desires it, and be given to the stupid masses? Ah, make her another time merciful within and so ugly without that she will be displeasing to me, and she will be the one to fall in love with me.

Madrigal, for 'the beautiful and cruel lady', 1536-46. *

147

— Deh dimmi, Amor, se l'alma di costei
fusse pietosa com'ha bell' il volto,
s'alcun saria sì stolto
ch'a sé non si togliessi e dessi a lei?
E io, che più potrei   5
servirla, amarla, se mi fuss'amica,
che, sendomi nemica,
l'amo più c'allor far non doverrei?
   — Io dico che fra voi, potenti dei,
convien c'ogni riverso si sopporti.   10
Poi che sarete morti
di mille 'ngiurie e torti,
amando te com'or di lei tu ardi,
far ne potrai giustamente vendetta.
Ahimè, lasso chi pur tropp'aspetta   15
ch'i' gionga a' suoi conforti tanto tardi!
Ancor, se ben riguardi,
un generoso, alter e nobil core
perdon' e porta a chi l'offend' amore.

148

Con più certa salute
men grazia, donna, mi terrie ancor vivo;
dall'uno e l'altro rivo
degli occhi il petto sarie manco molle.
Doppia mercé mie picciola virtute   5
di tanto vince che l'adombra e tolle;
né saggio alcun ma' volle,
se non sé innalza e sprona,
di quel gioir ch'esser non può capace.
Il troppo è vano e folle;   10
ché modesta persona
d'umil fortuna ha più tranquilla pace.
Quel c'a vo' lice, a me, donna, dispiace:
chi si dà altrui, c'altrui non si prometta,
d'un superchio piacer morte n'aspetta.   15

147

'Ah, tell me, Love: if that lady's soul were as pitying as her face is beautiful, would there be anyone so stupid as not to renounce his liberty and give himself to her? As for me, how could I serve and love her more if she were friendly to me, since, when she is hostile, I now love her more than I ought then to do?'

'I declare that among you, powerful gods, every reverse should be patiently borne. Then, when through a thousand wrongs and injuries you are dead, and she loves you as you now burn for her, you can justly take revenge for them. Alas, wretched is he who foolishly goes on waiting for me to come and bring him comfort so late on! Besides, you really ought to know that a generous, proud and noble heart pardons and bears love towards one who hurts it.'

Madrigal, for 'the beautiful and cruel lady', 1536–46. *

148

Less graciousness, lady, would keep me alive still, and in stronger health; my breast would be less bathed by streams from both my eyes. Double pity so overcomes my weak powers that it darkens and destroys them; no wise man ever wished such measure of that joy as he could not receive, but only such as would raise and spur him on. Too much is vain and foolish, for a modest person finds more tranquil peace in a lowly lot. What lies within your power, lady, brings distress to me: whoever gives herself to another in a measure he does not look for may well bring about death from excessive pleasure.

Madrigal, very probably for Vittoria Colonna, probably late 1530s. *

149

Non posso non mancar d'ingegno e d'arte
a chi mi to' la vita
con tal superchia aita,
che d'assai men mercé più se ne prende.
D'allor l'alma mie parte   5
com'occhio offeso da chi troppo splende,
e sopra me trascende
a l'impossibil mie; per farmi pari
al minor don di donna alta e serena,
seco non m'alza; e qui convien ch'impari   10
che quel ch'i' posso ingrato a lei mi mena.
Questa, di grazie piena,
n'abonda e 'nfiamma altrui d'un certo foco,
che 'l troppo con men caldo arde che 'l poco.

150

Non men gran grazia, donna, che gran doglia
ancide alcun, che 'l furto a morte mena,
privo di speme e ghiacciato ogni vena,
se vien subito scampo che 'l discioglia.
Simil se tuo mercé, più che ma' soglia,   5
nella miseria mie d'affanni piena,
con superchia pietà mi rasserena,
par, più che 'l pianger, la vita mi toglia.
Così n'avvien di novell'aspra o dolce:
ne' lor contrari è morte in un momento,   10
onde s'allarga o troppo stringe 'l core.
Tal tuo beltà, c'Amore e 'l ciel qui folce,
se mi vuol vivo affreni il gran contento,
c'al don superchio debil virtù muore.

151

Non ha l'ottimo artista alcun concetto
c'un marmo solo in sé non circonscriva
col suo superchio, e solo a quello arriva
la man che ubbidisce all'intelletto.
Il mal ch'io fuggo, e 'l ben ch'io mi prometto,   5
in te, donna leggiadra, altera e diva,
tal si nasconde; e perch'io più non viva,
contraria ho l'arte al disïato effetto.

149

I cannot but be lacking in wit and skill regarding one who takes away my life by offering help so excessive that one would gain more from much less compassion. And so my soul takes its leave, like an injured eye from what shines too brightly, and rises above me to where I cannot reach; it does not raise me with itself to be equal to receiving the least gift from a lady lofty and serene; from this she must learn that it is my incapacity that makes me appear ungrateful before her. This lady, herself full of grace, distributes this so lavishly and inflames others with such a fire that its excess burns with less heat than would a little of it.

Madrigal, very probably for Vittoria Colonna, probably late 1530s. *

150

Great grace, lady, no less than great suffering can kill a thief being led to death, devoid of hope and paralysed in every vein, if the pardon granting him freedom is suddenly presented.

Likewise if your mercy, bestowed more generously than ever before on this misery of mine so full of woes, should with excessive compassion bring me peace, then it seems that this would take away not just my tears but life itself.

Such is what happens to us with harsh or sweet news: contrary though they be, both result in instant death, by causing the heart to expand or to contract too much.

And so your beauty, nourished here by Love and heaven, should restrain the great happiness it brings if it would have me live: for touched by an excessive gift a weak power dies.

Sonnet, very probably for Vittoria Colonna, probably late 1530s. *

151

The greatest artist does not have any concept which a single piece of marble does not itself contain within its excess, though only a hand that obeys the intellect can discover it.

The evil which I flee, and the good to which I aspire, gracious, noble and divine lady, lie hidden in you in just this way; but that I may not live hereafter, my art brings about the opposite of what I desire.

Amor dunque non ha, né tua beltate
o durezza o fortuna o gran disdegno,　　　　　　　10
del mio mal colpa, o mio destino o sorte;
　　se dentro del tuo cor morte e pietate
porti in un tempo, e che 'l mio basso ingegno
non sappia, ardendo, trarne altro che morte.

152

　　Sì come per levar, donna, si pone
in pietra alpestra e dura
una viva figura,
che là più cresce u' più la pietra scema;
tal alcun'opre buone,　　　　　　　5
per l'alma che pur trema,
cela il superchio della propria carne
co' l'inculta sua cruda e dura scorza.
Tu pur dalle mie streme
parti puo' sol levarne,　　　　　　　10
ch'in me non è di me voler né forza.

153

　　Non pur d'argento o d'oro
vinto dal foco esser po' piena aspetta,
vota d'opra prefetta,
la forma, che sol fratta il tragge fora;
tal io, col foco ancora　　　　　　　5
d'amor dentro ristoro
il desir voto di beltà infinita,
di coste' ch'i' adoro,
anima e cor della mie fragil vita.
Alta donna e gradita　　　　　　　10
in me discende per sì brevi spazi,
c'a trarla fuor convien mi rompa e strazi.

It is not Love, then, nor your beauty, nor harshness, nor fortune, nor haughty disdain that is to be blamed for my evil, nor my destiny nor fate,

if within your heart you carry at the same time death and mercy, and my low mind, in its burning, does not know how to draw forth from it anything but death.

Sonnet, for Vittoria Colonna, 1538–41/4.

152

Just as, lady, it is by removing that one places in hard, alpine stone a living figure, which grows greater precisely where the stone grows less, so the excess that is one's own flesh, with its coarse, rough, hard bark, hides some good works in the soul which trembles under this burden. You alone can so remove from my outer being, for in me there is regarding me neither will nor strength.

Madrigal, for Vittoria Colonna, 1538–41/4.

153

It is not unique, the mould which, empty of the work of art, finally stands ready to be filled by silver or gold melted by fire, and then brings forth the work only by being sundered; I, also, through the fire of love, replenish the desire within me, empty of infinite beauty, with her whom I adore, soul and heart of my fragile life. This noble and dear lady descends into me through such narrow spaces that, for her to be brought forth, I too must be broken and shattered.

Madrigal, for Vittoria Colonna, 1538–41/4. *

154

Tanto sopra me stesso
mi fai, donna, salire,
che non ch'i' 'l possa dire,
nol so pensar, perch'io non son più desso.
Dunche, perché più spesso,   5
se l'alie tuo mi presti,
non m'alzo e volo al tuo leggiadro viso,
e che con teco resti,
se dal ciel n'è concesso
ascender col mortale in paradiso?   10
Se non ch'i' sia diviso
dall'alma per tuo grazia, e che quest'una
fugga teco suo morte, è mie fortuna.

155

Le grazie tua e la fortuna mia
hanno, donna, sì vari
gli effetti, perch'i' 'mpari
in fra 'l dolce e l'amar qual mezzo sia.
Mentre benigna e pia   5
dentro, e di fuor ti mostri
quante se' bella al mie 'rdente desire,
la fortun' aspra e ria,
nemica a' piacer nostri,
con mille oltraggi offende 'l mie gioire;   10
se per avverso po' di tal martire,
si piega alle mie voglie,
tuo pietà mi si toglie.
Fra 'l riso e 'l pianto, en sì contrari stremi,
mezzo non è c'una gran doglia scemi.   15

154

You make me rise so high above myself, lady, that it is not just my power of speech but thought itself that fails to grasp what happens, for I am no longer myself. Why, then, if you give me wings, do I not more often raise myself and fly to your lovely face; and why may I not remain with you, if heaven has granted us to ascend to paradise with our mortal body? Yet I do recognize that it is my good fortune that, through your grace, I should be separated from my soul, and that it alone, being with you, should escape its death.

Madrigal, for Vittoria Colonna, 1538–41/4. *

155

Your favours and my fortune, lady, produce such different effects so that I may learn what it means to live between sweetness and bitterness. When you show yourself kind and compassionate within and to my burning desire how beautiful without, harsh and cruel fortune, hostile to our pleasures, with a thousand assaults attacks my joy; if it, then, bending to my wishes, reverses such a torment, you withdraw your favour from me. Between laughter and tears, at such opposite extremes, there is no mean that may lessen a great suffering.

Madrigal, possibly for 'the beautiful and cruel lady', 1536–46. *

156

A l'alta tuo lucente dïadema
per la strada erta e lunga,
non è, donna, chi giunga,
s'umiltà non v'aggiugni e cortesia:
il montar cresce, e 'l mie valore scema,   5
e la lena mi manca a mezza via.
Che tuo beltà pur sia
superna, al cor par che diletto renda,
che d'ogni rara altezza è ghiotto e vago:
po' per gioir della tuo leggiadria   10
bramo pur che discenda
là dov'aggiungo. E 'n tal pensier m'appago,
se 'l tuo sdegno presago,
per basso amare e alto odiar tuo stato,
a te stessa perdona il mie peccato.   15

157

Pietosa e dolce aita
tuo, donna, teco insieme,
per le mie parte streme
spargon dal cor gli spirti della vita,
onde l'alma, impedita   5
del suo natural corso
pel subito gioir, da me diparti.
Po' l'aspra tuo partita,
per mie mortal soccorso,
tornan superchi al cor gli spirti sparti.   10
S'a me veggio tornarti,
dal cor di nuovo dipartir gli sento;
onde d'equal tormento
e l'aita e l'offesa mortal veggio:
el mezzo, a chi troppo ama, è sempre il peggio. 15

156

There is no one, lady, who may reach your high, shining crown by mounting the long, steep road, unless you also reach down to him with humility and kindness: the ascent steepens, my strength fails, and my breath gives out halfway along the road. That your beauty should indeed be so exalted seems to bring delight to my heart which longs eagerly for all that is rare and sublime; but then to enjoy your loveliness I also crave that you descend to where I may reach. And I content myself with this thought: that when your reproachful insight reveals my sin to you, of loving your state as low and hating it as high, you will pardon yourself for having been its cause.

*Madrigal, very probably for Vittoria Colonna, probably late 1530s or early 1540s.**

157

When I am with you, lady, your compassionate and sweet help scatters from my heart through my extremities the spirits of life; and so my soul, prevented from its natural activity by sudden joy, departs from me. Then, at your harsh parting, the scattered spirits return to my heart in such excess that the aid they bring threatens to be fatal. If I see you returning to me, I feel them once more departing from my heart; and so I see that both help and hurt are equally fatal torment: to have each half the time is, for one who loves too much, to live always in the worst state possible.

*Madrigal, possibly for 'the beautiful and cruel lady', 1536-46.**

158

Amor, la morte a forza
del pensier par mi scacci,
e con tal grazia impacci
l'alma che, senza, sarie più contenta.
Caduto è 'l frutto e secca è già la scorza,   5
e quel, già dolce, amaro or par ch'i' senta;
anzi, sol mi tormenta,
nell'ultim'ore e corte,
infinito piacere in breve spazio.
Sì, tal mercé, spaventa   10
tuo pietà tardi e forte,
c'al corpo è morte, e al diletto strazio;
ond'io pur ti ringrazio
in questa età: ché s'i' muoio in tal sorte,
tu 'l fai più con mercé che con la morte.   15

159

Per esser manco, alta signora, indegno
del don di vostra immensa cortesia,
prima, all'incontro a quella, usar la mia
con tutto il cor volse 'l mie basso ingegno.
Ma visto poi, c'ascendere a quel segno   5
propio valor non è c'apra la via,
perdon domanda la mie audacia ria,
e del fallir più saggio ognor divegno.
E veggio ben com'erra s'alcun crede
la grazia, che da voi divina piove,   10
pareggi l'opra mia caduca e frale.
L'ingegno, l'arte, la memoria cede:
c'un don celeste non con mille pruove
pagar del suo può già chi è mortale.

160

S'alcun legato è pur dal piacer molto,
come da morte altrui tornare in vita,
qual cosa è che po' paghi tanta aita,
che renda il debitor libero e sciolto?

158

Love, it seems that you drive death forcibly from my thoughts, and impede the soul with the kind of grace that it would in fact be happier without. The fruit is fallen and the rind already dry, and that fruit which once was sweet now seems bitter to my taste; indeed it only torments me in these last, short hours to have an infinite pleasure in a brief space. In showing such mercy, this late, powerful pity of yours so frightens me that it causes death to my body and torment to my delight; and yet I thank you at my age: for if I die in this state, you shall have brought it about through mercy rather than through death.

Madrigal, for 'the beautiful and cruel lady', 1536–46. *

159

To be less unworthy, high lady, of the gift of your immense courtesy, my lowly mind at first tried wholeheartedly to reciprocate in kind.

But having seen then that my own powers can make no headway towards ascending to such a goal, I ask pardon for my wicked boldness, and through that fault grow constantly wiser.

And I see clearly how wrong it is to believe that my fleeting and frail activity could match that divine grace which rains down from you.

Mind, skill and memory give way: for one still mortal cannot repay a heavenly gift from his own resources, not even if he tries a thousand times.

Sonnet, for Vittoria Colonna, of uncertain date, possibly c. 1541. *

160

If someone is truly bound to another through having received a great favour, such as being brought back to life from death, what could possibly so repay such help as to render the debtor discharged and free?

E se pur fusse, ne sarebbe tolto   5
il soprastar d'una mercé infinita
al ben servito, onde sarie 'mpedita
da l'incontro servire, a quella volto.
   Dunche, per tener alta vostra grazia,
donna, sopra 'l mie stato, in me sol bramo   10
ingratitudin più che cortesia:
   ché dove l'un dell'altro al par si sazia,
non mi sare' signor quel che tant'amo:
ché 'n parità non cape signoria.

                    161

   Per qual mordace lima
discresce e manca ognor tuo stanca spoglia,
anima inferma? or quando fie ti scioglia
da quella il tempo, e torni ov'eri, in cielo,
candida e lieta prima,   5
deposto il periglioso e mortal velo?
C'ancor ch'i' cangi 'l pelo
per gli ultim'anni e corti,
cangiar non posso il vecchio mie antico uso,
che con più giorni più mi sforza e preme.   10
Amore, a te nol celo,
ch'i' porto invidia a' morti,
sbigottito e confuso,
sì di sé meco l'alma trema e teme.
Signor, nell'ore streme,   15
stendi ver' me le tuo pietose braccia,
tomm'a me stesso e famm'un che ti piaccia.

And even were this possible, it would take, from him who had served well, the continual care of an infinite mercy, since this cannot exist where service has been given in return.

So, lady, to keep your graciousness high above my state, I yearn only that there seem to be in me ingratitude rather than courtesy,

for if each of us were equally to satisfy the other, you whom I so love could not then be my lord: for in equality there is no place for lordship.

Sonnet, for Vittoria Colonna, of uncertain date, possibly c. 1541.

161

What biting file makes your tired hide wear away and fail, weak soul? Oh when will time free you from it, so that, having laid aside your dangerous and mortal veil, you may return to heaven where you once were, pure and happy? For though I change my skin in these last, short years, I cannot change my old, habitual way of life, which with each passing day binds and oppresses me all the more. Love, I will not hide from you that in my frightened and confused state I bear envy towards the dead, so greatly does my soul while still with me fear and tremble for its fate. Lord, in my last hours, stretch out to me your merciful arms, take me from myself and make me one who is pleasing to you.

Madrigal, for Vittoria Colonna, c. 1538–41.

162

Ora in sul destro, ora in sul manco piede
variando, cerco della mie salute.
Fra 'l vizio e la virtute
il cor confuso mi travaglia e stanca,
come chi 'l ciel non vede,   5
che per ogni sentier si perde e manca.
Porgo la carta bianca
a' vostri sacri inchiostri,
c'amor mi sganni e pietà 'l ver ne scriva:
che l'alma, de sé franca,   10
non pieghi agli error nostri
mie breve resto, e che men cieco viva.
Chieggio a voi, alta e diva
donna, saper se 'n ciel men grado tiene
l'umil peccato che 'l superchio bene.   15

163

Quante più fuggo e odio ognor me stesso,
tanto a te, donna, con verace speme
ricorro; e manco teme
l'alma di me, quant'a te son più presso.
A quel che 'l ciel promesso   5
m'ha nel tuo volto aspiro
e ne' begli occhi, pien d'ogni salute:
e ben m'accorgo spesso,
in quel c'ogni altri miro,
che gli occhi senza 'l cor non han virtute.   10
Luci già mai vedute!
né da vederle è men che 'l gran desio;
ché 'l veder raro è prossimo a l'oblio.

164

Per fido esemplo alla mia vocazione
nel parto mi fu data la bellezza,
che d'ambo l'arti m'è lucerna e specchio.
S'altro si pensa, è falsa opinione.
Questo sol l'occhio porta a quella altezza   5
c'a pingere e scolpir qui m'apparecchio.

162

Sometimes on my right foot, sometimes on my left, shifting from one to the other, I go in search of my salvation. Moving between vice and virtue, my confused heart troubles and wearies me, like one who does not see heaven, which along every path becomes lost from view and disappears. I hold out a blank page for your sacred ink, that your love may show how I deceive myself and your compassion may there write the truth, so that my soul, made master of itself, may not bend to our errors what little of my life remains, and I may live less blindly. I beg to know from you, high and divine lady, whether in heaven the humble sinner will hold a lesser rank than he who is perfectly good.

Madrigal, for Vittoria Colonna, c. 1538–41. *

163

The more I flee and hate myself with each passing hour, the more, lady, I have recourse to you with lively hope; and my soul has less fear of me the closer I am to you. I aspire to what heaven has promised me in your face and in your beautiful eyes, full of all salvation; and I often realize clearly, from what I see in every other face, that the eyes without the heart possess no power. Lights never seen before! and see them I ought, no less than I greatly desire, for to see them rarely is to risk forgetting them.

Madrigal, for Vittoria Colonna, c. 1538–44, probably 1541–4. *

164

From birth I was given beauty as a faithful guide to my vocation; it is a light and mirror for me in both the arts. If anyone thinks otherwise, he is quite mistaken. This alone carries the eye to those heights which here I set myself to paint and sculpt.

S'e' giudizi temerari e sciocchi
al senso tiran la beltà, che muove
e porta al cielo ogni intelletto sano,
dal mortale al divin non vanno gli occhi   10
infermi, e fermi sempre pur là d'ove
ascender senza grazia è pensier vano.

165

Se 'l commodo degli occhi alcun constringe
con l'uso, parte insieme
la ragion perde, e teme;
ché più s'inganna quel c'a sé più crede:
onde nel cor dipinge   5
per bello quel c'a picciol beltà cede.
Ben vi fo, donna, fede
che 'l commodo né l'uso non m'ha preso,
sì di raro e' mie veggion gli occhi vostri
circonscritti ov' a pena il desir vola.   10
Un punto sol m'ha acceso,
né più vi vidi c'una volta sola.

166

Ben posson gli occhi mie presso e lontano
veder dov'apparisce il tuo bel volto;
ma dove loro, ai pie', donna, è ben tolto
portar le braccia e l'una e l'altra mano.
    L'anima, l'intelletto intero e sano   5
per gli occhi ascende più libero e sciolto
a l'alta tuo beltà; ma l'ardor molto
non dà tal previlegio al corp' umano
    grave e mortal, sì che mal segue poi,
senz'ali ancor, d'un'angioletta il volo,   10
e 'l veder sol pur se ne gloria e loda.
    Deh, se tu puo' nel ciel quante tra noi,
fa' del mie corpo tutto un occhio solo;
né fie poi parte in me che non ti goda.

If those of rash and foolish judgement drag down beauty to the senses, though it moves and carries every healthy mind to heaven, let them realize that eyes that are infirm do not move from the mortal to the divine sphere, but remain forever firmly fixed there whence to think of rising without grace is a vain hope.

Double sestet, for Vittoria Colonna, possibly 1541–4.

165

If the pleasure given to the eyes together with familiarity come to dominate someone, he loses his judgement partly and becomes fearful: for he who most trusts himself most deceives himself; as a result he paints as beautiful in his heart what is inferior even to something of little beauty. I give you my word, lady, that I have been taken neither by pleasure nor by familiarity, so rarely do my eyes see yours, which are confined to where desire can fly only with difficulty. A single moment was enough to set me on fire, and I have not looked on you other than as you were that one time.

Madrigal, for Vittoria Colonna, possibly 1541–4.

166

My eyes can certainly see near or far where your beautiful face appears; but it is certainly beyond the power of my feet to carry my arms and hands to where my eyes can reach.

The soul, the whole and healthy intellect, more free and unbound ascends by means of the eyes to your high beauty; but burning ardour gives no such privilege to the human body,

heavy and mortal, so that, still lacking wings, it cannot follow the flight even of a little angel, and sight alone may pride itself and rejoice in doing so.

Ah, if you have as much power in heaven as you have among us, make of my entire body a single eye; and may there then be no part of me which does not rejoice in you.

Sonnet, for Vittoria Colonna, possibly 1541–4. *

167

La morte, Amor, del mie medesmo loco,
del qual, già nudo, trïonfar solevi
non che con l'arco e co' pungenti strali,
ti scaccia e sprezza, e col fier ghiaccio il foco
tuo dolce ammorza, c'ha dì corti e brevi.   5
In ogni cor veril men di le' vali;
e se ben porti l'ali,
con esse mi giugnesti, or fuggi e temi,
c'ogni età verde è schifa a' giorni stremi.

168

Perché 'l mezzo di me che dal ciel viene
a quel con gran desir ritorna e vola,
restando in una sola
di beltà donna, e ghiaccio ardendo in lei,
in duo parte mi tiene   5
contrarie sì, che l'una all'altra invola
il ben che non diviso aver devrei.
Ma se già ma' costei
cangia 'l suo stile, e c'a l'un mezzo manchi
il ciel, quel mentre c'a le' grato sia,   10
e' mie sì sparsi e stanchi
pensier fien tutti in quella donna mia;
e se 'lor che m'è pia,
l'alma il ciel caccia, almen quel tempo spero
non più mezz'esser, ma suo tutto intero.   15

169

Nel mie 'rdente desio,
coste' pur mi trastulla,
di fuor pietosa e nel cor aspra e fera.
Amor, non tel diss'io,
ch'e' no' ne sare' nulla   5
e che 'l suo perde chi 'n quel d'altri spera?
Or s'ella vuol ch'i' pèra,
mie colpa, e danno s'ha prestarle fede,
com'a chi poco manca a chi più crede.

167

Death scornfully drives you out, Love, from that very place in me over which you used to triumph unaided, not just when armed with your bow and piercing arrows; and with fierce ice it extinguishes your sweet fire, whose days are short and few. In every manly heart you have less power than death; and though you bear wings with which you once reached me, with these you now flee in fear: for the entire green age is loathsome to our last days.

Madrigal, possibly 1541-4. *

168

Since the half of me that comes from heaven flies back there with great desire, my remaining bound to a lady unique in beauty, and burning in her who is as ice, keeps me in two parts so contrary that one steals from the other the good which, were I undivided, I should have. But were it ever to happen that she should change her attitude, and heaven fail to draw the other half, then while I should be pleasing to her, my thoughts, till now so scattered and weary, would all be directed to that lady of mine; and so if when she were compassionate to me heaven should drive my soul away, for that time at least I should hope to be hers not by half, but whole and entire.

Madrigal, for 'the beautiful and cruel lady', 1536-46. *

169

While I burn with desire, this woman merely toys with me, outwardly merciful but in her heart harsh and cruel. Love, did I not tell you that for me there was nothing to be gained from her, and that he who places his hopes in what belongs to another loses even what is his? So if she wishes me to die, the fault is mine, and the harm comes from having put my trust in her, for little blame attaches to one who is too much believed.

Madrigal, possibly for 'the beautiful and cruel lady', 1536-46. *

170

   Spargendo gran bellezza ardente foco
per mille cori accesi,
come cosa è che pesi,
c'un solo ancide, a molti è lieve e poco.
Ma, chiuso in picciol loco,   5
s'il sasso dur calcina,
che l'acque poi il dissolvon 'n un momento,
come per pruova il sa chi 'l ver dicerne:
così d'una divina
de mille il foco ho drento   10
c'arso m'ha 'l cor nelle mie parte interne;
ma le lacrime etterne
se quel dissolvon già sì duro e forte,
fie me' null'esser c'arder senza morte.

171

   Nella memoria delle cose belle
morte bisogna, per tor di costui
il volto a lei, com'a vo' tolto ha lui;
se 'l foco in ghiaccio e 'l riso volge in pianto,
con tale odio di quelle,   5
che del cor voto più non si dien vanto.
Ma se rimbotta alquanto
i suo begli occhi nell'usato loco,
fien legne secche in un ardente foco.

170

Great beauty that scatters burning fire over a thousand hearts is like a heavy weight which if it bears down on one man alone kills him but if borne by many is easy and light. Yet just as fire when enclosed in a small space reduces hard stone to lime which water can then dissolve in an instant, as he can testify who has seen this process in action, so I have within me the fire of a thousand lovers for a divine woman which has burnt my heart in my innermost parts; yet if my unceasing tears dissolve what was once so hard and strong, it will be better to become nothing than to burn without dying.

Madrigal, possibly for 'the beautiful and cruel lady', 1536–46. *

171

Death must penetrate the memory of beautiful things to take away his face from your memory as it has taken him from you, since it turns fire to ice and laughter to tears, causing such hatred of beautiful things that they can no longer boast over the empty heart. But if he should bring back his eyes to that customary place even for a short time, they would be like dry wood to a burning fire.

Madrigal, possibly for 'the beautiful and cruel lady', 1536–46. *

172

Costei pur si delibra,
indomit' e selvaggia,
ch'i' arda, mora e caggia
a quel c'a peso non sie pure un'oncia;
e 'l sangue a libra a libra   5
mi svena, e sfibra e 'l corpo all'alma sconcia.
La si gode e racconcia
nel suo fidato specchio,
ove sé vede equale al paradiso;
po', volta a me, mi concia   10
sì, c'oltr'all'esser vecchio,
in quel col mie fo più bello il suo viso,
ond'io vie più deriso
son d'esser brutto; e pur m'è gran ventura,
s'i' vinco, a farla bella, la natura.   15

173

Se dal cor lieto divien bello il volto,
dal tristo il brutto; e se donna aspra e bella
il fa, chi fie ma' quella
che non arda di me com'io di lei?
Po' c'a destinguer molto   5
dalla mie chiara stella
da bello a bel fur fatti gli occhi mei,
contr'a sé fa costei
non men crudel che spesso
dichi: — Dal cor mie smorto il volto viene. —   10
Che s'altri fa se stesso,
pingendo donna, in quella
che farà poi, se sconsolato il tiene?
Dunc'ambo n'arien bene
ritrarla col cor lieto e 'l viso asciutto: 15
sé farie bella e me non farie brutto.

172

Untamed and wild, she deliberately decides that I should burn, die and turn into something which weighs not even an ounce; and from my veins she draws my blood pint by pint, and weakens me and makes my body unfit for my soul. She rejoices in herself and adorns herself before her faithful mirror, where she sees herself equal to paradise; then, turning to me, she so upsets me that my face, in addition to being old, by contrast makes hers in the mirror more beautiful still, so that I am scorned even more for being ugly; and yet I consider it my great good fortune that, by increasing her beauty, I surpass nature.

Madrigal, possibly for 'the beautiful and cruel lady', 1536-46. *

173

If one's face becomes beautiful from having a happy heart, and ugly from a sad one; and if it is made to be the latter by a harsh and beautiful woman, what woman is there who would not burn for me as I for her? Since through the influence of my bright star my eyes were so formed as to be able to distinguish clearly one beauty from another, she acts no less cruelly towards herself in often making me say: 'My downcast face comes from my heart.' For if an artist represents himself in painting a woman, what will he represent in painting her, if she keeps him disconsolate? So it would be for both our good if while portraying her I could have a happy heart and dry face: she would then make herself beautiful and not make me ugly.

Madrigal, possibly for 'the beautiful and cruel lady', 1536-46. *

174

Per quel che di vo', donna, di fuor veggio,
quantunche dentro al ver l'occhio non passi,
spero a' mie stanchi e lassi
pensier riposo a qualche tempo ancora;
e 'l più saperne il peggio,   5
del vostro interno, forse al mie mal fora.
Se crudeltà dimora
'n un cor che pietà vera
co' begli occhi prometta a' pianti nostri,
ben sarebb'ora l'ora,   10
c'altro già non si spera
d'onesto amor, che quel ch'è di fuor mostri.
Donna, s'agli occhi vostri
contraria è l'alma, e io, pur contro a quella,
godo gl'inganni d'una donna bella.   15

175

No' salda, Amor, de' tuo dorati strali
fra le mie vecchie ancor la minor piaga,
che la mente, presaga
del mal passato, a peggio mi traporti.
Se ne' vecchi men vali,   5
campar dovria, se non fa' guerra a' morti.
S'a l'arco l'alie porti
contra me zoppo e nudo,
con gli occhi per insegna,
c'ancidon più che'e' tuo più feri dardi,   10
chi fia che mi conforti?
Elmo non già né scudo,
ma sol quel che mi segna
d'onor, perdendo, e biasmo a te, se m'ardi.
Debile vecchio, è tardi   15
la fuga e lenta, ov'è posto 'l mie scampo;
e chi vince a fuggir, non resti in campo.

174

Although my eyes cannot pass within to see how you truly feel, I hope to find peace a little while longer for my tired and unhappy thoughts, lady, from what I see of you outwardly; to know more of your internal state might perhaps only make my troubles worse. If cruelty dwells in a heart that through beautiful eyes promises true pity to our tears, now would certainly be the time truly to display what outwardly appears, for nothing less is expected of virtuous love. But if, lady, your soul is the opposite of your eyes, then, despite its opposition, I shall go on enjoying the deceptions of a beautiful lady.

Madrigal, for 'the beautiful and cruel lady', 1536–46. *

175

Not even the least of the old wounds I received from your golden arrows, Love, has closed when you turn my mind to foreseeing worse harm even than that suffered in the past. Since you have less power over those who are old, I ought to flee, provided you do not wage war on the dead. If against me, who am lame and defenceless, you add wings to your bow, fighting under the standard of those eyes which kill more surely than your cruellest arrows, what might offer me protection? Neither helmet nor shield will be of use, but only what will mark me with honour in defeat, and bring you reproof, if you burn me. Flight, my only hope of escape, is late and slow for a frail, old man; but he who wins by fleeing ought not to linger on the battlefield.

Madrigal, for 'the beautiful and cruel lady', 1536–46.

176

Mestier non era all'alma tuo beltate
legar me vinto con alcuna corda;
ché, se ben mi ricorda,
sol d'uno sguardo fui prigione e preda:
c'alle gran doglie usate   5
forz'è c'un debil cor subito ceda.
Ma chi fie ma' che 'l creda,
preso da' tuo begli occhi in brevi giorni,
un legno secco e arso verde torni?

177

In noi vive e qui giace la divina   10
beltà da morte anz'il suo tempo offesa.
Se con la dritta man face' difesa,
campava. Onde nol fe'? Ch'era mancina.

178

La nuova alta beltà che 'n ciel terrei
unica, non c'al mondo iniquo e fello
(suo nome dal sinistro braccio tiello
il vulgo, cieco a non adorar lei),
    per voi sol nacque; e far non la saprei   5
con ferri in pietra, in carte col pennello;
ma 'l vivo suo bel viso esser può quello
nel qual vostro sperar fermar dovrei.
    E se, come dal sole ogni altra stella
è vinta, vince l'intelletto nostro,   10
per voi non di men pregio esser dovea.
    Dunche, a quetarvi, è suo beltà novella
da Dio formata all'alto desir vostro;
e quel solo, e non io, far lo potea.

176

It was not necessary for your sublime beauty to bind me, once overcome, with any cord, because, if I remember rightly, I was made prisoner and prey by a single look; for a frail heart must straightaway yield to the renewed onslaught of great suffering. But who would ever have believed that, taken by your beautiful eyes, in a few, brief days a piece of withered, burnt-out wood would become green once more?

Madrigal, possibly for 'the beautiful and cruel lady', 1536–46. *

177

In us there lives and here there lies the divine beauty struck down by death before her time. If she had defended herself with her right hand, she would have escaped. Why did she not do this? Because she was left-handed.

Quatrain, for Gandolfo Porrino on the death of Fausta Mancini Attavanti, 1543. *

178

The fresh, noble beauty that I would deem unique in heaven itself, not just in this evil and treacherous world (the common people named her after her left hand, being blind not to adore her),

was born for you alone; I should not be able to fashion it with tools in stone, or on paper with the brush: it could be only with the living beauty of her face that I could satisfy your hope.

And if she surpasses our intellect, as every other star is surpassed by the sun, she must have been no less highly prized by you.

So to bring you peace her beauty has been formed afresh by God to fulfil your noble desire; and he alone, not I, could have done this.

Sonnet: see poem 177. *

179

Se qui son chiusi i begli occhi e sepolti
anzi tempo, sol questo ne conforta:
che pietà di lor vivi era qua morta;
or che son morti, di lor vive in molti.

180

Deh serbi, s'è di me pietate alcuna
che qui son chiuso e dal mondo disciolto,
le lacrime a bagnarsi il petto e 'l volto
per chi resta suggetto alla fortuna.

181

— Perché ne' volti offesi non entrasti
dagli anni, Morte, e c'anzi tempo i' mora?
— Perché nel ciel non sale e non dimora
cosa che 'nvecchi e parte il mondo guasti.

182

Non volse Morte non ancider senza
l'arme degli anni e de' superchi giorni
la beltà che qui giace, acciò c'or torni
al ciel con la non persa sua presenza.

183

La beltà che qui giace al mondo vinse
di tanto ogni più bella creatura,
che morte, ch'era in odio alla natura,
per farsi amica a lei, l'ancise e stinse.

179

If here his beautiful eyes are closed and buried before their time, this alone brings us comfort: that pity for them while they were alive was dead here; but now that they are dead, it is alive in many.

Quatrain, first of a series of fifty epitaphs for Cecchino [Francesco] Bracci, sent to Luigi del Riccio in the course of 1544.

180

Ah, if there is anyone who feels pity for me who am here enclosed and freed from the world, let him reserve the tears which bathe his breast and face for those who remain subject to fortune.

See poem 179.

181

'Why did you not enter into faces worn by the years, Death, and why should I die before my time?'
'Because whatever grows old and is in the process wasted by the world does not rise to heaven and there find its dwelling.'

See poem 179.

182

Death did not wish to kill with the weapons of the years and of excessive days the beauty that lies here, so that it may now return to heaven with its comeliness unspoiled.

See poem 179.

183

The beauty that lies here so far surpassed all the most beautiful creatures in the world that death, which nature viewed with hate, killed and extinguished that beauty to gain nature's friendship.

See poem 179.

184

Qui son de' Bracci, deboli a l'impresa
contr'a la morte mia per non morire;
meglio era esser de' piedi per fuggire
che de' Bracci e non far da lei difesa.

185

Qui son sepulto, e poco innanzi nato
ero: e son quello al qual fu presta e cruda
la morte sì, che l'alma di me nuda
s'accorge a pena aver cangiato stato.

186

Non può per morte già chi qui mi serra
la beltà, c'al mortal mie largir volse,
renderla agli altri tutti a chi la tolse,
s'alfin com'ero de' rifarmi in terra.

187

L'alma di dentro di fuor non vedea,
come noi, il volto, chiuso in questo avello:
che se nel ciel non è albergo sì bello,
trarnela morte già ma' non potea.

188

Se dalla morte è vinta la natura
qui nel bel volto, ancor vendetta in cielo
ne fie pel mondo, a trar divo il suo velo
più che mai bel di questa sepoltura.

184

Here am I, one of the Arms family, which was too weak in the struggle against death to prevent my dying; it would have been better to be a Foot and be able flee death, than an Arm, that did not defend me against it.

See poem 179.

185

Here I am buried, yet it is only a short time since was I born: I am one to whom death was so quick and cruel that my soul, stripped of me, scarcely notices that it underwent a change of state.

See poem 179.

186

He who shuts me in here cannot now through death give back the beauty that he took from all others and generously bestowed on my mortal part, if he must finally make me again as I once was on earth.

See poem 179.

187

The soul within did not see outside, as we did, the face enclosed in this tomb; but if in heaven there were not a dwelling-place so beautiful, death could certainly never have drawn forth the soul from this one.

See poem 179.

188

If here in his beautiful face nature has been conquered by death, revenge will none the less be taken in heaven, for the world's sake, through his divine veil's being drawn forth from this tomb more beautiful than ever.

See poem 179.

189

Qui son chiusi i begli occhi, che aperti
facén men chiari i più lucenti e santi;
or perché, morti, rendon luce a tanti,
qual sie più 'l danno o l'util non siàn certi.

190

Qui son morto creduto; e per conforto
del mondo vissi, e con mille alme in seno
di veri amanti; adunche a venir meno,
per tormen' una sola non son morto.

191

Se l'alma vive del suo corpo fora,
la mie, che par che qui di sé mi privi,
il mostra col timor ch'i' rendo a' vivi:
che nol po far chi tutto avvien che mora.

192

S'è ver, com'è, che dopo il corpo viva,
da quel disciolta, c'a mal grado regge
sol per divina legge,
l'alma e non prima, allor sol è beata;
po' che per morte diva   5
è fatta sì, com'a morte era nata.
Dunche, sine peccata,
in riso ogni suo doglia
preschiver debbe alcun del suo defunto,
se da fragile spoglia   10
fuor di miseria in vera pace è giunto
de l'ultim'ora o punto.
Tant'esser de' dell'amico 'l desio,
quante men val fruir terra che Dio.

189

Here lie closed the beautiful eyes which, when open, made less bright other eyes most shining and holy; since now, when dead, they restore light to so many, one cannot be sure which is the greater, the loss or the gain.

See poem 179.

190

I am believed to be dead here; but I lived to bring comfort to the world, with the souls of a thousand true lovers in my breast; and so in passing away, by being deprived of only one of them, I am not dead.

See poem 179.

191

My soul, which seems here to have deprived me of itself, proves that the soul lives outside its body by the fear that I cause in the living: this he cannot do whose fate it is to die entirely.

See poem 179.

192

If it is true, as it is, that it is after the soul's time with the body, when freed from what it ruled unwillingly and only because of God's law, that it lives and not before, it is only then that the soul is happy; for it is through death that it is made divine, just as it was born for death. So everyone must, quite blamelessly, replace with laughter all his weeping for any dead person dear to him, since that person, leaving behind his fragile covering, has after his last hour or instant reached true peace beyond all misery. Desire for one's friend should be governed by the degree to which enjoying this world falls short of enjoying God.

Madrigal: see poem 179.

193

A pena prima aperti gli vidd'io
i suo begli occhi in questa fragil vita,
che, chiusi el dì dell'ultima partita,
gli aperse in cielo a contemplare Dio.
    Conosco e piango, e non fu l'error mio,   5
col cor sì tardi a lor beltà gradita,
ma di morte anzi tempo, ond'è sparita
a voi non già, m'al mie 'rdente desio.
    Dunche, Luigi, a far l'unica forma
di Cecchin, di ch'i' parlo, in pietra viva   10
etterna, or ch'è già terra qui tra noi,
    se l'un nell'altro amante si trasforma,
po' che sanz'essa l'arte non v'arriva,
convien che per far lui ritragga voi.

194

Qui vuol mie sorte c'anzi tempo i' dorma,
né son già morto; e ben c'albergo cangi,
resto in te vivo, c'or mi vedi e piangi,
se l'un nell'altro amante si trasforma.

195

— Se qui cent'anni t'han tolto due ore,
un lustro è forza che l'etterno inganni.
— No: che 'n un giorno è vissuto cent'anni
colui che 'n quello il tutto impara e muore.

196

Gran ventura qui morto esser mi veggio:
tal dota ebbi dal cielo, anzi che veglio;
ché, non possendo al mondo darmi meglio,
ogni altro che la morte era 'l mie peggio.

193

Scarcely had I seen his beautiful eyes open for the first time in this fragile life when, closed on the day of his final departure, he opened them in heaven to gaze on God.

I acknowledge and in my heart lament that I recognized too late their gracious beauty, but the error was not mine, it was untimely death's, through which it has vanished not indeed from you but from my burning desire.

So, Luigi, if I am to make eternal in living stone the unique form of him of whom I speak, Cecchino, now that here among us it is already earth,

I must portray you in order to make him, for one lover is transformed into the other, and without a model art cannot achieve its goal.

Sonnet: see poem 179.

194

Here my destiny wills that I should sleep before due time. I am not truly dead; although I have indeed changed dwelling, I remain alive in you, who now see me and weep, for one lover is transformed into the other.

See poem 179.

195

'If here two hours have taken from you a hundred years, a lustrum would certainly cheat you of eternity.'

'No: for in one day he has lived a hundred years who in that day learns everything and dies.'

See poem 179.

196

It is my great good fortune to lie dead here, I see: I received this gift from heaven before I grew old, for, since it was unable to give me anything better in the world, all else apart from death would have been something worse for me.

See poem 179.

197

La carne terra, e qui l'ossa mie, prive
de' lor begli occhi e del leggiadro aspetto,
fan fede a quel ch'i' fu' grazia e diletto
in che carcer quaggiù l'anima vive.

198

Se fussin, perch'i' viva un'altra volta,
gli altru' pianti a quest'ossa carne e sangue,
sarie spietato per pietà chi langue
per rilegar lor l'alma in ciel disciolta.

199

Chi qui morto mi piange indarno spera,
bagnando l'ossa e 'l mie sepulcro, tutto
ritornarmi com'arbor secco al frutto;
c'uom morto non risurge a primavera.

200

S'i' fu' già vivo, tu sol, pietra, il sai,
che qui mi serri, e s'alcun mi ricorda,
gli par sognar: sì morte è presta e 'ngorda,
che quel ch'è stato non par fusse mai.

201

I' temo più, fuor degli anni e dell'ore
che m'han qui chiuso, il ritornare in vita,
s'esser può qua, ch'i' non fe' la partita;
po' c'allor nacqui ove la morte muore.

197

My flesh, being earth, and my bones deprived here of their beautiful eyes and lovely face, bear witness to him for whom I was a grace and delight what a prison the soul lives in here below.

See poem 179.

198

If the tears shed that I might once more be alive were to become flesh and blood for these bones, he would be pitiless out of pity who mourned that my soul might be bound to them again after being set free in heaven.

See poem 179.

199

It is in vain that those who weep here over my being dead hope by bathing my bones and tomb to restore me fully to life, like a withered tree to fruitfulness: for a dead man does not rise again to springtime.

See poem 179.

200

If I was ever alive you alone know it, oh stone, who here enclose me, for if anyone remembers me he seems merely to be dreaming: so ready and greedy is death that what once was seems never to have been.

See poem 179.

201

Being now beyond the years and hours that have here brought my life to a close, I should fear more to return to it, if that were possible here, than I did the leaving of it, since I was born at the very moment when death dies.

See poem 179.

202

I' fu de' Bracci, e se ritratto e privo
restai dell'alma, or m'è cara la morte,
po' che tal opra ha sì benigna sorte
d'entrar dipinto ov'io non pote' vivo.

203

De' Bracci nacqui, e dopo 'l primo pianto,
picciol tempo il sol vider gli occhi mei.
Qui son per sempre; né per men vorrei,
s'i' resto vivo in quel che m'amò tanto.

204

Più che vivo non ero, morto sono
vivo e caro a chi morte oggi m'ha tolto;
se più c'averne copia or m'ama molto,
chi cresce per mancar, gli è 'l morir buono.

205

Se morte ha di virtù qui 'l primo fiore
del mondo e di beltà, non bene aperto,
anzi tempo sepulto, i' son ben certo
che più non si dorrà chi vecchio muore.

206

Dal ciel fu la beltà mie diva e 'ntera,
e 'l corpo sol mortal dal padre mio.
Se morto è meco quel che ebbi d'Iddio
che dunche il mortal sol da morte spera?

202

I was a member of the Bracci family, and if, deprived of my soul, I remain in portrait form, death is now dear to me, for its work has this happy outcome that, as painted, I can enter where I could not when alive.

See poem 179.

203

I was born a Bracci, and after my first cry my eyes saw the sun for a short time only. I am here forever, and I would not wish for less, if I remain alive in him who so much loved me.

See poem 179.

204

More so than when I was alive, as dead I am alive and dear to him from whom death today has taken me; if he now loves me much more than when he had an abundance of me, then death is good for one who grows by fading away.

See poem 179.

205

If death has buried here the world's finest flower of virtue and of beauty before its time, not yet fully opened, I am quite certain that he will not be more sorely mourned who dies in his old age.

See poem 179.

206

From heaven came my beauty divine and whole, and only my mortal body from my father. If what I received from God has died with me, what then may my mortal part alone hope for from death?

See poem 179.

207

Per sempre a morte, e prima a voi fu' dato
sol per un'ora; e con diletto tanto
porta' bellezza, e po' lasciai tal pianto
che 'l me' sarebbe non esser ma' nato.

208

Qui chiuso è 'l sol di c'ancor piangi e ardi:
l'alma suo luce fu corta ventura.
Men grazia e men ricchezza assai più dura;
c'a' miseri la morte è pigra e tardi.

209

Qui sol per tempo convien posi e dorma
per render bello el mie terrestre velo;
ché più grazia o beltà non have 'l cielo,
c'alla natura fussi esempro e norma.

210

Se gli occhi aperti mie fur vita e pace
d'alcun, qui chiusi, or chi gli è pace e vita?
Beltà non già, che del mond'è sparita,
ma morte sol, s'ogni suo ben qui giace.

211

Se, vivo al mondo, d'alcun vita fui
che gli è qui terra or la bellezza mia,
mort'è non sol, ma crudel gelosia
c'alcun per me non mora innanzi a lui.

207

Forever given to death, I was first given to you only for an hour;
I brought beauty, which was a source of immense delight, then
left behind such mourning that it would have been better had I
never been born.

See poem 179.

208

Here is enclosed the sun for whom you still weep and burn: his
sublime light was a brief good fortune. Less grace, less richness
lasts much longer, for to the wretched death comes slow and late.

See poem 179.

209

Here I alone must before my time rest and sleep in order to give
back while beautiful my earthly veil; for heaven has no greater
grace or beauty that may for nature serve as norm and exemplar.

See poem 179.

210

If my eyes when open gave life and peace to someone, what will
bring him peace and life now that they are closed here? Not
beauty, certainly, for it has disappeared from the world, but death
alone, for his entire good lies here.

See poem 179.

211

If when alive in the world I meant life for someone for whom
now my beauty here is earth, it is not death alone that hurts him
cruelly, but jealous fear that someone else might die for me before
him.

See poem 179.

212

Perc'all'altru' ferir non ave' pari
col suo bel volto il Braccio che qui serro,
morte vel tolse e fecel, s'io non erro,
perc'a lei ancider toccava i men chiari.

213

Sepulto è qui quel Braccio, che Dio volse
corregger col suo volto la natura;
ma perché perso è 'l ben, c'altri non cura,
lo mostrò al mondo e presto sel ritolse.

214

Era la vita vostra il suo splendore:
di Cecchin Bracci, che qui morto giace.
Chi nol vide nol perde e vive in pace:
la vita perde chi 'l vide e non muore.

215

A la terra la terra e l'alma al cielo
qui reso ha morte; a chi morto ancor m'ama
ha dato in guardia mie bellezza e fama,
ch'etterni in pietra il mie terrestre velo.

216

Qui serro il Braccio e suo beltà divina,
e come l'alma al corpo è forma e vita,
è quello a me dell'opra alta e gradita;
c'un bel coltello insegna tal vagina.

212

Since the Arm whom I here shut in had no equal in striking people down with his beautiful face, death took him from you, and did so, if I am not mistaken, because it was its right alone to kill those less lovely.

See poem 179.

213

Here lies buried that Arm with whose face God wished to correct nature; but since a good to which people pay no need is wasted, God showed him to the world and quickly took him back to himself.

See poem 179.

214

His radiant beauty was your life: that of Cecchino Bracci, who here lies dead. Anyone who did not see him has not lost him, and lives in peace; he has lost his life who saw him, and has not died.

See poem 179.

215

Here death has restored earth to earth and the soul to heaven; to his safe-keeping who loves me still though I am dead, death has given my beauty and renown, that he may immortalize in stone my earthly veil.

See poem 179.

216

Here I enclose Bracci and his divine beauty; and as the soul gives form and life to the body, so does he to the noble and gracious work I am; for a sheath of like quality tells the beauty of the knife within.

See poem 179.

217

S'avvien come fenice mai rinnuovi
qui 'l bel volto de' Bracci di più stima,
fie ben che 'l ben chi nol conosce prima
per alcun tempo il perda e po' 'l ritruovi.

218

Col sol de' Bracci il sol della natura,
per sempre estinto, qui lo chiudo e serro:
morte l'ancise senza spada o ferro,
c'un fior di verno picciol vento il fura.

219

I' fui de' Bracci, e qui mie vita è morte.
Sendo oggi 'l ciel dalla terra diviso,
toccando i' sol del mondo al paradiso,
anzi per sempre serri le suo porte.

220

Deposto ha qui Cecchin sì nobil salma
per morte, che 'l sol ma' simil non vide.
Roma ne piange, e 'l ciel si gloria e ride,
che scarca del mortal si gode l'alma.

221

Qui giace il Braccio, e men non si desìa
sepulcro al corpo, a l'alma il sacro ufizio.
Se più che vivo, morto ha degno ospizio
in terra e 'n ciel, morte gli è dolce e pia.

217

If it should happen that, like the phoenix, the beautiful face of the Bracci here should one day be reborn more fully appreciated, it will be good that whoever before failed to recognize the good should have lost it for a time and then found it once more.

See poem 179.

218

Here I enclose and lock away with the sun of the Bracci the sun of nature forever extinguished; death killed him without sword or steel, for it takes but a little wind to carry off a winter flower.

See poem 179.

219

I was a Bracci, and here death for me is life. Since today heaven is cut off from the earth, because I alone of those in the world attained to paradise, heaven may indeed forever close its gates.

See poem 179.

220

Here in death Cecchino has laid down a corpse so noble that the sun has never seen its like before. So Rome weeps, but heaven glories and makes merry, for it enjoys his soul unburdened of what is mortal.

See poem 179.

221

Here Bracci lies, lacking nothing as regards a tomb for his body or sacred rites for his soul. If on earth and in heaven he has a worthier home when dead than when alive, then death for him has been sweet and kind.

See poem 179.

222

Qui stese il Braccio e colse acerbo il frutto
morte, anz'il fior, c'a quindici anni cede.
Sol questo sasso il gode che 'l possiede,
e 'l resto po' del mondo il piange tutto.

223

I' fu' Cecchin mortale e or son divo:
poco ebbi 'l mondo e per sempre il ciel godo.
Di sì bel cambio e di morte mi lodo,
che molti morti, e me partorì vivo.

224

Chiusi ha qui gli occhi, e 'l corpo e l'alma sciolta
di Cecchin Bracci morte, e la partita
fu 'nanz' al tempo per cangiar suo vita
a quella c'a molt'anni spesso è tolta.

225

I' fu' de' Bracci, e qui dell'alma privo
per esser da beltà fatt'ossa e terra:
prego il sasso non s'apra, che mi serra,
per restar bello in chi m'amò già vivo.

226

Che l'alma viva, i' che qui morto sono
or ne son certo e che, vivo, ero morto.
I' fu' de' Bracci, e se 'l tempo ebbi corto,
chi manco vive più speri perdono.

222

Here death stretched out its Arm and gathered the unripe fruit, indeed the flower, which yields at fifteen years. Only this stone which possesses him rejoices, while all the rest of the world weeps for him.

See poem 179.

223

I, Cecchino, once was mortal but am now divine; I had the earth for a little time, but delight forever in heaven. I rejoice in a change so wonderful and I rejoice in death, which has given birth to many dead, but to me alive.

See poem 179.

224

Death has here enclosed the eyes and body of Cecchino Bracci, and freed his soul from his body; the separation was before due time, that he might change his life for a life often denied to those of many years.

See poem 179.

225

I was a Bracci, and here I lie deprived of my soul, now that my beauty has been turned to bones and earth. I beg the stone which locks me up not to open, that I may remain beautiful in him who loved me when I was still alive.

See poem 179.

226

I who here am dead am now quite certain that the soul lives on, and that alive I was dead. I was a Bracci, and no matter that my time was short, for he who lives less may hope more for pardon.

See poem 179.

227

Ripreso ha 'l divin Braccio il suo bel velo:
non è più qui, c'anz'al gran dì l'ha tolto
pietà di terra; che s'allor sepolto
fussi, lu' sol sarie degno del cielo.

228

Se 'l mondo il corpo, e l'alma il ciel ne presta
per lungo tempo, il morto qui de' Bracci
qual salute fie mai che 'l soddisfacci?
Di tanti anni e beltà creditor resta.

229

Occhi mie, siate certi
che 'l tempo passa e l'ora s'avvicina,
c'a le lacrime triste il passo serra.
Pietà vi tenga aperti,
mentre la mie divina   5
donna si degna d'abitare in terra.
Se grazia il ciel disserra,
com'a' beati suole,
questo mie vivo sole
se lassù torna e partesi da noi,   10
che cosa arete qui da veder poi?

230

Perché tuo gran bellezze al mondo sièno
in donna più cortese e manco dura,
prego se ne ripigli la natura
tutte quelle c'ognor ti vengon meno,
e serbi a riformar del tuo sereno   5
e divin volto una gentil figura
del ciel, e sia d'amor perpetua cura
rifarne un cor di grazia e pietà pieno.
E serbi poi i mie sospiri ancora,
e le lacrime sparte insieme accoglia   10
e doni a chi quella ami un'altra volta.

227

The divine Braccio has taken back his beautiful veil; it is no longer here, for pity has taken it from earth before the great day; for were it then still buried, it alone would be worthy of heaven.

See poem 179.

228

Since it is for a long time that the world lends us the body and heaven the soul, what benefit could ever compensate the dead Bracci who lies here? To him are owing still so many years, and so much beauty.

See poem 179.

229

My eyes, be certain that time is passing and the hour is approaching that will close the outlet for sorrowful tears. May compassion keep you open while my divine lady deigns to live on earth. If grace should unlock heaven, as is its custom for the blessed, and this my living sun return there above and part from us, what will you have then to gaze on here?

Madrigal, probably for Vittoria Colonna, 1544–6. *

230

That your great beauties may again be present to the world in a woman more courteous and less harsh, I pray that nature may once more take all those beauties which from you are fading hour by hour,

and preserve them to refashion from your serene and divine face a noble heavenly figure, and that it may be love's continual concern to make for it a new heart full of grace and pity.

And may it likewise preserve my sighs, and gather together my scattered tears, and give them to someone who will love that woman in another time.

Forse a pietà chi nascerà in quell'ora
la moverà co' la mie propia doglia,
né fie persa la grazia c'or m'è tolta.

231

Non è più tempo, Amor, che 'l cor m'infiammi,
né che beltà mortal più goda o tema:
giunta è già l'ora strema
che 'l tempo perso, a chi men n'ha, più duole.
Quante 'l tuo braccio dammi,   5
morte i gran colpi scema,
e ' sua accresce più che far non suole.
Gl'ingegni e le parole,
da te di foco a mio mal pro passati,
in acqua son conversi;   10
e Die 'l voglia c'or versi
con essa insieme tutti e' mie peccati.

232

Non altrimenti contro a sé cammina
ch'i' mi facci alla morte,
chi è da giusta corte
tirato là dove l'alma il cor lassa;
tal m'è morte vicina,   5
salvo più lento el mie resto trapassa.
Né per questo mi lassa
Amor viver un'ora
fra duo perigli, ond'io mi dormo e veglio:
la speme umile e bassa   10
nell'un forte m'accora,
e l'altro parte m'arde, stanco e veglio.
Né so il men danno o 'l meglio:
ma pur più temo, Amor, che co' tuo sguardi
più presto ancide quante vien più tardi.   15

Perhaps he who is born in that hour will move her to pity with my very suffering, and the grace will not then be wanting which is now denied to me.

Sonnet, probably for 'the beautiful and cruel lady' in the final version, c. 1542-6.*

231

It is no longer time, Love, for you to inflame my heart, nor for me to enjoy or fear mortal beauty; the final hour has now come, when time lost most pains him to whom least remains. However many blows your arm may deal me, death lessens their great force, and increases his beyond its usual strength. The thoughts and words transformed into fire by you to my great harm have been turned into water; and God grant that I now pour out with it all my sins.

Madrigal, possibly for 'the beautiful and cruel lady', 1544-5.*

232

No more unwillingly does a man condemned by a court of justice walk to where the soul leaves the heart than I do to death; this is as close to me, except that the time that remains to me passes more slowly. But that does not make Love leave me in peace for a single hour between two dangers that threaten me, whether I wake or sleep: on the one hand my hope's being weak and scanty grieves me greatly; on the other Love burns me, old and weary though I am. And I do not know which is the more harmful, which the better: yet I do fear you more, Love, who with your glances kill more quickly the later you appear.

Madrigal, possibly for 'the beautiful and cruel lady', 1544-5.*

233

Se da' prim'anni aperto un lento e poco
ardor distrugge in breve un verde core,
che farà, chiuso po' da l'ultim'ore,
d'un più volte arso un insaziabil foco?
Se 'l corso di più tempo dà men loco   5
a la vita, a le forze e al valore,
che farà a quel che per natura muore
l'incendio arroto d'amoroso gioco?
Farà quel che di me s'aspetta farsi:
cenere al vento sì pietoso e fero,   10
c'a' fastidiosi vermi il corpo furi.
Se, verde, in picciol foco i' piansi e arsi,
che, più secco ora in un sì grande, spero
che l'alma al corpo lungo tempo duri?

234

Tanto non è, quante da te non viene,
agli occhi specchio, a che 'l cor lasso cede;
che s'altra beltà vede,
gli è morte, donna, se te non somiglia,
qual vetro che non bene   5
senz'altra scorza ogni su' obbietto piglia.
Esempro e maraviglia
ben fie a chi si dispera
della tuo grazia al suo 'nfelice stato,
s'e' begli occhi e le ciglia   10
con la tuo pietà vera
volgi a far me sì tardi ancor beato:
a la miseria nato,
s'al fier destin preval grazia e ventura,
da te fie vinto il cielo e la natura.   15

233

If a slow, slight burning destroys in a short time a green heart made open by its early years, what will an insatiable fire do to a heart, now closed in by its final hours, which has many times been burned?

If the passing of many years gives less space to one's life, one's powers and strength, what will the added fire of a teasing love make of one whom nature carries towards death?

It will make of him what I expect it to make of me: ashes scattered by a wind so merciful yet fierce, that it will steal the body from the nauseating worms.

For if, when green, I wept and burned in a small fire, how can I now, drier and in a fire so great, hope that my soul may last much longer in my body?

Sonnet, possibly for 'the beautiful and cruel lady', c. 1544-5. *

234

Whatever does not come from you cannot serve my eyes as a mirror, in which my weary heart may rest; for if it sees any beauty that does not resemble you, lady, this to it is dead, like glass which lacking any lining fails to catch properly any of the objects before it. It will indeed be a source of encouragement and wonder to one who despairs of your grace's touching his unhappy state, if with your true compassion you turn your beautiful eyes and brows to make me blessed, old as I am: if in me, who was born to misery, grace and good fortune prevail over harsh destiny, then by you heaven and nature will have been conquered.

Madrigal, very probably for Vittoria Colonna, c. 1545.

235

Un uomo in una donna, anzi uno dio
per la sua bocca parla,
ond'io per ascoltarla
son fatto tal, che ma' più sarò mio.
I' credo ben, po' ch'io   5
a me da lei fu' tolto,
fuor di me stesso aver di me pietate;
sì sopra 'l van desio
mi sprona il suo bel volto,
ch'i' veggio morte in ogni altra beltate.   10
O donna che passate
per acqua e foco l'alme a' lieti giorni,
deh, fate c'a me stesso più non torni.

236

Se ben concetto ha la divina parte
il volto e gli atti d'alcun, po' di quello
doppio valor con breve e vil modello
dà vita a' sassi, e non è forza d'arte.
Né altrimenti in più rustiche carte,   5
anz'una pronta man prenda 'l pennello,
fra ' dotti ingegni il più accorto e bello
pruova e rivede, e suo storie comparte.
Simil di me model di poca istima
mie parto fu, per cosa alta e prefetta   10
da voi rinascer po', donna alta e degna.
Se 'l poco accresce, e 'l mie superchio lima
vostra mercé, qual penitenzia aspetta
mie fiero ardor, se mi gastiga e 'nsegna?

237

Molto diletta al gusto intero e sano
l'opra della prim'arte, che n'assembra
i volti e gli atti, e con più vive membra,
di cera o terra o pietra un corp' umano.
Se po' 'l tempo ingiurioso, aspro e villano   5
la rompe o storce o del tutto dismembra,
la beltà che prim'era si rimembra,
e serba a miglior loco il piacer vano.

235

A man in a woman, indeed a god speaks through her mouth, and so in listening to her I have become such that I shall never again be mine. I firmly believe, now that I have been taken from myself by her, that from outside myself I shall have pity on myself; so far above vain desire does her beautiful face spur me that I see death in every other beauty. Oh lady who passes souls through water and fire to happy days, bring this about, I beg you: that I may never again return to my own self.

Madrigal, for Vittoria Colonna, 1544/5-6.

236

If man's divine part has well conceived someone's face and gestures, it then through that double power, using a slight and lowly model, gives life to stones – and this is not the result of mere craftsmanship.

It operates no differently with regard to the roughest designs: before a ready hand may lift the brush, the divine part tries out and reworks the most interesting and beautiful of its fine ideas, then arranges its figures into a pattern.

So, too, with me: from birth I was made a model of little value, that I might then through you, noble and virtuous lady, be reborn as something noble and perfect.

If your kindness is to make the little I have increase, and file away my excess, what penitence awaits my fierce ardour, if it is to chastise and teach me?

Sonnet, for Vittoria Colonna, 1544/5-6, revised 1546-50.

237

To one whose taste is healthy and unspoiled, the work of the first art brings great delight: in wax or clay or stone it makes a likeness for us of the face, the gestures, the whole human body, and indeed gives greater life to the body's members.

If destructive, harsh and boorish time then breaks, distorts or dismembers such a work, the beauty which first existed is remembered, and keeps for a better place the pleasure that here proved vain.

Partial sonnet, possibly for Vittoria Colonna, c. 1545.

238

Non è non degna l'alma che n'attende
etterna vita, in cui si posa e quieta,
per arricchir dell'unica moneta
che 'l ciel ne stampa, e qui natura spende.

239

Com'esser, donna, può quel c'alcun vede
per lunga sperïenza, che più dura
l'immagin viva in pietra alpestra e dura
che 'l suo fattor, che gli anni in cener riede?
La causa a l'effetto inclina e cede,   5
onde dall'arte è vinta la natura.
I' 'l so, che 'l pruovo in la bella scultura,
c'all'opra il tempo e morte non tien fede.
Dunche, posso ambo noi dar lunga vita
in qual sie modo, o di colore o sasso,   10
di noi sembrando l'uno e l'altro volto;
sì che mill'anni dopo la partita,
quante voi bella fusti e quant'io lasso
si veggia, e com'amarvi i' non fu' stolto.

240

Sol d'una pietra viva
l'arte vuol che qui viva
al par degli anni il volto di costei.
Che dovria il ciel di lei,
sendo mie questa, e quella suo fattura,   5
non già mortal, ma diva,
non solo agli occhi mei?
E pur si parte e picciol tempo dura.
Dal lato destro è zoppa suo ventura,
s'un sasso resta e pur lei morte affretta.   10
Chi ne farà vendetta?
Natura sol, se de' suo nati sola
l'opra qui dura, e la suo 'l tempo invola.

238

A soul is not unworthy of looking forward to eternal life, in which it will find rest and peace, if it enriches itself with the unique money that heaven mints for us, and nature spends down here.

Quatrain, possibly for Vittoria Colonna, c. 1545.

239

How can it be, lady, that, as long experience clearly shows, the living image in hard, alpine stone lasts longer than its maker, whom the years reduce again to dust?

The cause bows and yields to the effect, and so nature is conquered by art. This I know, who prove it in beautiful sculpture, that confronted with a work of art time and death fail in their task.

So I can give us both long life in either medium, whether in paint or stone, making a likeness of each of our faces;

so that a thousand years after we are gone people will be able to see how beautiful you were and how wretched I, and how in loving you I was not foolish.

Sonnet, probably for Vittoria Colonna, c. 1545. *

240

Art wills that only in a living stone may the face of that woman live here as long as time will last. This being my creation, what ought heaven to do for her, who is its creation, since she is not just mortal but divine, and not in my eyes only? And yet she will depart, after lasting but a little time. Good fortune is lacking to her more noble part, since a rock remains and death hurries off even her. Who will avenge this? Nature alone, for it is her children's work alone that lasts here below, though her own are carried off by time.

Madrigal, possibly for Vittoria Colonna, possibly c. 1544–5. *

241

Negli anni molti e nelle molte pruove,
cercando, il saggio al buon concetto arriva
d'un'immagine viva,
vicino a morte, in pietra alpestra e dura;
c'all'alte cose nuove   5
tardi si viene, e poco poi si dura.
Similmente natura,
di tempo in tempo, d'uno in altro volto,
s'al sommo, errando, di bellezza è giunta
nel tuo divino, è vecchia, e de' perire: 10
onde la tema, molto
con la beltà congiunta,
di stranio cibo pasce il gran desire;
né so pensar né dire
qual nuoca o giovi più, visto 'l tuo 'spetto,   15
o 'l fin dell'universo o 'l gran diletto.

242

S'egli è che 'n dura pietra alcun somigli
talor l'immagin d'ogni altri a se stesso,
squalido e smorto spesso
il fo, com'i' son fatto da costei.
E par ch'esempro pigli   5
ognor da me, ch'i' penso di far lei.
Ben la pietra potrei,
per l'aspra suo durezza,
in ch'io l'esempro, dir c'a lei s'assembra;
del resto non saprei,   10
mentre mi strugge e sprezza,
altro sculpir che le mie afflitte membra.
Ma se l'arte rimembra
agli anni la beltà per durare ella,
farà me lieto, ond'io le' farò bella.   15

243

Ognor che l'idol mio si rappresenta
agli occhi del mie cor debile e forte,
fra l'uno e l'altro obbietto entra la morte,
e più 'l discaccia, se più mi spaventa.

241

After many years and after many attempts, the wise artist succeeds in realizing a fine idea in a living image of hard, alpine stone only when he is near to death: for he comes late to fashioning what is noble and original, and he remains there for but a short time. So too with nature: if it has attained the height of beauty in your divine face only through trial and error, going from one period to the next, from one face to another, it is old and must soon perish. And so fear, closely linked to beauty, feeds my great desire with strange food; and I can neither know nor say whether, at the sight of your beautiful face, I am more harmed by the prospect of the end of the universe or helped by my great delight.

Madrigal, possibly for Vittoria Colonna, c. 1542-5. *

242

Since it is the case that, working in hard stone, the artist sometimes makes the image of everyone else resemble himself, I often make that woman's bleak and drear, as I am made by her. It seems that I always take myself as model when I set myself to fashion her. I could say that in its harsh hardness the very stone in which I model her resembles her; whatever about that, I simply am not able, while she destroys and despises me, to sculpt anything other than my afflicted features. But since art records beauty down the ages, if she wishes to endure she will make me happy, so that I may make her beautiful.

Madrigal, possibly for 'the beautiful and cruel lady', c. 1545. *

243

Every time my lady's image reappears before the eyes of my heart, which is weak yet strong, death enters between these two objects, and the more it terrifies me the more it drives that image away.

L'alma di tale oltraggio esser contenta   5
più spera che gioir d'ogni altra sorte;
l'invitto Amor, con suo più chiare scorte,
a suo difesa s'arma e s'argomenta:
  Morir, dice, si può sol una volta,
né più si nasce; e chi col mie 'mor muore,   10
che fie po', s'anzi morte in quel soggiorna?
  L'acceso amor, donde vien l'alma sciolta,
s'è calamita al suo simile ardore,
com'or purgata in foco, a Dio si torna.

244

Se 'l duol fa pur, com'alcun dice, bello,
privo piangendo d'un bel volto umano,
l'essere infermo è sano,
fa vita e grazia la disgrazia mia:
ché 'l dolce amaro è quello   5
che, contr'a l'alma, il van pensier desia.
Né può fortuna ria
contr'a chi basso vola,
girando, trïonfar d'alta ruina;
ché mie benigna e pia   10
povertà nuda e sola,
m'è nuova ferza e dolce disciplina:
c'a l'alma pellegrina
è più salute, o per guerra o per gioco,
saper perdere assai che vincer poco.   15

My soul has greater hope of being made happy by this outrage than of finding joy from anything else that might befall it; but Love, undaunted, calling on his strongest arguments, arms himself for his own defence, and reasons thus:

'Everyone', he says, 'can die only once, and no one is born a second time; and if someone dwells in my love before death, what will happen to him when he dies through that same love?

'The love enkindled, by which the soul is freed, will act like a magnet to draw the ardour that is similar to itself, and so the soul, like gold purified by fire, will return to God.'

Sonnet, c. 1545.

244

If, as some say, suffering even makes a person beautiful, then since I am deprived of the sight of a beautiful human face, my being ill is healthy, my ungracious fate brings life and grace: for that sweetness is bitter which vain thought desires, contrary to the soul's good. Nor can evil fortune, turning its wheel, enjoy the triumph of casting down to ruin from a great height someone who flies low; for my naked and lonely poverty is yet kind and merciful, being a fresh whip and a sweet discipline: because to the pilgrim soul there is greater benefit, whether in war or in play, in knowing how to lose much than how to gain little.

Madrigal, c. 1545.

245

— Se 'l volto di ch'i' parlo, di costei,
no' m'avessi negati gli occhi suoi,
Amor, di me qual poi
pruova faresti di più ardente foco,
s'a non veder me' lei   5
co' suo begli occhi tu m'ardi e non poco?
— La men parte del gioco
ha chi nulla ne perde,
se nel gioir vaneggia ogni desire:
nel sazio non ha loco   10
la speme e non rinverde
nel dolce che preschive ogni martire —.
— Anzi di lei vo' dire:
s'a quel c'aspiro suo gran copia cede,
l'alto desir non quieta tuo mercede.   15

246

Te sola del mie mal contenta veggio,
né d'altro ti richieggio amarti tanto;
non è la pace tua senza il mio pianto,
e la mia morte a te non è 'l mie peggio.
Che s'io colmo e pareggio   5
il cor di doglia alla tua voglia altera,
per fuggir questa vita,
qual dispietata aita
m'ancide e strazia e non vuol poi ch'io pera?
Perché 'l morir è corto   10
al lungo andar di tua crudeltà fera.
Ma chi patisce a torto
non men pietà che gran iustizia spera.
Così l'alma sincera
serve e sopporta e, quando che sia poi,   15
spera non quel che puoi:
ché 'l premio del martir non è tra noi.

245

'If the face of which I am speaking, her face, had not denied to me its eyes, Love, what further trial would you have set for me in a more fiercely burning fire, since even without my seeing more of her you burn me, and not a little, with her beautiful eyes?'

'He gains least from playing who in doing so loses nothing, for when joy is attained all desire disappears: in complete fulfilment there is no room for hope, which cannot flower again in the sweetness that banishes all suffering.'

'But in her case I wish to say: if she were to grant in great abundance what I aspire to, this reward from you would not quieten my high desire.'

Madrigal, c. 1545–7.

246

I see you alone made happy by my woe, even though I ask of you only that I may love you; you find no peace except in my weeping, and for you my death would not be the worst that could befall me. And so if to flee this life I fill my heart with suffering that matches your haughty will, what pitiless help is this that kills me and tears me apart, but does not wish me then to perish? For dying would be short compared to the long course of your fierce cruelty. But whoever wrongly suffers hopes for compassion no less than for full justice. So the steadfast soul serves and endures, and hopes to receive, whenever it may be, that which you cannot give: for the reward of martyrdom is not found here among us.

Madrigal, c. 1546, from a capitolo of 1524–34. *

247

Caro m'è 'l sonno, e più l'esser di sasso,
mentre che 'l danno e la vergogna dura;
non veder, non sentir m'è gran ventura;
però non mi destar, deh, parla basso.

248

Dal ciel discese, e col mortal suo, poi
che visto ebbe l'inferno giusto e 'l pio,
ritornò vivo a contemplare Dio,
per dar di tutto il vero lume a noi.
Lucente stella, che co' raggi suoi   5
fe' chiaro a torto el nido ove nacqu'io,
né sare' l' premio tutto 'l mondo rio;
tu sol, che la creasti, esser quel puoi.
Di Dante dico, che mal conosciute
fur l'opre suo da quel popolo ingrato   10
che solo a' iusti manca di salute.
Fuss'io pur lui! c'a tal fortuna nato,
per l'aspro esilio suo, co' la virtute,
dare' del mondo il più felice stato.

249

— Per molti, donna, anzi per mille amanti
creata fusti, e d'angelica forma;
or par che 'n ciel si dorma,
s'un sol s'appropia quel ch'è dato a tanti.
Ritorna a' nostri pianti   5
il sol degli occhi tuo, che par che schivi
chi del suo dono in tal miseria è nato.
— Deh, non turbate i vostri desir santi,
ché chi di me par che vi spogli e privi,
col gran timor non gode il gran peccato;   10
ché degli amanti è men felice stato
quello, ove 'l gran desir gran copia affrena,
c'una miseria di speranza piena.

247

Dear to me is sleep, dearer still being made of stone, while harm and shame last; not to see, not to hear, to me is a great boon; so do not waken me, ah, speak but softly.

Quatrain, c. 1545–6. *

248

He came down from heaven, and in his mortal body, after seeing both the just and the merciful hell, returned alive to contemplate God, that he might give to us true light regarding all that he had seen.

A shining star, who with his rays made undeservedly famous the nest where I was born: for him the whole wicked world would not be adequate reward; you alone, who created him, can be such.

I speak of Dante, whose works were ill recognized by that ungrateful people which fails to bestow favour only on the just.

Oh that I were he! for were I born to such a destiny, I should exchange for his harsh exile, together with his virtue, the happiest state in all the world.

Sonnet, c. 1545–6. *

249

'For many lovers, lady, indeed for thousands, were you created, with your angelic form; but now it seems that heaven has fallen asleep, for one man alone has appropriated what was given to so many. In answer to our tears restore the sun of your eyes, for it seems that you shun those born to the misery of being deprived of such a gift.'

'Ah, do not be troubled in your holy desires, for he who seems to despoil and deprive you of me is prevented by great fear from enjoying his great sin, because for lovers that state is less happy in which great abundance stifles great desire than that in which misery is full of hope.'

Madrigal, c. 1545–6. *

250

Quante dirne si de' non si può dire,
ché troppo agli orbi il suo splendor s'accese;
biasmar si può più 'l popol che l'offese,
c'al suo men pregio ogni maggior salire.

Questo discese a' merti del fallire   5
per l'util nostro, e poi a Dio ascese;
e le porte, che 'l ciel non gli contese,
la patria chiuse al suo giusto desire.

Ingrata, dico, e della suo fortuna
a suo danno nutrice; ond'è ben segno   10
c'a' più perfetti abonda di più guai.

Fra mille altre ragion sol ha quest'una:
se par non ebbe il suo exilio indegno,
simil uom né maggior non nacque mai.

251

Nel dolce d'una immensa cortesia,
dell'onor, della vita alcuna offesa
s'asconde e cela spesso, e tanto pesa
che fa men cara la salute mia.

Chi gli omer' altru' 'mpenna e po' tra via   5
a lungo andar la rete occulta ha tesa,
l'ardente carità d'amore accesa
là più l'ammorza ov'arder più desia.

Però, Luigi mio, tenete chiara
la prima grazia, ond'io la vita porto,   10
che non si turbi per tempesta o vento.

L'isdegno ogni mercé vincere impara,
e s'i' son ben del vero amico accorto,
mille piacer non vaglion un tormento.

250

All that should be said of him cannot be said, for too brightly did his splendour burn for our blind eyes; we can more easily reprove the people that wronged him than we can rise, even the greatest among us, to speak of his least merit.

For our good this man descended to where transgression has its just deserts, and then ascended to God; but the gates which heaven did not hold barred against him his native land closed to his just desire.

Ungrateful I declare that land, and nourisher of its destiny to its own harm; of which a clear sign is that it lavishes most troubles on those who are most perfect.

Among a thousand proofs that might be given let this alone suffice: just as no exile was ever less deserved than his, so no one of like worth or greater was ever born.

Sonnet, c. 1545–6. *

251

Within the sweetness of an immense kindness there often lurks concealed some offence to one's honour and one's life; and this so weighs on me that it makes my good health less precious.

Anyone who gives wings to another's shoulders, and then along the way gradually spreads out a hidden net, extinguishes completely the ardent charity enkindled by love precisely where it most desires to burn.

So, my Luigi, keep shining clear that first graciousness, to which I owe my life, that it may not be troubled by storm or wind.

Offence manages to outweigh all kindness shown, and if I do indeed understand true friendship, then a thousand pleasures count less than a single torment.

Sonnet, for Luigi del Riccio, 1545–6.

252

Perch'è troppo molesta,
ancor che dolce sia,
quella mercé che l'alma legar suole,
mie libertà di questa
vostr'alta cortesia   5
più che d'un furto si lamenta e duole.
E com'occhio nel sole
disgrega suo virtù ch'esser dovrebbe
di maggior luce, s'a veder ne sprona,
così 'l desir non vuole   10
zoppa la grazia in me, che da vo' crebbe.
Ché 'l poco al troppo spesso s'abbandona,
né questo a quel perdona:
c'amor vuol sol gli amici, onde son rari,
di fortuna e virtù simili e pari.   15

253

S'i' fussi stato ne' prim'anni accorto
del fuoco, allor di fuor, che m'arde or drento,
per men mal, non che spento,
ma privo are' dell'alma il debil core
e del colpo, or ch'è morto;   5
ma sol n'ha colpa il nostro prim'errore.
Alma infelice, se nelle prim'ore
alcun s'è mal difeso,
nell'ultim' arde e muore
del primo foco acceso: 10
ché chi non può non esser arso e preso
nell'età verde, c'or c'è lume e specchio,
men foco assai 'l distrugge stanco e vecchio.

252

Sweet though it be, that favour is too costly whose effect is to bind the soul; and so my freedom laments and suffers over this noble kindness of yours more than over a theft. And as the eye loses its power by looking at the sun, even though it ought thereby to be made capable of receiving greater light, since the sun spurs us to look, so my desire to be grateful, which was increased by you, does not like being lame. But what is little often collapses before what is great, and the latter cannot tolerate the former: love in fact requires that they only can be friends who are alike in fortune and equal in virtue – which is why friends are so rare.

Madrigal, for Luigi del Riccio, 1545–6. *

253

If in my first years I had been wise regarding the fire which then burned me only on the outside but does so now within, then to receive less harm I should not simply have extinguished that fire but should have deprived my feeble heart of my soul, and so of that blow that has now killed it; but the blame for this must be borne by our first error alone. Unhappy soul, if anyone in his first hours defends himself badly, in his last he will burn and die from the first fire kindled; for he who does not know how to avoid being burned and taken in his green season, which is now a light and mirror to us, is destroyed by a much lesser fire when he is tired and old.

Madrigal, possibly 1546. *

254

Donn', a me vecchio e grave,
ov'io torno e rientro
e come a peso il centro,
che fuor di quel riposo alcun non have,
il ciel porge le chiave.   5
Amor le volge e gira
e apre a' iusti il petto di costei;
le voglie inique e prave
mi vieta, e là mi tira,
già stanco e vil, fra ' rari e semidei.   10
Grazie vengon da lei
strane e dolce e d'un certo valore,
che per sé vive chiunche per le' muore.

255

Mentre i begli occhi giri,
donna, ver' me da presso,
tanto veggio me stesso
in lor, quante ne' mie te stessa miri.
Dagli anni e da' martiri   5
qual io son, quegli a me rendono in tutto,
e ' mie lor te più che lucente stella.
Ben par che 'l ciel s'adiri
che 'n sì begli occhi i' mi veggia sì brutto,
e ne' mie brutti ti veggia sì bella; 10
né men crudele e fella
dentro è ragion, c'al core
per lor mi passi, e quella
de' tuo mi serri fore.
Perché 'l tuo gran valore   15
d'ogni men grado accresce suo durezza,
c'amor vuol pari stato e giovanezza.

254

Heaven offers to me, heavy with years, the keys of the lady to whom I turn and go back, as a weight does to the centre because nowhere else can it find repose. Love fits and turns them, and opens the heart of that lady to those who are just: she forbids me to have evil and depraved desires, and draws me up, tired and worthless though I am, among the godlike few. From her come graces strange and sweet and of such power that whoever dies for her lives for himself.

*Madrigal, possibly for Vittoria Colonna, possibly 1546.**

255

When you turn your beautiful eyes to me from nearby, lady, I see myself as clearly in your eyes as you do yourself in gazing into mine. Your eyes reflect me back to myself just as I am, marked by the years and by my sufferings, while mine to them reflect you, more brilliant than any star. It seems indeed to anger heaven that I who am so ugly should be seen in eyes so beautiful, and you who are so beautiful be seen in my ugly eyes; and what is done within is no less cruel and sad, for while through my eyes you pass to my heart, you within yours shut me out. This happens because your great virtue always increases in hardness when faced by what is inferior: for love requires equality of condition and youth.

*Madrigal, c. 1546.**

256

S'alcuna parte in donna è che sie bella,
benché l'altre sien brutte,
debb'io amarle tutte
pel gran piacer ch'i' prendo sol di quella?
La parte che s'appella,   5
mentre il gioir n'attrista,
a la ragion, pur vuole
che l'innocente error si scusi e ami.
Amor, che mi favella
della noiosa vista,   10
com'irato dir suole
che nel suo regno non s'attenda o chiami.
E 'l ciel pur vuol ch'i' brami,
a quel che spiace non sie pietà vana:
ché l'uso agli occhi ogni malfatto sana.   15

257

Perché sì tardi e perché non più spesso
con ferma fede quell'interno ardore
che mi lieva di terra e porta 'l core
dove per suo virtù non gli è concesso?
    Forse c'ogn' intervallo n'è promesso   5
da l'uno a l'altro tuo messo d'amore,
perc'ogni raro ha più forz'e valore
quant'è più desïato e meno appresso.
    La notte è l'intervallo, e 'l dì la luce:
l'una m'agghiaccia 'l cor, l'altro l'infiamma   10
d'amor, di fede e d'un celeste foco.

256

If in a woman there is some part that is beautiful, though the others are ugly, ought I to love them all because of the great pleasure I take in that part alone? The part which diminishes our joy appeals none the less to reason, and makes the plea that the innocent fault be excused and loved. But when Love speaks to me of the distressing sight, it usually says in angry tones that in his kingdom no attention should be paid to reason, no call made to it. Yet heaven wills that I should burn for her, and that pity should not be lacking towards what displeases: because familiarity to our eyes heals all defects.

Madrigal, 1545–6 or later.

257

Why does it come so slowly and why not more often, that inner ardour full of firm faith, which lifts me from earth and bears my heart to where by its own power it is not permitted to go?

Perhaps every interval between one message of your love and the next is allotted us because everything rare has greater strength and value the more it is desired and the less near.

The interval is night, the light is day: one freezes my heart, the other inflames it with love, with faith and with a heavenly fire.

Partial sonnet, possibly for Vittoria Colonna, possibly 1546.

258

Quantunche sie che la beltà divina
qui manifesti il tuo bel volto umano,
donna, il piacer lontano
m'è corto sì, che del tuo non mi parto,
c'a l'alma pellegrina   5
gli è duro ogni altro sentiero erto o arto.
Ond' il tempo comparto:
per gli occhi il giorno e per la notte il core,
senza intervallo alcun c'al cielo aspiri.
Sì 'l destinato parto   10
mi ferm'al tuo splendore,
c'alzar non lassa i mie ardenti desiri,
s'altro non è che tiri
la mente al ciel per grazia o per mercede:
tardi ama il cor quel che l'occhio non vede.   15

259

Ben può talor col mie 'rdente desio
salir la speme e non esser fallace,
ché s'ogni nostro affetto al ciel dispiace,
a che fin fatto arebbe il mondo Iddio?
    Qual più giusta cagion dell'amart'io   5
è, che dar gloria a quella eterna pace
onde pende il divin che di te piace,
e c'ogni cor gentil fa casto e pio?
    Fallace speme ha sol l'amor che muore
con la beltà c'ogni momento scema,   10
ond'è suggetta al variar d'un bel viso.
    Dolce è ben quella in un pudico core,
che per cangiar di scorza o d'ora strema
non manca, e qui caparra il paradiso.

260

Non è sempre di colpa aspra e mortale
d'una immensa bellezza un fero ardore,
se poi sì lascia liquefatto il core,
che 'n breve il penetri un divino strale.

258

Although it is true that your beautiful human face shows forth the divine beauty here, lady, my delight in that distant beauty is for me so fleeting that I cannot part from my delight in you, for to my pilgrim soul every other path, being steep and narrow, is too difficult. So I divide my time thus: my day is given to your eyes, by night my heart is with you, leaving no interval at all in which I may aspire to heaven. The destiny accorded me at birth so binds me to your splendour that it does not allow me to raise my burning desires, if there be nothing else to draw my mind to heaven by grace or mercy: the heart is slow to love what the eye does not see.

Madrigal, possibly for Vittoria Colonna, possibly 1546. *

259

Hope can indeed at times ascend on high with my burning desire and not prove false, for if all our emotions were displeasing to heaven, to what end would God have made the world?

What juster reason for my loving you can there be, than to give glory to that eternal peace from which derives the divine element in you that brings pleasure, and that makes every noble heart pure and devout?

False hope is harboured only by that love which dies with the beauty that is worn away by each passing minute, and so is subject to the variation wrought in a beautiful face.

Sweet indeed is the hope found in a chaste heart: it does not fail because of changes caused in the husk or brought by the final hour, and is here below a pledge of paradise.

Sonnet, possibly for Tommaso Cavalieri, c. 1546. *

260

To burn fiercely for an immense beauty is not always a harsh and deadly fault, if it so softens the heart that a divine arrow may then easily pierce it.

Amore isveglia e desta e 'mpenna l'ale,   5
né l'alto vol preschive al van furore;
qual primo grado c'al suo creatore,
di quel non sazia, l'alma ascende e sale.

L'amor di quel ch'i' parlo in alto aspira;
donna è dissimil troppo; e mal conviensi   10
arder di quella al cor saggio e verile.

L'un tira al cielo, e l'altro in terra tira;
nell'alma l'un, l'altr'abita ne' sensi,
e l'arco tira a cose basse e vile.

261

Se 'l troppo indugio ha più grazia e ventura
che per tempo al desir pietà non suole,
la mie, negli anni assai, m'affligge e duole,
ché 'l gioir vecchio picciol tempo dura.

Contrario ha 'l ciel, se di no' sente o cura,   5
arder nel tempo che ghiacciar si vuole,
com'io per donna; onde mie triste e sole
lacrime peso con l'età matura.

Ma forse, ancor c'al fin del giorno sia,
col sol già quasi oltr'a l'occaso spento,   10
fra le tenebre folte e 'l freddo rezzo,

s'amor c'infiamma solo a mezza via,
né altrimenti è, s'io vecchio ardo drento,
donna è che del mie fin farà 'l mie mezzo.

Love arouses and awakens us, and gives us feathered wings; it does not prevent vain passion from becoming a flight on high: this serves as a first step towards the creator for the soul, which, not satisfied with it, rises and ascends to him.

The love of which I am speaking aspires to the heights; it is too unlike a woman, and to burn for one ill becomes a wise and manly heart.

The former shoots towards heaven, the latter shoots on earth; one dwells in the soul, the other in the senses, and looses the bow at low and worthless things.

Sonnet, probably for Tommaso Cavalieri, 1546–7.

261

Though long delay brings more grace and good fortune than is the case when mercy is shown early to desire, their coming to me only in my late years afflicts and grieves me, since joy found in old age lasts but a short time.

Heaven, if it feels or cares for us, must be displeased at one's burning, as I do for a woman, at that time of life when one should freeze; and so I have the burden of my sad and lonely tears along with my advanced age.

But perhaps, though I am at the end of my days, with the sun already almost set below the horizon, so that I live in dense darkness and cold shade,

this woman may be one who will make of my life's end its middle, if love inflames us only when we are in midlife and if it is not otherwise in my case, since when old I burn within.

Sonnet, c. 1546. *

262

Amor, se tu se' dio,
non puo' ciò che tu vuoi?
Deh fa' per me, se puoi,
quel ch'i' fare' per te, s'Amor fuss'io.
Sconviensi al gran desio   5
d'alta beltà la speme,
vie più l'effetto a chi è press'al morire.
Pon nel tuo grado il mio:
dolce gli fie chi 'l preme?
Ché grazia per poc'or doppia 'l martire.   10
Ben ti voglio ancor dire:
che sarie morte, s'a' miseri è dura,
a chi muor giunto a l'alta suo ventura?

263

La nuova beltà d'una
mi sprona, sfrena e sferza;
né sol passato è terza,
ma nona e vespro, e prossim'è la sera.
Mie parto e mie fortuna,   5
l'un co' la morte scherza,
né l'altra dar mi può qui pace intera.
I' c'accordato m'era
col capo bianco e co' molt'anni insieme,
già l'arra in man tene' dell'altra vita,   10
qual ne promette un ben contrito core.
Più perde chi men teme
nell'ultima partita,
fidando sé nel suo propio valore
contr'a l'usato ardore: 15
s'a la memoria sol resta l'orecchio,
non giova, senza grazia, l'esser vecchio.

262

Love, if you are a god, can you not do what you wish? Ah do for me, if you can, what I should do for you, if I were Love. In one who is close to death, it is not right that hope should nourish his great desire for high beauty, much less that this should be fulfilled. Make my will yours: can what oppresses someone become sweet for him? For a grace that is short-lived is a double torment. Indeed, I wish to say more to you: if death is hard even for those who are wretched, what will it be for one who dies at the height of his good fortune?

Madrigal, c. 1546–7.

263

The fresh beauty of a woman spurs me, lets loose my reins, and whips me; and this not only when Terce has passed, but Nones and Vespers too, and night is near. As for my age and for my fortune in love, of these one toys with death, and the other cannot bring me complete peace here. I, who had come to terms with my white hair and with my many years, already held in my hands a pledge of the other life, such as a truly contrite heart promises us. He loses most who fears least in the final parting, by trusting in his own powers against habitual passion: for if there remain even an echo of this in his memory, being old will be of no help, where grace is lacking.

Madrigal, c. 1547.

264

Come portato ho già più tempo in seno
l'immagin, donna, del tuo volto impressa,
or che morte s'appressa,
con previlegio Amor ne stampi l'alma,
che del carcer terreno   5
felice sie 'l dipor suo grieve salma.
Per procella o per calma
con tal segno sicura,
sie come croce contro a' suo avversari;
e donde in ciel ti rubò la natura,   10
ritorni, norma agli angeli alti e chiari,
c'a rinnovar s'impari
là sù pel mondo un spirto in carne involto,
che dopo te gli resti il tuo bel volto.

265

Per non s'avere a ripigliar da tanti
quell'insieme beltà che più non era,
in donna alta e sincera
prestata fu sott'un candido velo,
c'a riscuoter da quanti   5
al mondo son, mal si rimborsa il cielo.
Ora in un breve anelo,
anzi in un punto, Iddio
dal mondo poco accorto
se l'ha ripresa, e tolta agli occhi nostri.   10
Né metter può in oblio,
benché 'l corpo sie morto,
i suo dolci, leggiadri e sacri inchiostri.
Crudel pietà, qui mostri,
se quanto a questa il ciel prestava a' brutti,   15
s'or per morte il rivuol, morremo or tutti.

266

Qual meraviglia è, se prossim'al foco
mi strussi e arsi, se or ch'egli è spento
di fuor, m'affligge e mi consuma drento,
e 'n cener mi riduce a poco a poco?

264

Just as for many years, lady, I have carried in my heart the image of your face impressed there, so now that death approaches may Love as a special privilege stamp it on your soul, that this may happily lay down the heavy corpse of its earthly prison. May your soul in storm or calm proceed safely with such a sign, like a cross warding off its adversaries; and may it return to heaven, whence nature stole you, to act as model for the high, shining angels, that there above they may learn to recreate for the world's good a spirit clothed in flesh, so that when you are gone your beautiful face may yet be present here.

Madrigal, possibly for the dying Vittoria Colonna, c. 1547. *

265

To avoid having to recover from a multitude that complete beauty when it has ceased to exist, heaven lent it in the form of the white veil of a pure and noble lady, for if heaven had to collect it from as many people as there are in the world then it would be badly reimbursed. Now in one short breath, indeed in an instant, God has gathered it back to himself from a world little aware of it, and taken it from our eyes. But though her body be dead, the world cannot cast into oblivion her sweet, graceful and holy writings. Cruel mercy, in this you show that if heaven had lent to the ugly all that it had to her, and were now claiming it back through death, we should all now die.

Madrigal, on the death of Vittoria Colonna, 1547.

266

What wonder is it if I, who when near the fire was destroyed and burned up by it, should now, when it has been extinguished outside of me, be tormented and consumed by it within, and little by little reduce myself to ashes?

Vedea ardendo sì lucente il loco   5
onde pendea il mio greve tormento,
che sol la vista mi facea contento,
e morte e strazi m'eran festa e gioco.

Ma po' che del gran foco lo splendore
che m'ardeva e nutriva, il ciel m'invola,   10
un carbon resto acceso e ricoperto.

E s'altre legne non mi porge amore
che lievin fiamma, una favilla sola
non fie di me, sì 'n cener mi converto.

267

I' sto rinchiuso come la midolla
da la sua scorza, qua pover e solo,
come spirto legato in un'ampolla:

e la mia scura tomba è picciol volo,
dov'è Aragn' e mill'opre e lavoranti,   5
e fan di lor filando fusaiuolo.

D'intorn'a l'uscio ho mete di giganti,
ché chi mangi'uva o ha presa medicina
non vanno altrove a cacar tutti quanti.

I' ho 'mparato a conoscer l'orina   10
e la cannella ond'esce, per quei fessi
che 'nanzi dì mi chiamon la mattina.

Gatti, carogne, canterelli o cessi,
chi n'ha per masserizi' o men vïaggio
non vien a vicitarmi mai senz'essi.   15

L'anima mia dal corpo ha tal vantaggio,
che se stasat' allentasse l'odore,
seco non la terre' 'l pan e 'l formaggio.

La toss' e 'l freddo il tien sol che non more;
se la non esce per l'uscio di sotto,   20
per bocca il fiato a pen' uscir può fore.

Dilombato, crepato, infranto e rotto
son già per le fatiche, e l'osteria
è morte, dov'io viv' e mangio a scotto.

La mia allegrezz' è la maninconia,   25
e 'l mio riposo son questi disagi:
che chi cerca il malanno, Dio gliel dia.

Chi mi vedess' a la festa de' Magi
sarebbe buono; e più, se la mia casa
vedessi qua fra sì ricchi palagi.   30

In my burning state, I used to see so radiant the place which was the source of my heavy torment that the very sight of it made me happy, and death and anguish were to me holiday and sport.

But now that heaven has robbed me of the splendour of that great fire which set me on fire yet nourished me, I am an ember burning still but buried.

And if love does not grant me fresh wood to raise a flame, then not a single spark will be left of me, so quickly am I turning myself to ashes.

Sonnet, on the death of Vittoria Colonna, 1547.

267

I am shut in like a marrow by its skin, poor and alone here, like a genie trapped in a bottle,

and it would take little time to fly round my dark tomb, where Arachne and a thousand of her works and workers are, who as they spin make bobbins of themselves.

Around my doorway I have giant dung-heaps, for those who have eaten grapes or taken a laxative go nowhere else to dump the lot.

I have learned to become well acquainted with urine and the spout from which it comes, because of those cracks which before daybreak announce the morning to me.

Cats' corpses, turds, chamberpots or their contents, no one ever comes to visit me without leaving these, as offerings for the house or to save themselves a further journey.

My soul is so at ease in my body that if this were unstopped and let out its smell, I should not be able to keep my soul in it, even if I offered a good meal.

Only my coughs and colds prevent my body from dying; if my soul cannot get out the lower exit, my breath itself can scarcely get out through my mouth.

I am by now worn out, ruptured, crushed and broken by my labours, and death is my tavern, where I eat and stay at a price.

I find my happiness in melancholy, and my rest in these discomforts: so may whoever seeks misfortune be granted it by God.

Were anyone to see me at the feast of the Ugly Old Woman, he would think I'd do very well for the part; and all the more if he saw my house set here among such rich palaces.

Fiamma d'amor nel cor non m'è rimasa;
se 'l maggior caccia sempre il minor duolo,
di penne l'alma ho ben tarpata e rasa.
    Io tengo un calabron in un orciuolo,
in un sacco di cuoio ossa e capresti,   35
tre pilole di pece in un bocciuolo.
    Gli occhi di biffa macinati e pesti,
i denti come tasti di stormento
c'al moto lor la voce suoni e resti.
    La faccia mia ha forma di spavento;   40
i panni da cacciar, senz'altro telo,
dal seme senza pioggia i corbi al vento.
    Mi cova in un orecchio un ragnatelo,
ne l'altro canta un grillo tutta notte;
né dormo e russ' al catarroso anelo.   45
    Amor, le muse e le fiorite grotte,
mie scombiccheri, a' cemboli, a' cartocci,
agli osti, a' cessi, a' chiassi son condotte.
    Che giova voler far tanti bambocci,
se m'han condotto al fin, come colui   50
che passò 'l mar e poi affogò ne' mocci?
    L'arte pregiata, ov'alcun tempo fui
di tant'opinïon, mi rec'a questo,
povero, vecchio e servo in forz' altrui,
    ch'i' son disfatto, s'i' non muoio presto.   55

268

    Perché l'età ne 'nvola
il desir cieco e sordo,
con la morte m'accordo,
stanco e vicino all'ultima parola.
L'alma che teme e cola   5
quel che l'occhio non vede,
come da cosa perigliosa e vaga,
dal tuo bel volto, donna, m'allontana.
Amor, c'al ver non cede,
di nuovo il cor m'appaga   10
di foco e speme; e non già cosa umana
mi par, mi dice, amar ...

No flame of love is to be found now in my heart; since greater suffering casts out the lesser, my soul has been well and truly clipped and shorn of its wings.

I possess a hornet in a jug, bones and sinews in a leather sack, and three pills of pitch in a little bottle.

My eyes are a bluish colour, as if they had been ground and pounded; my teeth are like the keys of an instrument, for as they move my voice sounds out and ceases.

My face is fit to terrify; my clothes, without further weapons, would be enough to scatter to the winds crows feeding on seeds in a dry field.

A cobweb sits brooding in one ear, in the other a cricket sings all night; and I cannot sleep and snore for my catarrhal breathing.

My scribblings about love, the muses, flowery grottoes have ended up on tambourines, or as waste-paper in inns, latrines and brothels.

What was the good of having set myself to make so many rag-dolls, if they have led me to such an end, like someone who crossed the sea only to drown in snot?

The esteemed art, through which at one time I was held in such high regard, has brought me to this: I am poor, old, and a slave in others' power,

so that I shall be a human wreck, if death does not come soon.

Capitolo, *1546–50*.

268

Since old age steals from us blind and deaf desire, I come to terms with death, tired as I am and near to my last word. The soul which fears and reverences what the eye cannot see makes me keep my distance from your beautiful face, lady, as from something dangerous yet alluring. Love, which will not bow to truth, once more fills my heart with fire and hope, and seems to say to me that love is not something merely human ...

Incomplete madrigal, probably 1547 or later.

269

Or d'un fier ghiaccio, or d'un ardente foco,
or d'anni o guai, or di vergogna armato,
l'avvenir nel passato
specchio con trista e dolorosa speme;
e 'l ben, per durar poco,   5
sento non men che 'l mal m'affligge e preme.
Alla buona, alla rie fortuna insieme,
di me già stanche, ognor chieggio perdono:
e veggio ben che della vita sono
ventura e grazia l'ore brieve e corte,   10
se la miseria medica la morte.

270

Tu mi da' di quel c'ognor t'avanza
e vuo' da me le cose che non sono.

271

Di te con teco, Amor, molt'anni sono
nutrito ho l'alma e, se non tutto, in parte
il corpo ancora; e con mirabil arte
con la speme il desir m'ha fatto buono.
Or, lasso, alzo il pensier con l'alie e sprono   5
me stesso in più sicura e nobil parte.
Le tuo promesse indarno delle carte
e del tuo onor, di che piango e ragiono,
. . . .

272

Tornami al tempo, allor che lenta e sciolta
al cieco ardor m'era la briglia e 'l freno;
rendimi il volto angelico e sereno
onde fu seco ogni virtù sepolta,
e ' passi spessi e con fatica molta,   5
che son sì lenti a chi è d'anni pieno;
tornami l'acqua e 'l foco in mezzo 'l seno,
se vuo' di me saziarti un'altra volta.

269

With sad and painful hope I see my future reflected in my past, armed sometimes with fierce ice, sometimes with burning fire, sometimes with fears and woes, sometimes with shame; and I feel that the good, because it lasts but a little time, afflicts and oppresses me no less than the bad. I ask pardon every hour of good and evil fortune alike, both now tired of me; and I clearly see that in life to have short, brief hours is a grace and blessing, since it is death alone that cures our misery.

Madrigal, probably 1547 or later.

270

You give me only from what you have left over, and ask from me the things I do not have.

Unrhymed couplet, probably 1547 or later.

271

For many years now, Love, with your help I have nourished my soul on you, and my body too, if not completely, at least in part; and with wonderful skill, desire together with hope has made me strong.

Now, tired out, I raise my thoughts on wings and spur myself towards a safer and more noble place. The promises that you vainly made on paper and on your honour, over which I weep and ponder, ...

Unfinished sonnet, 1546–50, possibly 1547.

272

Take me back to the time when, at the urging of blind ardour, my bit was lightly held, my reins loose; bring back to me the serene, angelic face whose burial meant also the loss of every virtue;

bring back the frequent steps I made, with strenuous effort, which come now so slowly to one weighed down by years; give back to me, to my innermost breast, the water and the fire, if you wish once more to sate yourself on me.

E s'egli è pur, Amor, che tu sol viva
de' dolci amari pianti de' mortali,   10
d'un vecchio stanco oma' puo' goder poco;
 ché l'alma, quasi giunta a l'altra riva,
fa scudo a' tuo di più pietosi strali:
e d'un legn'arso fa vil pruova il foco.

273

 Se sempre è solo e un quel che sol muove
il tutto per altezza e per traverso,
non sempre a no' si mostra per un verso,
ma più e men quante suo grazia piove.
 A me d'un modo e d'altri in ogni altrove: 5
più e men chiaro o più lucente e terso,
secondo l'egritudin, che disperso
ha l'intelletto a le divine pruove.
 Nel cor ch'è più capace più s'appiglia,
se dir si può, 'l suo volto e 'l suo valore;   10
e di quel fassi sol guida e lucerna.
. . . .
. . . .
truova conforme a la suo parte interna.

274

 Deh fammiti vedere in ogni loco!
Se da mortal bellezza arder mi sento,
appresso al tuo mi sarà foco ispento,
e io nel tuo sarò, com'ero, in foco.
 Signor mie caro, i' te sol chiamo e 'nvoco   5
contr'a l'inutil mie cieco tormento:
tu sol puo' rinnovarmi fuora e drento
le voglie e 'l senno e 'l valor lento e poco.
 Tu desti al tempo, Amor, quest'alma diva
e 'n questa spoglia ancor fragil e stanca   10
l'incarcerasti, e con fiero destino.
 Che poss'io altro che così non viva?
Ogni ben senza te, Signor, mi manca;
il cangiar sorte è sol poter divino.

But if it is indeed true, Love, that you live only from the bitter-sweet tears of mortals, you can by now get little pleasure from a weary old man;

for my soul, which has almost reached the other bank, makes a shield of more merciful arrows to ward off yours; and fire has little to gain from a burned-out piece of wood.

Sonnet, c. 1547.

273

Though he remains always one and the same who alone governs the universe in all its height and breadth, he does not always show himself to us in the same way, but more and less according as his grace rains down.

In one way to me and in other ways in every other place: more clearly and less so, or more brightly and distinctly and less so, in accordance with the sickness that has enfeebled man's intellect with regard to the signs of God's presence.

It is in the heart that is more open that his face and power are better grasped, if one can so put it; and only of such does he make himself guide and lantern.

. . . .

. . . . he finds suited to his inner part.

Unfinished sonnet, c. 1547.

274

Ah make me see you present everywhere! If I feel myself burning for mortal beauty, that will be for me like a spent fire compared to yours, and in yours I shall be on fire, as I was before.

My dear Lord, you alone do I call on and invoke against my blind, futile torment; you alone can renew inside and out my will, my mind and my sluggish, feeble strength.

You, Love, awakened into time this divine soul, and in this covering, now fragile and weary, you imprisoned it, allotting it a harsh destiny.

What else can I do that I may not live this way? Every good without you, Lord, will fail me: to change a person's state belongs to divine power alone.

Sonnet, 1547.

275

Dagli alti monti e d'una gran ruina,
ascoso e circunscritto d'un gran sasso,
discesi a discoprirmi in questo basso,
contr'a mie voglia, in tal lapedicina.
    Quand'el sol nacqui, e da chi il ciel destina,   5
. . . .

276

Passa per gli occhi al core in un momento
qualunche obbietto di beltà lor sia,
e per sì larga e sì capace via
c'a mille non si chiude, non c'a cento,
    d'ogni età, d'ogni sesso; ond'io pavento,   5
carco d'affanni, e più di gelosia;
né fra sì vari volti so qual sia
c'anzi morte mi die 'ntero contento.
    S'un ardente desir mortal bellezza
ferma del tutto, non discese insieme   10
dal ciel con l'alma; è dunche umana voglia.
    Ma se pass'oltre, Amor, tuo nome sprezza,
c'altro die cerca; e di quel più non teme
c'a lato vien contr'a sì bassa spoglia.

277

Se con lo stile o coi colori avete
alla natura pareggiato l'arte,
anzi a quella scemato il pregio in parte,
che 'l bel di lei più bello a noi rendete,
    poi che con dotta man posto vi sete   5
a più degno lavoro, a vergar carte,
quel che vi manca, a lei di pregio in parte,
nel dar vita ad altrui, tutta togliete.
    Che se secolo alcuno omai contese
in far bell'opre, almen cedale, poi   10
che convien c'al prescritto fine arrive.

275

From a great ravine, high in the mountains, hidden and enclosed within a great boulder, I came down to find myself in this low place, against my will, among this heap of stones.

When the sun was born, and by him whom heaven destines,

....

Unfinished sonnet, late, possibly 1547–50.

276

Any object that appears beautiful to my eyes passes through them to my heart in an instant, and by a path so wide and spacious that it would not be blocked by a thousand such, never mind a hundred,

of every age and of each sex; this makes me fearful, weighed down by troubles as I am, and even more by envy; nor do I know any face among so many different ones that might before death bring me complete happiness.

If mortal beauty entirely arrests an ardent desire, such a desire did not descend from heaven along with the soul; it is, therefore, a human willing.

But if it passes beyond, Love, it scorns your name, for it seeks another god; and it no longer fears the fact that you are at our side warring against such a miserable covering.

Sonnet, late, possibly 1547–50.

277

If with your stylus and your colours you have made art equal to nature, and indeed in part surpassed its achievement by making more beautiful for us the beauty found in it,

now that you have set yourself with learned hand to a more noble task, to writing, you have completely gained, by giving life to others, what was lacking in you and was nature's sole advantage.

For if any century has ever vied with nature in making works of beauty, it has always had to concede this to it, that all must finally arrive at their prescribed end.

Or le memorie altrui, già spente, accese
tornando, fate or che fien quelle e voi,
malgrado d'esse, etternalmente vive.

278

Chi non vuol delle foglie
non ci venga di maggio.

279

La forza d'un bel viso a che mi sprona?
C'altro non è c'al mondo mi diletti:
ascender vivo fra gli spirti eletti
per grazia tal, c'ogni altra par men buona.
Se ben col fattor l'opra suo consuona,   5
che colpa vuol giustizia ch'io n'aspetti,
s'i' amo, anz'ardo, e per divin concetti
onoro e stimo ogni gentil persona?

280

L'alma inquieta e confusa in sé non truova
altra cagion c'alcun grave peccato
mal conosciuto, onde non è celato
all'immensa pietà c'a' miser giova.
I' parlo a te, Signor, c'ogni mie pruova   5
fuor del tuo sangue non fa l'uom beato:
miserere di me, da ch'io son nato
a la tuo legge; e non fie cosa nuova.

281

Arder sole' nel freddo ghiaccio il foco;
or m'è l'ardente foco un freddo ghiaccio,
disciolto, Amor, quello insolubil laccio,
e morte or m'è, che m'era festa e gioco.

Yet by rekindling the memories of men which had once been extinguished, you now bring it about that they, and you, despite nature, are eternally alive.

Sonnet, for Giorgio Vasari, 1550.

278

Whoever does not like leaves ought not to come here in May.

Unrhymed couplet, late.

279

To what am I spurred by the power of a beautiful face? Since there is nothing else in the world that brings me delight: to ascend, while still alive, among the blessed spirits by a grace so great that every other seems inferior.

If every work is truly similar to its maker, what blame would justice have me expect, if I love, indeed burn, and honour and esteem every noble person as being divinely conceived?

Partial sonnet, late.

280

The troubled and confused soul will find within itself no other cause of its state than some grave sin only dimly understood, which does not mean that it is hidden to the boundless mercy that brings help to the wretched.

I turn to you, Lord, for no effort of mine without your blood can gain man blessedness; have mercy on me, for I was born subject to your law; and it will not be for the first time.

Partial sonnet, late.

281

The fire used to burn even in the freezing ice; but now that those thongs which defied escape have been undone, Love, the burning fire itself has become for me freezing ice, and what was for me fun and games is now death to me.

Quel primo amor che ne diè tempo e loco,   5
nella strema miseria è greve impaccio
a l'alma stanca...

282

Con tanta servitù, con tanto tedio
e con falsi concetti e gran periglio
dell'alma, a sculpir qui cose divine.

283

Non può, Signor mie car, la fresca e verde
età sentir, quant'a l'ultimo passo
si cangia gusto, amor, voglie e pensieri.
     Più l'alma acquista ove più 'l mondo perde;
l'arte e la morte non va bene insieme: 5
che convien più che di me dunche speri?

284

S'a tuo nome ho concetto alcuno immago,
non è senza del par seco la morte,
onde l'arte e l'ingegno si dilegua.
     Ma se, quel c'alcun crede, i' pur m'appago
che si ritorni a viver, a tal sorte   5
ti servirò, s'avvien che l'arte segua.

285

Giunto è già 'l corso della vita mia,
con tempestoso mar, per fragil barca,
al comun porto, ov'a render si varca
conto e ragion d'ogni opra trista e pia.
     Onde l'affettüosa fantasia   5
che l'arte mi fece idol e monarca
conosco or ben com'era d'error carca
e quel c'a mal suo grado ogn'uom desia.

That first love which opened up time and space for us is in our
final misery a heavy burden to the tired soul ....
....

Unfinished sonnet, late.

282

To sculpt divine things here can be done only with great slavery
and great tedium, with false ideas and with grave danger to the
soul.

Unrhymed tercet, c. 1552.

283

The fresh, green age cannot grasp, my dear Lord, how greatly
at the final step one changes taste, love, desires and thoughts.

The soul gains more the more it loses the world; art and death
do not go well together: in what, then, should I place my greatest
hope?

Partial sonnet, c. 1552.

284

If in your name I have conceived some image, this never happens
without death likewise appearing with it, which makes my powers
of art and intellect fade away.

But if I too were happy to believe, as some do, that man returns
to this life, I should in that case serve you, provided that my
artistic powers come back with me.

Partial sonnet, c. 1552.

285

My life's journey has finally arrived, after a stormy sea, in a
fragile boat, at the common port, through which all must pass to
render an account and explanation of their every act, evil and
devout.

So I now fully recognize how my fond imagination which made
art for me an idol and a tyrant was laden with error, as is that
which all men desire to their own harm.

Gli amorosi pensier, già vani e lieti,
che fien or, s'a duo morte m'avvicino?　　　　10
D'una so 'l certo, e l'altra mi minaccia.
　　Né pinger né scolpir fie più che quieti
l'anima, volta a quell'amor divino
c'aperse, a prender noi, 'n croce le braccia.

286

Gl'infiniti pensier mie d'error pieni,
negli ultim'anni della vita mia,
ristringer si dovrien 'n un sol che sia
guida agli etterni suo giorni sereni.
　　Ma che poss'io, Signor, s'a me non vieni　　5
coll'usata ineffabil cortesia?

287

Di giorno in giorno insin da' mie prim'anni,
Signor, soccorso tu mi fusti e guida,
onde l'anima mia ancor si fida
di doppia aita ne' mie doppi affanni.

288

Le favole del mondo m'hanno tolto
il tempo dato a contemplare Iddio,
né sol le grazie suo poste in oblio,
ma con lor, più che senza, a peccar volto.
　　Quel c'altri saggio, me fa cieco e stolto　　5
e tardi a riconoscer l'error mio;
manca la speme, e pur cresce il desio
che da te sia dal propio amor disciolto.
　　Ammezzami la strada c'al ciel sale,
Signor mie caro, e a quel mezzo solo　　　　10
salir m'è di bisogno la tuo 'ita.
　　Mettimi in odio quante 'l mondo vale
e quante suo bellezze onoro e colo,
c'anzi morte caparri eterna vita.

What will now become of my former thoughts of love, empty yet happy, if I am now approaching a double death? Of one I am quite certain, and the other threatens me.

Neither painting nor sculpting can any longer quieten my soul, turned now to that divine love which on the cross, to embrace us, opened wide its arms.

Sonnet, 1552–4.

286

My infinite thoughts, full of error, ought in the last years of my life to reduce themselves to one which may guide it towards its serene, eternal days.

But what can I do, Lord, if you do not come to me with your customary ineffable kindness?

Partial sonnet, late, possibly 1552–4.

287

Day after day from my very earliest years, Lord, you have been my aid and guide, and so my soul trusts even now that it will receive double help in my double woes.

Quatrain, late, possibly 1552–4.

288

The fables of this world have taken from me the time given for contemplating God; and not only have I disregarded God's graces, but, because of these, I have more fully turned to sin than had I lacked them.

What makes others wise makes me blind and foolish, and slow to recognize the error of my ways; hope fades, and yet my desire increases that by you I may be freed from selfish love.

Halve for me the road that climbs to heaven, my dear Lord; and even to climb that half I have need of your help.

Make me hate all that the world values, and all its beauties that I honour and revere, so that before death I may lay hold of life eternal.

Sonnet, sent to Monsignor Ludovico Beccadelli in March 1555.

289

Non è più bassa o vil cosa terrena
che quel che, senza te, mi sento e sono,
onde a l'alto desir chiede perdono
la debile mie propia e stanca lena.
 Deh, porgi, Signor mio, quella catena   5
che seco annoda ogni celeste dono:
la fede, dico, a che mi stringo e sprono;
né, mie colpa, n'ho grazia intiera e piena.
 Tanto mi fie maggior, quante più raro
il don de' doni, e maggior fia se, senza,   10
pace e contento il mondo in sé non have.
 Po' che non fusti del tuo sangue avaro,
che sarà di tal don la tuo clemenza,
se 'l ciel non s'apre a noi con altra chiave?

290

Scarco d'un'importuna e greve salma,
Signor mie caro, e dal mondo disciolto,
qual fragil legno a te stanco rivolto
da l'orribil procella in dolce calma.
 Le spine e ' chiodi e l'una e l'altra palma   5
col tuo benigno umil pietoso volto
prometton grazia di pentirsi molto,
e speme di salute a la trist'alma.
 Non mirin co' iustizia i tuo sant'occhi
il mie passato, e 'l gastigato orecchio;   10
non tenda a quello il tuo braccio severo.
 Tuo sangue sol mie colpe lavi e tocchi,
e più abondi, quant'i' son più vecchio,
di pronta aita e di perdono intero.

291

Penso e ben so c'alcuna colpa preme,
occulta a me, lo spirto in gran martire;
privo dal senso e dal suo propio ardire
il cor di pace, e 'l desir d'ogni speme.

289

No earthly thing is more base and vile than I feel myself to be, and am, without you, and so my own weak and tired breath begs pardon of you, who are supremely to be desired.

Ah, hold out to me, my Lord, that chain which comes bound round with every heavenly gift: faith, I mean, to which I press and spur myself, but of which through my own fault I lack the grace whole and entire.

This gift of gifts will be to me all the greater for being so rare, and greater still since, without it, the world cannot in itself find peace and happiness.

Though you were not sparing of your blood, what good will be your mercy shown in such a gift, if heaven does not open itself to us with another key?

Sonnet, 1555.

290

Relieved of a troublesome and heavy burden, my dear Lord, and freed from the world, I turn wearily to you, like a fragile boat passing from a terrible storm to a pleasant calm.

The thorns and nails and both your palms, together with your kind, humble, merciful face, promise to the sinful soul the grace of deep repentance and the hope of salvation.

May your holy eyes and pure ears not respond with rigorous justice to my past life; may your severe arm not stretch out towards it.

May your blood alone cleanse and remove my sins; and may it more abound the older I am, with ready help and with complete forgiveness.

Sonnet, late, possibly 1555 or after.

291

I think, indeed I know, that some guilt, hidden from me, oppresses my soul to the point of great torment, while by the senses and by its own boldness my heart is deprived of peace and my desire of all hope.

Ma chi è teco, Amor, che cosa teme   5
che grazia allenti inanzi al suo partire?

292

Ben sarien dolce le preghiere mie,
se virtù mi prestassi da pregarte:
nel mio fragil terren non è già parte
da frutto buon, che da sé nato sie.
Tu sol se' seme d'opre caste e pie,   5
che là germuglian, dove ne fa' parte;
nessun propio valor può seguitarte,
se non gli mostri le tuo sante vie.

293

Carico d'anni e di peccati pieno
e col trist'uso radicato e forte,
vicin mi veggio a l'una e l'altra morte,
e parte 'l cor nutrisco di veleno.
Né propie forze ho, c'al bisogno sièno   5
per cangiar vita, amor, costume o sorte,
senza le tuo divine e chiare scorte,
d'ogni fallace corso guida e freno.
Signor mie car, non basta che m'invogli
c'aspiri al ciel sol perché l'alma sia,   10
non come prima, di nulla, creata.
Anzi che del mortal la privi e spogli,
prego m'ammezzi l'alta e erta via,
e fie più chiara e certa la tornata.

294

Mentre m'attrista e duol, parte m'è caro
ciascun pensier c'a memoria mi riede
il tempo andato, e che ragion mi chiede
de' giorni persi, onde non è riparo.
Caro m'è sol, perc'anzi morte imparo   5
quant'ogni uman diletto ha corta fede;
tristo m'è, c'a trovar grazi' e mercede
negli ultim'anni a molte colpe è raro.

But if someone is close to you, Love, what can he fear that may weaken grace before his passing?

Partial sonnet, late, possibly 1555 or after.

292

My prayers would indeed be sweet if you would lend me power to pray to you; in my poor soil there is nowhere that by itself can produce good fruit.

You alone are the seed of pure and pious deeds, which spring up wherever you sow yourself; no man's own strength is sufficient to follow you, if you do not show him your holy ways.

Partial sonnet, late, possibly 1555 or after.

293

Burdened by years and full of sins and with my evil habits rooted and strong, I see myself close to both deaths, and still I nourish my heart with poison.

And I do not have powers of my own sufficient to change my life, love, conduct or condition, without your clear, divine help, which is guide and restraint for every treacherous journey.

My dear Lord, it is not enough for you simply to implant in me the will through which one aspires to heaven for my soul to be recreated, and not simply, as it was before, created from nothing.

Before you deprive and strip it of what is mortal, I beg you to halve for me the high, steep road, so that my return may be more clear and sure.

Sonnet, late, possibly 1555 or after.

294

While I am saddened and pained by each one of them, those thoughts are yet dear to me that call to mind the time gone by and require me to give account of the lost days, which cannot be made up.

Dear to me only because I learn before death how short-lived is the promise given by every human pleasure; sad for me, because it is rare to find grace and mercy for many sins in one's final years.

Ché ben c'alle promesse tua s'attenda,
sperar forse, Signore, è troppo ardire   10
c'ogni superchio indugio amor perdoni.
    Ma pur par nel tuo sangue si comprenda,
se per noi par non ebbe il tuo martire,
senza misura sien tuo cari doni.

295

Di morte certo, ma non già dell'ora,
la vita è breve e poco me n'avanza;
diletta al senso, è non però la stanza
a l'alma, che mi prega pur ch'i' mora.
    Il mondo è cieco e 'l tristo esempro ancora   5
vince e sommerge ogni prefetta usanza;
spent'è la luce e seco ogni baldanza,
trionfa il falso e 'l ver non surge fora.
    Deh, quando fie, Signor, quel che s'aspetta
per chi ti crede? c'ogni troppo indugio   10
tronca la speme e l'alma fa mortale.
    Che val che tanto lume altrui prometta,
s'anzi vien morte, e senza alcun refugio
ferma per sempre in che stato altri assale?

296

S'avvien che spesso il gran desir prometta
a' mie tant'anni di molt'anni ancora,
non fa che morte non s'appressi ognora,
e là dove men duol manco s'affretta.
    A che più vita per gioir s'aspetta,   5
se sol nella miseria Iddio s'adora?
Lieta fortuna, e con lunga dimora,
tanto più nuoce quante più diletta.
    E se talor, tuo grazia, il cor m'assale,
Signor mie caro, quell'ardente zelo   10
che l'anima conforta e rassicura,
    da che 'l propio valor nulla mi vale,
subito allor sarie da girne al cielo:
ché con più tempo il buon voler men dura.

For though one does rely on your promises, it is perhaps daring too much to hope, Lord, that love may pardon all excessive delay.

But still it seems that in your blood we are given to understand that, as for us your torment had no equal, so too your dear gifts may be without limit.

Sonnet, late, possibly after 1555.

295

Certain of death, but not yet of its hour, I know that life is short and little of it left to me; though to remain here is delightful for the senses, it is not so for the soul, which indeed begs me to die.

The world is blind, and evil example still conquers and overwhelms even the noblest conduct; the light has been extinguished, and with it all valour; falsehood triumphs and truth does not rise clear.

Ah, Lord, when will that happen which everyone who believes in you awaits? For all excessive delay cuts off hope and makes the soul mortal.

What good is it that you promise us such great light, if in the meantime death overcomes us and forever binds us in that state in which it strikes us down?

Sonnet, late, possibly after 1555.

296

If it often happens that strong desire promises my advanced years many years more, this does not mean that death does not draw closer every hour, or that it hastens more slowly to him who is less troubled by it.

Why does one look for longer life to enjoy oneself, if it is only in misery that God is adored? Good fortune together with long life bring greater harm the more they bring delight.

And if at times through your grace, my dear Lord, that burning zeal assails my heart which comforts and reassures the soul,

since my own powers do not afford me any help at all, then would be the very moment to rise to heaven: for with more time good will in us lasts less.

Sonnet, late, 1555 or after.

297

Se lungo spazio del trist'uso e folle
più temp'il suo contrario a purgar chiede,
la morte già vicina nol concede,
né freno il mal voler da quel ch'e' volle.

298

Non fur men lieti che turbati e tristi
che tu patissi, e non già lor, la morte,
gli spirti eletti, onde le chiuse porte
del ciel, di terra a l'uom col sangue apristi.

    Lieti, poiché, creato, il redemisti   5
dal primo error di suo misera sorte;
tristi, a sentir c'a la pena aspra e forte,
servo de' servi in croce divenisti.

    Onde e chi fusti, il ciel ne diè tal segno
che scurò gli occhi suoi, la terra aperse,   10
tremorno i monti e torbide fur l'acque.

    Tolse i gran Padri al tenebroso regno,
gli angeli brutti in più doglia sommerse;
godé sol l'uom, c'al battesmo rinacque.

299

Al zucchero, a la mula, a le candele,
aggiuntovi un fiascon di malvagia,
resta sì vinta ogni fortuna mia,
ch'i' rendo le bilance a san Michele.

    Troppa bonaccia sgonfia sì le vele,   5
che senza vento in mar perde la via
la debile mie barca, e par che sia
una festuca in mar rozz'e crudele.

    A rispetto a la grazia e al gran dono,
al cib', al poto e a l'andar sovente   10
c'a ogni mi' bisogno è caro e buono,

    Signor mie car, ben vi sare' nïente
per merto a darvi tutto quel ch'i' sono:
ché 'l debito pagar non è presente.

297

If a long time spent in an evil, foolish way of life requires for its purging a greater period spent in a contrary way, my death's being already near does not allow this, indeed I do not even rein in my evil will from what it willed.

Quatrain, late, after 1555.

298

The blessed spirits were no less glad than troubled and sad that you, not they themselves, suffered death, by which with your blood you opened from on earth to man the closed gates of heaven.

Glad, because you redeemed man, created by you, from his wretched state caused by the first sin; sad, in knowing that it was through harsh and bitter pain that you became servant of the servants on the cross.

Whence you came and who you were, heaven showed us through these signs: it darkened its own eyes, and opened the earth, the mountains trembled and the waters were convulsed.

It took the great patriarchs from the realm of darkness, and buried the vile angels in deeper suffering; only man rejoiced, for he was reborn through baptism.

Sonnet, late.

299

The sugar, the mule, the candles, to which was added a flagon of malmsey: these so outweigh all my resources that I am handing back the scales to St Michael.

Too much calm weather has taken the wind from my sails so completely that my fragile boat lies lost on a windless sea, or seems like a wisp of straw on a rough and cruel sea.

Compared with your kindness and your great gifts – the food, the drink, the means of moving readily around, which is something very welcome and helpful for all my needs –

my dear lord, I should count as nothing in terms of merit, even were I to give you all that I am: for it is no present to repay a debt.

Sonnet, possibly for Giorgio Vasari, late.

300

Per croce e grazia e per diverse pene
son certo, monsignor, trovarci in cielo;
ma prima c'a l'estremo ultimo anelo,
goderci in terra mi parria pur bene.

    Se l'aspra via coi monti e co 'l mar tiene   5
l'un da l'altro lontan, lo spirto e 'l zelo
non cura intoppi o di neve o di gelo,
né l'alia del pensier lacci o catene.

    Ond'io con esso son sempre con voi,
e piango e parlo del mio morto Urbino,   10
che vivo or forse saria costà meco,

    com'ebbi già in pensier. Sua morte poi
m'affretta e tira per altro cammino,
dove m'aspetta ad albergar con seco.

301

Di più cose s'attristan gli occhi mei,
e 'l cor di tante quant'al mondo sono;
se 'l tuo di te cortese e caro dono
non fussi, della vita che farei?

    Del mie tristo uso e dagli esempli rei,   5
fra le tenebre folte, dov'i' sono,
spero aita trovar non che perdono,
c'a chi ti mostri, tal prometter dei.

302

Non più per altro da me stesso togli
l'amor, gli affetti perigliosi e vani,
che per fortuna avversa o casi strani,
ond'e' tuo amici dal mondo disciogli,

    Signor mie car, tu sol che vesti e spogli,   5
e col tuo sangue l'alme purghi e sani
da l'infinite colpe e moti umani,

. . . .

300

Through the cross and grace and through our various sufferings, I am certain, monsignor, that we shall meet in heaven; but I am quite sure that it is right, before we finally breathe our last, to go on enjoying one another on earth.

If a harsh journey over mountain and sea keeps us far from each other, the spirit and ardent love care nothing for such obstacles as snow and ice, nor do the wings of thought know snares or chains.

So in thought I am always with you, and with you I weep as I speak of my dead Urbino, who, were he still alive, would perhaps be over there with me now,

as I once had in mind. But instead his death hurries and draws me along another path, to where he is waiting for me to lodge with him.

Sonnet, for Monsignor Ludovico Beccadelli, probably 1556.

301

My eyes are saddened by many things, and my heart by as many as the whole world holds; were it not for your gracious and dear gift of yourself, what should I make of life?

I hope to find not only pardon for my evil habits but help against the evil examples that surround me in the dense darkness in which I find myself, for such you must promise to those to whom you show yourself.

Partial sonnet, 1560 or later.

302

There is no longer any other way for you to rid me of love, of dangerous and empty affections, than by adverse fortune or by strange occurrences, through which you set your friends free from the world,

my dear Lord, you who alone clothe and strip souls, and with your blood purify and heal them of their infinite sins and human urgings, ...

Unfinished sonnet, 1560 or later.

APPENDIX

Poetic fragments

F1

La morte è 'l fin d'una prigione scura.

F2

La voglia invoglia e ella ha poi la doglia.

F3

Davitte colla fromba e io coll'arco.
                    Michelangolo

F4

Rott'è l'alta colonna e 'l verde lauro.

F5

Al dolce mormorar d'un fiumicello
c'aduggia di verd'ombra un chiaro fonte
c'a star il cor (?) . . .

F6

Vidi donna bella
ch'i' . . . la sorte mia . . .
io mi senti' tutto consolato
. . . .

F7

. . . dolce stanza nell'inferno.

FI

Death is the end of a dark prison

c. 1501.

F2

Desire engenders desire and then must suffer.

c. 1501.

F3

David with the sling and I with the bow.
Michelangelo

c. 1501–2.

F4

The high column and the green laurel are broken.

c. 1501–2.

F5

At the sweet murmuring of a little stream which a clear spring
darkens with green shadows, which a heart to remain
....

c. 1501–2.

F6

I saw a beautiful lady whom I ... my fate ... I felt myself
completely consoled ....

Early.

F7

... a sweet abode in hell.

1503–4.

F8

... Dio devotamente.

F9

Deus in nomine tuo salvum me fac.

F10

... che Febo alle ... nora
... ti del suo vago e bel soggiorno
... do all'ombra mi refugi' el giorno
del suo lume le campagne indora (?)
... dove sie d'una (?) mi addolora
... mo .... discolora.

F11

Raccoglietele al piè del tristo cesto.

F12

In omo Dio tu se'.
In pensier ...

F13

L'ardente nodo ov'io fu' d'ora in ora,
contando anni ventuno ardendo preso,
morte disciolse; né già mai tal peso
provai, né credo c'uom ...

F8

... God devoutly.

1503–4.

F9

God, save me through your power.

1503–4.

FIO

... which Phoebus to the ... you of its pleasant and beautiful rest ... I take refuge in the shade during the day, when with its light it makes the fields golden ... wherever it may be it makes me suffer over one ... discolours.

1503–4.

FII

Gather them up at the foot of the wretched bush.

c. 1505–6.

FI2

You, God, are in man. In thought ....

c. 1505–6.

FI3

Death dissolved the burning knot in which I had been bound hour upon hour, held burning for a space of twentyone years; never before had I experienced such a burden, nor do I believe that man ....

c. 1505–6.

F14

Di pensier...
Chi dire' ch'ella f...
di mie mano
Di pensier in pensier...

F15

Laudate parvoli
el Signore nostro,
laudate sempre.

F16

Febbre, fianchi, dolor, morbi, occhi e denti.

F17

La m'arde e lega e temmi e parm'un zucchero.

F18

Però amando m'affatico
che la vittoria fie quant'è 'l nemico.

F19

Agli occhi, alla virtù, al tuo valore
. . . .

F20

c'altro piacer non hanno,
ove se vivo (?) ... ove morto io defunto,
e di niente so' fatto appunto appunto.

F14

From thought ... Who would say that she ... by my hand ...
From thought to thought ....

c. 1505–6.

F15

Praise our Lord, little ones, praise him always.

c. 1505–6.

F16

Fever, flanks, pains, diseases, eyes and teeth.

Early.

F17

She burns, binds and holds me and seems to me like sugar.

c. 1507.

F18

And so I grow weary in love, for victory turns out to be like an enemy.

1520–5.

F19

To your eyes, your virtue and your strength ....

1520–5.

F20

... for they have no other pleasure, whether I live ... or whether I am dead and buried, and made into absolutely nothing at all.

1520–5.

F21

Dentr'a me giugne al cor, già fatto tale,

F22

Valle locus clausa toto mihi nullus in orbe.

F23

L'una di par sen va con la mia sorte,
l'altra mirando pur mi porge aita.

F24

Non altrimenti Dedal si riscosse,
non altrimenti el sol l'ombra discaccia.

F25

... o e stanco anelo
... o el tempo rio
... luce al gioir mio
... in tenebre e gelo
... ombra discaccia
... e l'altra penna
... terno porta
... el ciel conforta.

F26

Che mal si può amar ben chi non si vede.

F21

It reaches right inside me to my heart, already made such . . . .

c. 1520.

F22

No place in all the world [was more pleasing] to me than Vaucluse.

1513–30.

F23

One of the two departs with my fate, while the other, looking on, offers me help.

c. 1523.

F24

In just this way did Daedalus free himself, in just this way does the sun chase the shadows away.

c. 1524.

F25

. . . and a tired yearning . . . the evil time . . . in darkness and ice . . . light bringing me joy . . . chases away the shadows . . . and the other wing . . . carries . . . heaven comforts.

Probably 1520s.

F26

For one can scarcely love well someone one does not see.

c. 1524–6.

F27

… ser può che d'ogni angoscia e tedio
… sie sol rimedio
… fra noi non è già cosa umana
… r po' el cor, la mente l'alma sana
… mal d'ogni errore
… sdegno e furore
… discaccia e l'una e l'altra morte
… nella mi' sorte.

F28

… va e fera
… al fiore s'appressa amore
… donna altiera
passar per li occhi al core.

F29

Fatto arsicciato e cotto dal sole e da maggior caldi.

F30

Così dentro o di fuor da' raggi suoi,
nel foco son, che m'arde 'l corpo debile,
e so…
Così colmo di grazia e d'amar pieno,
un occulto pensier mi mostra e dice:
A veder lei t'aspetto un'altra volta:
quel che fie rivedella in tristo aspetto.

F31

Signore, io fallo e veggio el mio fallire,
ma fo com'uom che arde e 'l foco ha 'n seno,
ché 'l duol pur cresce, e la ragion vien meno
ed è già quasi vinta dal martire.
Sole' spronare el mio caldo desire
per non turbare el bel viso sereno:
non posso più; di man m'ha' tolto 'l freno,
e l'alma disperando ha preso ardire.

F27

... can who by every agony and weariness ... may be the only remedy ... among us it is certainly not a human thing ... then the healthy soul heals the heart and mind ... evil of every error ... anger and fury ... chases away both forms of death ... in my fate.

c. 1525.

F28

... and cruel ... to the flower love comes close ... proud woman ... to pass through the eyes to the heart.

1524–8.

F29

Parched and baked by the sun and by greater forms of heat.

c. 1532.

F30

So inside and out through her rays I am in the fire, which burns my weak body, and I know ... So brimming with grace and full of love, a hidden thought appears to me and says: 'I wait on you to see her another time: this will make you see her with a sad face.'

c. 1532.

F31

Lord, I transgress and I see my transgression, but I act like a man who burns with a fire inside his breast, for my suffering keeps increasing, and my reason grows weaker and is almost overcome by my torment.

I used to spur my burning desire in order not to darken her clear and beautiful face: I no longer can; you have taken the reins from my hands, and my soul in desperation has started to be bold.

Possibly c. 1534.

F32

Du' occhi asciutti, e' mie, fan tristi el mondo.

F33

. . . .
un'altra sera, ché stasera piove,
e mal può dir chi è 'spettato altrove.

F34

Nulla già valsi
. . . .
il tuo volto nel mio
ben può veder, tuo grazia e tuo mercede,
chi per superchia luce te non vede.

F35

Non ha l'abito intero
prima alcun, c'a l'estremo
dell'arte e della vita.

F36

In tal misero stato, il vostro viso
ne presta, come 'l sol, tenebre e luce.

F37

Se ben talor tuo gran pietà m'assale,
non men che tuo durezza curo o temo,
ché l'uno e l'altro stremo
è ne' colpi d'amor piaga mortale.

F32

Two dry eyes, mine, make the world sad.

Possibly 1545.

F33

... some other evening, for this evening it is raining, and he who is awaited elsewhere can scarcely say.

Possibly 1545.

F34

I had no strength at all ... whoever cannot see you because of an excess of light can clearly see your face in mine, thanks to your grace and kindness.

Before 1547.

F35

No one acquires full mastery until he has reached the limit of his skill and of his life.

Before 1547.

F36

In such a wretched state, your face lends us, like the sun, darkness and light.

Before 1547.

F37

Although indeed from time to time your great mercy strikes me, I am on my guard and fear it no less than your hardness, for each of these extremes is, in love's blows, a fatal wound.

Before 1547.

F38

Né so se d'altro stral già mai s'avviene,
....
ma mie fortuna vinse il suo costume.

F39

Che posso o debbo o vuoi ch'io pruovi ancora,
Amore, anzi ch'io mora?
....
....
Dille che sempre ognora
suo pietà vinta da tuo fera stella,
....

F40

Non vi si pensa quanto sangue costa.

F41

Mal fa chi tanta fé sì tosto oblia.

F38

Nor do I know if it ever happens through another arrow, ...
but his way of acting conquered my fortune.

Before 1547.

F39

What can I or should I or what do you want me still to undergo,
Love, before I die? ... Tell her that every single hour her mercy,
overcome by your cruel star ....

Before 1547.

F40

No one thinks how much blood it costs.

c. 1546.

F41

He does wrong who forgets so quickly such great faithfulness.

c. 1557.

NOTES

These Notes aim principally to do the following: to record the comments Michelangelo made on some of his own poems; to supply background information essential for the understanding of the poetry; to clarify the thought of the poems when this is not immediately evident; and, on a number of disputed points, to indicate briefly alternative interpretations and the attitude of the commentary tradition to them. Although literary influences on Michelangelo are occasionally indicated here, it would have exceeded the scope of this book to have attempted to trace these in any detail. When reference is made to Michelangelo's letters, the numbers in both Poggi's edition and Ramsden's translation (if applicable) are given; when the Notes refer to other works in foreign languages, only translations are cited. When standard translations exist, these have been used (see the Bibliography of Works Cited, pp. 343–5); in other cases, the translations are my own.

Abbreviations

The following abbreviations are used for the authors most commonly referred to in the Notes. Details of the works whose authors are referred to in abbreviated form, and of other works referred to in the Notes (by the name of the authors), are to be found in the Bibliography; page references are not given when the work cited is a commentary.

B	Barelli
C	Ceriello
Ca	*Il carteggio di Michelangelo*
Con	Condivi
Cont	Contini
D	Dobelli
F	Frey
G	Girardi (critical edition of 1960)

Gu   Guasti
M   Michelangelo
Ma   Mastrocola
R   Rizzi
Ra   Ramsden
S   Saslow
V   Vasari

1

The normal rhyme-scheme for M's quatrains, whether within the sonnets or as independent pieces, is ABBA (see p. xxi); this suggests that lines 5–6 here (BA) were intended to be lines 7–8 of a complete sonnet.

5, Cosa mobil non è che sotto el sole: an early, notable example of M's frequent tendency to invert the normal word order, which here would be (ignoring poetic considerations): *Non è cosa mobil sotto el sole che ....* M's linguistic liberty, amounting at times to violence, helps to give the poetry its dense, rugged force.

2

3, e: adversative, as quite frequently in M: see, e.g., 45:21, 50:3, 92:10.

3

When M's early poetry merely laments the evils of love, as here, it often has an artificial air. In his early poetry M's dependence on the poetic tradition, particularly on his favourite authors, Dante and Petrarch, was often heavy. Con states that around 1503 M spent much time 'reading Italian poets and orators' (p. 24), and later testifies to M's particular predilection for the two greatest of the early Italian poets (p. 68).

9–14: the change of addressee, from Love in the quatrains to ladies in the tercets, is more evident in Italian with the shift from a singular to a plural verb.

11, morir: changed by G from *morire* of the original, for the sake of metre.

4

This poem is often described as dedicated to 'the beautiful Bolognese woman', from its manuscript location on a letter written to M in 1507, when he was living in Bologna. There is no evidence, however, that M had a romantic attachment while he was there. The poem is unique in its detailed description of the beloved's dress and ornaments; elsewhere in M's love poetry few physical details of any kind are given, and no clear physical picture of the beloved can be gained. In this poem, as in much of M's art, the clothing serves to reveal rather than conceal the lines of the body.

4, 'as if all … the first to kiss her head': so also R, Piccoli, C and S; or: 'though only the first will actually kiss her head' (so G and Ma). The former interpretation seems grammatically more natural.

5

A self-mocking lament by M on his troubles as he painted the ceiling of the Sistine Chapel (on which he worked from 1508–12). On the verso M wrote: 'To Giovanni, to him who is from Pistoia'; it seems highly likely that the person in question was Giovanni di Benedetto da Pistoia, who later became a servant of the Medici regime and a member of the Florentine academy; he may also have been the recipient of poems 10 and 71, and certainly sent M a number of poems. The tailed sonnet form (so called from the presence of one or more additional tercets) is unusual in M's work; there are only two other instances, 25 and 71. The form was popularized by Francesco Berni (1497/8–1535: see poem 85), and became associated with the burlesque style, of which Berni was a master. Although clearly M cannot in this poem have been influenced by Berni, the poem's humour is patent, the bitterness which lies just beneath the surface never being allowed to dominate; this is all the more admirable in that we know M deeply resented being taken from sculpture, his first (and last) love, by Pope Julius II who commissioned the painting of the Sistine Ceiling (see Con, pp. 32–3, and V, pp. 349–50). The poem's humour is delightfully pointed up by the tiny sketch of himself in the posture described in the poem which M scribbled at the side of the autograph.

1, 'In this difficult position': or, 'at this drudgery' (so S).

2, 'peasants': this is the meaning of *gatti* suggested by Cont, principally on the basis of dialect use; such an interpretation makes better sense than the normal 'cats'.

4, 'for it … chin': the translation assumes (with G and B) that *c'* signifies *ché*; if it is to be understood as *che*, introducing a relative clause, then line 4 may refer to the water spoken of in the previous two lines (so Cont).

11, *e ' passi*: i.e., *e [i] passi*: this is clearly the reading in Girardi's edition of 1967; his earlier edition might be read as *e' passi*.

14, 'Syrian bow': a semicircular bow; see also 20:14.

18, 'dead': in the striking adjective *morta*, so at odds with the reality of the work it describes, M may well be contrasting painting with sculpture, which he often characterized as 'living' (*viva*): see, e.g., poems 152:3, 237:3, 239:3, 236:1–4.

20, 'nor indeed a painter': M complained to his father while working on the Sistine Ceiling that painting was not his profession (*Ca* LXII / Ra 45). He always regarded himself principally as a sculptor, and indeed in his early years often signed himself 'Michelagniolo scultore'. Many letters also amply testify to M's single-minded, not to say obsessive, dedication to his work at this time, and to the physical and financial difficulties he suffered: see, e.g., *Ca* LXII, LXIV, LXX, LXXV / Ra 45–6, 51, 53.

6

A vigorous complaint against a patron by whom M felt himself betrayed. Although it is impossible to determine with certainty the identity of the patron, two details of the poem suggest Pope Julius II (1503–13): see notes to lines 10 and 14 below. We know that M's relationship with that pontiff was stormy (see notes to poem 5), and even late in life he complained of the treatment he had received at Julius's hands: *Ca* MI / Ra 227.

10, 'the powerful sword': these words may simply continue the reference to justice, since justice is often portrayed as a figure carrying scales in one hand and a sword in the other. It is possible, though, that they refer to Julius II: that pope was famous, or infamous, for the energy he spent in pursuing militarily the temporal claims of the papacy to the point of leading the papal troops in battle. Both Con (p. 32) and V (p. 349) report that, when M suggested to Julius that, in casting the bronze statue of the pope on which he was working, he should represent Julius as carrying a book, the pope scorned the idea, declaring that he should be shown carrying a sword.

11, *ecco*: so Girardi's edition of 1967, an improvement on *eco* of his 1960 edition, possibly made at the suggestion of Cont; the MSS read *echo* (to rhyme with *secho* at line 14).

14, 'a withered tree': this may be a pun on Julius II's family name, della Rovere (*rovere* = oak tree).

8

The unrhymed penultimate line and the heptasyllabic final line need not necessarily be signs that the madrigal is incomplete or at least unpolished (as Ma and S suggest).

4, 'that she might be closer': as frequently in M's poetry (see, e.g., among the earliest poems, 2, 7, 9 and 15), the gender of M's beloved is not specified; in the translation the female is preferred, since none of M's earliest poems is certainly directed to a man, while poems 3–4 and 11–12 undoubtedly envisage a woman.

9

3, 'qualities': *cose*, literally, 'things'. *Cose* obviously has a wide range of reference: 'qualities' fits the context here, and accords with the clear meaning of *cose* at 41:7.

4, 'with his divine art': i.e., in M's beloved.

10

On Giovanni da Pistoia, see the introductory note to poem 5. In a recent study Bardeschi Ciulich (pp. 17–18), on the basis of the poem's spelling, dates it to much earlier, 1497, after the excommunication of Savonarola by the libertine Alexander VI; however, the pontificate of Julius II (see poems 5–6), with its direct involvement in military matters, would seem to fit better the subject matter of the poem. In this vigorous lament M is not concerned principally, as he was in poem 6, with his personal situation, but with the general condition of Rome (where the poem was written). He signed the poem 'Your Michelangelo in Turkey', an ironic reference to the similarity between Rome and the non-Christian power which then threatened the very existence of Western Christendom.

1, *elmi di calici e spade*: a notable instance of M's characteristic freedom with word order; here the poet separates the word *elmi* from its partner *spade*, and delays the latter to the end of the line, thus enabling him to accentuate the bellicosity of papal Rome, which was the main target of his criticism.

2, 'by the bucketful': this echoes the plebeian tone of *a giumelle* (literally, 'in double handfuls', i.e., in great quantities).

4, 'and still Christ shows patience': so also D, R, Cont and S; or (with Gu, Piccoli, C, G and B), 'and even Christ is losing patience'. The former interpretation is favoured by the following: *pur* signifying 'even' seems anachronistic, and *cade* has the meaning 'comes from heaven' in one of M's favourite authors, Petrarch, e.g., *Rime* 9:3 (so Cont); the latter interpretation would seem to call for some evidence of Christ's impatience, which the poem does not offer.

9–10: obscure lines, whose general import seems to be that M is facing poverty on account of the lack of, or the withdrawal of, a commission. This description might well have fitted M after he had completed the painting of the Sistine Ceiling, since by that time Julius II had lost interest in his earlier commission to M to construct a massive tomb which would in due course house his remains in St Peter's Basilica. That project, still in abeyance at Julius's death, was, through the pressures of Julius's heirs, to plague M for much of his life, being finally (though not happily) settled in 1547, with the unveiling of a much reduced memorial monument in the Church of S. Pietro ad Vincula in Rome.

10, 'now is the time': some such phrase is needed to complete the sense.

11, *può*: changed by G (following Gu) from *e' può* of the original, for the sake of metre.

11, 'he who wears the mantle': the pope (*il gran manto* = the papal mantle).

11, 'can do what Medusa did in Mauritania': petrify through neglect or hostility. The Gorgon Medusa was reputed to be able to turn people into stone by her stare, and to have done so to the Titan Atlas, thus creating the Atlas range of mountains in North Africa. It is a notable feature of M's poetry that it in fact makes little use of classical mythology.

12, *alto in cielo*: *alto* here may be an adverb, or it may be an adjective qualifying 'heaven', since M often anticipates for effect.

13, 'the great restoration of our state': this may refer either to the spiritual renewal of Rome on earth, or to the reversal of the earthly social hierarchy in heaven, where poverty will be rewarded.

14, 'another standard': a reference either to war (as most commentators would understand), or to money (so Cont). In the latter case, M is adding a further criticism of papal Rome, that of venality.

14, 'other life': the life of the soul, which will find true fulfilment only in eternity.

12

The poem (in a slightly different form) was set to music and published in 1518 by Bartolomeo Tromboncino; this suggests that it was originally composed several years before that date.
8, 'since': *se* often has this meaning in M's poetry: see, e.g., 192:10, 242:1.

13

Found on sheets of drawings for the Medici tombs in the New Sacristy, this and poem 14 are in many older editions of M's poetry, following F, set out in the form of free verse. In both cases, however, the words seem at most prose drafts for poems that M may have intended but never realized.
tiene gli epitaffi a giacere: the meaning of this phrase, and indeed of the draft as a whole, is obscure.
'they are dead': this phrase retains the ambiguity of the Italian, *son morti*: these words may refer either to epitaphs or, more plausibly (if M is speaking elliptically, as he often does), to those to whom the epitaphs refer.

14

See introductory note to poem 13 above. The figures of Day and Night were eventually placed on the sarcophagus under the effigy of Giuliano de' Medici, Duke of Nemours (1478–1516). The statue of Night later occasioned a laudatory quatrain from Giovanni di Carlo Strozzi, to which M penned a tart reply (poem 247 below).
'And his revenge is this: that ... had lived?': the basic sentiment, rather preciously formulated, seems to be that if the world was left a poorer place for Giuliano's passing after a short life, he would have enriched it much more had he lived longer.
tolta: G's *tolto* is a printer's error, corrected in his later edition.

15

This poem is often described as a madrigal or a part of a madrigal (so, e.g., Gu, F, C, B and Ma), and normally set out (as also in G) in two blocks of 4 and 6 lines. However, the metre (hendecasyllabic throughout) and the rhyme-scheme (ABBA + CDE × 2) suggest rather that it was cast in the form of the last 10 lines of a sonnet (so also D and S): see p. xxi. Partial sonnets are quite frequently found in M's poetry both before and after (though seldom during) his great central period of poetic creativity which lasted from 1532–47.

2, 'to heaven whence I derive': the idea that the human being (or more specifically the spiritual element in him, his 'soul') comes into the direct presence of God at death is common to many forms of religion, not least to the Catholic Christianity in which M was raised and in which he remained a devout believer. However, the specific formulation of this passing as a *return* to God, with the premise, stated or implied, that the soul had in some sense enjoyed knowledge and love of God before its earthly life in a human body, is characteristic of Neoplatonic philosophy, which had a wide vogue in educated circles in M's time (see pp. xxii–xxiii). This poem, with its references to the poet's origin in heaven (a periphrasis for God) and to the lure of beauty, may be the first expression in poetry of M's Neoplatonic views.

8, 'a soul ... more worthy': reason as such will always be attracted more towards what is objectively better.

16

Gilbert prints this poem and a third line found on the same sheet (here F21 in the Appendix) as a single poem, in view of the fact that the third line rhymes with the second line of the present poem. The evidence does not seem persuasive.

1, 'fleeting': literally 'pilgrim' (*pellegrino*): the human being's time on earth is a journey towards the goal of eternity, compared with which that time is but a moment.

2, 'a fountain of mercy': i.e., one who should be this but is not.

17

4, 'springtime': this interpretation of *dolce verno* (literally, 'sweet winter') seems to give the best sense, despite Alexander's criticism.

18

Although these lines are normally described either as an incomplete madrigal (so F) or simply as a group of lines or hendecasyllables (so B, S and Ma), it seems more likely that they form the quatrain and tercet of a sonnet: all seven lines are hendecasyllabic, and have the rhyme-scheme: ABAB + CCD. Although the rhyme-scheme in the tercet is certainly irregular, the scheme ABAB in the quatrain is not: see p. xxi.

2, 'ancient': *prestina* (literally, 'pristine'), a unique usage in M; it may refer to the biblical story of Adam and Eve, or to the Neo-platonic idea of the soul's original emanation from God: see note to 15:2.

4, 'The sea, the mountain and the fire with the sword': these are clearly allegorical, but there is no evident single matrix that would explain their meaning; the most likely candidate for such a role would seem to be Dante's *Purgatorio*, in which all four appear at various stages. The words may symbolize torments (C), obstacles (G) or remedies (Ma).

6, 'the one who has deprived me': Love, or the beloved. S would relate this poem and others (22, 27, 32 and 36) to M's close relationship to a young man, Gherardo Perini, in the early 1520s (see *Ca* DL–DLI, DLIX–DLX / *Ra* 151). However, there is no solid evidence for any such poetic links, and it militates against this hypothesis that the poems in question are for the most part flat and conventional in tone. Clements at several points asserts that M's relationship to Perini was homosexual, and suggests that a number of poems may reflect this relationship; but he only once links it to a specific poem, 27 (p. 112).

19

8, 'from a greater cause …': a fine example of M's terseness of expression; here, as not infrequently elsewhere, a philosophical maxim is adopted or coined to illuminate the experience of love.

20

Not the least value of this mock love poem is that it reminds us that M had a strong comic element in his character, and that he was capable of viewing the passions of love with irony. This suggests that many of his love poems which make heavy use of conventional imagery ought not to be taken with anything like total seriousness. M was greatly influenced by the poetry of the latter part of the fifteenth century, particularly by two major poets with whom he had contact in his youth, Poliziano and Lorenzo de' Medici. As S points out, M may in this poem be indebted to 'Una vecchia mi vagheggia' of the former, and 'La Nencia di Barberino' of the latter.

1, 'must': i.e., new wine.

6, 'theriac': a medicinal salve of a yellowish ('treacle') colour, thought to be an antidote to poison.

8, 'so I shall die ...': this was a frequent cry in conventional love poetry, but here contrasts strikingly with the bizarre images which precede and follow. It is lines such as this which make it impossible to believe that in this poem M was not intending to parody the Petrarchan love poetry common to his time, which readily lent itself to extreme expressions of sentiment. For a more extended (though incomplete) companion piece, see poem 54.

9–10: such paintings were in fact often rough and unsightly, a point M will later cleverly exploit in self-mockery: see 85:31–6.

13, 'by smoke from': some such phrase seems necessarily implied.

14, 'a Syrian bow': see poem 5:14, and note there.

20, 'hoe': symbolic of hard work, and an indication, if such were needed, of the peasant background of the speaker.

21–4: these lines, with their classical reference and their allusion to the sculpting ability of the speaker, seem poetically rather a lapse: they fit ill with the rough image of the lover in the rest of the poem, as conveyed not least by the immediately preceding line.

21, *s'avessi ancor la bella coppa*: the meaning is clear enough: 'if I were still young and handsome'. *Coppa* may, however, be understood in two quite different ways: if, as seems likely, it has its common meaning of 'cup', then the reference here is to the cup of beauty of classical mythology, which contained the ambrosian nectar that eternally renewed the youth of the gods. It is possible, though, as Ma suggests, that *coppa* here has the unusual sense of 'nape, neck' (as, e.g., at Dante's *Inferno* 25:22), with the neck symbolizing the speaker's beauty in general. The latter reading would have the advantage of exonerating M from the first of the two charges made in the note to lines 21–4 above.

23, 'so': the reading of Girardi's 1967 edition, *dunche*, seems much preferable to the unintelligible *di che* of his earlier edition.

23, 'blocks of stone': Girardi's hesitation about *massi* in his 1960 edition disappears in his later edition. Although *masso* could refer simply to a massive piece of rock, it was also used specifically of large blocks of stone (including marble) which had been made ready for use in building or (as here) sculpting. M normally refers to marble merely by words for stone, whether *sasso* (63:1, 236:4), or, more frequently, *pietra* (e.g., 152:2, 193:10).

21

In metre and imagery this poem is reminiscent of the songs used in carnival processions to remind revellers of the fleetingness of life. This theme is a constant in M's poetry and often, as here, moved him to poetry of a very high order. It is indicative both of the continuity of this subject and of the quality of poetry here that until G's edition this poem was commonly regarded as among M's final works. The darkly penitential view of life expressed in this and similar poems may have been due in part to the influence on M of Savonarola, the apocalyptic Dominican friar who dominated much of Florentine life between 1494 and 1498. Condivi's biography, which appears to have been based on lengthy conversations with M (see also the introductory note to poem 277), testifies to the profound and abiding influence of the friar on M: 'Michelangelo has similarly with great diligence and attention read the holy scriptures . . . as well as the writings of those who have busied themselves with their study, such as Savonarola for whom he has always had a strong affection, and the memory of whose living voice he still carries in his mind' (p. 68).

8, 'we were men': it first becomes clear here that the words of the poem are being spoken by the dead from the tombs. This gives in retrospect a particular edge to line 6 ('*our* ancient lineages . . .'), since the noble and wealthy, who could afford tombs, are those who in life might well have paid least attention to the kind of sentiment expressed in this poem.

22

On a suggested connection of this poem with Gherardo Perini, see the note to poem 18:6. This is M's first attempt at a long poem, of more than 25 lines; the stanzas are not of uniform length. A lament against Love, it has many of the faults that characterize most of M's longer poetry, which tends to be digressive in thought and flat in tone.

1–4: these lines, which are outside the stanza series, serve as an introduction, announcing the theme and specifying the addressee.

10, *per pruova*: this phrase is normally understood to refer to the fact that it is through his past experience that the speaker is able to resist Love's blandishments (so R, G and Ma). S, however, would see it as referring to future torments, to give the reading: 'for there's no room in me for love's ordeals'.

24-6, *cagion di tanti mali, ... // ... né fortuna*: grammatically these words may refer either to death, the subject of the main clause, or to Love, the implicit topic of the immediately preceding words. R and S prefer the latter, but the former (adopted here, with C and G) makes for an easier transition to the next verse.

28, 'with it': or 'with itself' (*seco*).

31, 'the journey ... in imagination': or 'the journey it sees before it in its mind's eye' (so C and G).

48, *or*: changed by G (following Gu) from *ora* of the original, for the sake of metre.

50, 'cruel revenge': presumably God's eternal punishment of sin after death.

54, *Che 'l dì ...*: a problematic line; the clause *che mi bisogna* seems to have the sense that the poet's last day ought to be one that will bring him eternal happiness, which it will not do if he is dominated by Love.

23

3, *mie colpa*: the phrase echoes the Latin *mea culpa*, which would have been familiar to the first readers of M's poetry from its threefold repetition in the *Confiteor*, the prayer of repentance said at the beginning of the Eucharist (the principal religious service in Catholic Christianity).

3, 'white-haired': a symbolic phrase: M in fact retained his black hair into old age (Con, p. 73, and V, p. 431).

4, 'shall I now ... take up again': it unjustifiably weakens the force of *riprenderò* to understand it in a passive sense, as M's being taken by Love (as do G and S).

12-14: exceptionally elliptic lines, even by M's standards, although the general sense is clear: there is nothing to be gained by a saw, a worm or Love, in the situations envisaged.

25

On the tailed sonnet see the introductory note to poem 5, although the present poem is undoubtedly serious.

1-8: the thought of the quatrains turns on the untranslatable *uso*, whose repetition (at lines 3, 5 and 8) the translation tries to signal in 'accustomed ... custom ... accustomed'.

15–20: the additional tercets expressly repudiate the view that M had voiced in poems 23 and 24 (found on the same sheet as poem 25). The contrary view put forward in those two poems and elsewhere in M, that love ill becomes old age, may be regarded as a commonplace.

17, 'something divine': the identification of *cosa divina* with *cose di natura* (line 19) is striking, and important for understanding M's frequently positive attitude to human love as bearing a crucial religious role.

26

G accepts F's reconstruction of this poem.

5, 'taken by one ...': it is not clear whether this refers to Love or to a specific person.

27

Clements (p. 112) and S would see this poem as connected with M's relationship with Gherardo Perini, but see the note to poem 18:6.

8, 'game': love is often so described in M's poetry, with bitterness.

28

12–17, 'whoever will come later ... beautiful eyes': this highly strained conceit suggests that, like several love poems of this period, this madrigal was written rather as a verbal and conceptual exercise than as an expression of real love.

29

A variant on the well known Virgilian dictum, *Omnia vincit Amor* (*Eclogues*, 10:69).

1, *forza*: a force from outside, constraining a person against his will: see also 22:41, 267:54.

2, *fortuna*: although this word can (like its English counterpart) be used neutrally to indicate all the vagaries of life whether good or bad, quite frequently in M it has, even without a qualifying adjective, a negative import: see, e.g., 1:6, 151:10, 180:4.

31

The left edge of the sheet on which this poem is found has been cut, and G's reconstruction of the beginning of each line can be only tentative.

32

On the dedication, see the note to poem 18:6; F also suggests that this poem might be directed to Perini. S's claim that this is 'the first time [that] M introduces his acute sense of sin as a concomitant of love' seems ill founded: there is no specific mention of love in this poem, and poem 22 has already repeatedly presented love as a threat to goodness and salvation.

5–6, 'my mortal part ... a god for me': S, possibly following D, presents a different dynamic here: 'my godly part [has been] made mortal for me.' The interpretation given in the translation, which accords with that of most commentators, harmonizes more readily with the common biblical notion that sin is tantamount to the worshipping of what is finite and transitory. It must be said in favour of S's interpretation that it makes the movement of the first and second parts of the sentence identical in direction, from high to low: from freedom to servitude, from what is divine to what is mortal.

33

9–10: when making paired statements, M not infrequently anticipates an element from the second member of the pair; although this technique often enables him to highlight a key idea, it also frequently makes the sense difficult to penetrate. The normal order in the present instance (ignoring poetic considerations) would be: '*e sie l'alma rinnovata in vita e tolta dal costume e d'ogni cosa umana*'.

14, '*n ogni loco*: G understands this to mean 'all around me', but the thrust of the entire poem is to emphasize M's own evil ways.

16, 'your rock': a most unusual image to associate with love; indeed Quaglio (p. 118) would suggest a different reading: *colle pietose tuo* .... The image of God as a rock, however, is common in the Old Testament, and its use here emphasizes the identification of Love with God in this poem: cp. the addressees at lines 13 and 20. This identification occurs occasionally elsewhere in M's poetry; more frequently, though, when Love is accorded a religious role, it is viewed (implicitly) as an intermediary between the divine and the human, below God but above man (and, presumably, the angels): see, e.g., 34:5–8 and 37. As so conceived, Love does not fit into the traditional Christian hierarchy of being.

17–18, *c'ogni altra cosa /... in brieve tolta*: obscure lines; with Ma, the translation takes them to refer to the fact that M's major difficulty with regard to living virtuously is himself, compared to which every other obstacle is as nothing. G and B (and similarly S) would interpret them thus: 'for every other impediment, if suddenly removed, is as if it had never been'.

34

A strikingly positive view of human love as the means of entrée to the divine, a view shared by several poems of this period (e.g., 33 and 38–9); this view will later animate many of M's finest love poems, particularly those dedicated to Tommaso Cavalieri.

1, 'heart': M oscillates considerably in his attitude to the heart in human love: sometimes, as here, it is contrasted with the soul, and portrayed as the locus of what is purely mortal and transitory and at least potentially evil; elsewhere it is viewed positively, as cooperating with the soul in enabling man to reach God, principally perhaps because it is viewed as the locus of man's image of beauty, through which the soul rises to contact with infinite beauty or God; see e.g., 38:9–11 and 40.

7–8, 'that part ... dies': to one of M's beliefs, the soul is by its very nature immortal. Marsilio Ficino (1433–99), the most influential Neoplatonist of the Renaissance, devoted one of his major treatises to defending belief in the immortality of the soul, which was in any case an intrinsic part of Christian doctrine.

8, 'my great desire': in M's poetry (as in religious thought generally) man's supreme desire is said to be for God or, what amounts to the same, the supreme perfection of beauty, goodness, etc.

10, 'the eternal beauty': God, or the perfect idea of beauty in God's mind.

11, 'whoever': or, more broadly, 'whatever'; *chi* sometimes means 'what' rather than 'who' in M: see, e.g., 45:12, 149:6, 262:9.

13, 'where I first loved you': i.e., in heaven, a clear example of M's adopting the Neoplatonic belief that human souls exist before their earthly life in a body: see note to 15:2.

35

A unique instance in M's poetry of a minute description of an individual 'object'. No doubt as an artist M had a particular interest in the eye; as a love poet he was also fascinated by it, as the means through which the soul of the beloved manifests itself and through which love enters the lover (via the image of the beloved). Several of the details of the description in this poem are obscure.

9, *aopre*: G's rendering (following Gu) of the mysterious *arupre* of the original.

36

See the introductory note to poem 18. M seems to echo Petrarch particularly closely here: see *Rime*, 112.

3, 'his': the translation assumes that the beloved spoken of in this poem is male, on the basis of *colui* at line 8; this masculine pronoun may, however, refer simply to *amor* (line 1, masculine in Italian), understood throughout the poem as a synonym for the beloved.

37

The rhyme-scheme is that of the tercets in the vast majority of M's sonnets: CDE × 2 (see p. xxi). The addressee of this poem is not specified: it cannot be God, who is referred to in the third person at line 6; it seems to be personified Love, conceived as a quasi-creative intermediary between the divine and the human, as at 34:5 (see also the note to 33:16).

5–6: D, C and G seem to understand these lines as referring to the soul's life after death, in eternity. This would unduly restrict their meaning: M repeatedly in his poetry, including that written in this period, expresses his belief that the soul, through love, can even in this life rise to what can perhaps best be termed mystical knowledge of God: see, e.g., from the poetry of this period, 39: 7–11, 40:1, and cf. 34:9–14, 38:1–2. The phrase *contemplare Dio* recurs at 288:2, where it clearly refers to knowing God in this life. *Contemplare* was, in any case, frequently used of such knowledge in the religious tradition with which M was familiar.

38

The quatrains have an unusual rhyme-scheme, ABAB × 2: see introductory note to poem 1.

9–11: an important, if dense and elliptic, expression of M's positive view of love. The phrase *concetto di bellezza* seems to indicate not only that Love, as a concept of beauty, belongs properly to the soul, but that it *results from* the image of beauty in the heart: it is that image's conception or offspring. See the note to 34:1.

39

See the note to 33:16.

1–2: i.e., the only normal remedy would be death.

7–8, 'for mortal beings ... to heaven': a strong expression of Neoplatonism: see pp. xxii–xxiii.

40

6, 'my soul ... against me': or, with G, 'my soul which laments at being alone with me'.

41

One of the clearest expressions of M's delight in human beauty in its fullness, physical and spiritual. M is particularly deeply indebted here to Petrarch: see, e.g., *Rime*, 53:1–3.

1, 'Well-born spirit': a literal translation of *ben nato* has the merit of drawing attention to what is emphasized in the opening quatrain: M's beloved has been physically blessed, through a happy conjunction of the twin causes of man as physical, i.e., of *natura*, the physical forces of this earth (acting, according to the physiognomy of the time, through the male seed only), and of *'l ciel*, the heavens. The following quatrain and the first tercet will describe his beloved's spiritual qualities.

9, 'love takes me, and beauty binds me': often quoted as a summary of the basic dynamics of M's life; *prende*, as befits a spiritual subject, has a lighter tone than *lega*.

10–11: 'compassion and kindness ...': after the mention of 'love' at line 9, these lines describe the effect of the other two members of the triad spoken of at line 7.

12, 'What pattern or law ...': it is not clear to what *uso* and *governo* refer; M seems to be offering two possible sources for the undeniable fact of the universality of death: either blind fate (*uso*) or a divine law (*governo*).

42

2, 'the beauty that I long for': i.e., perfect, unlimited beauty, to be identified with God. M usually reserves the term *aspirare* for his yearning for God or heaven, as at 93:10, 163:6, 258:9; cp., by contrast, 245:14.

10, 'a better place': the mind or soul.

12–13: essential to the logic of these lines is the idea that the soul is by its very nature immortal, to which quality the other three (being divine, virtuous and beautiful) are inextricably linked: see note to 34:7–8.

14, 'goes before': see also Gu, D and R; this seems to make better sense of *precorre* than 'first leaps to' or 'first meets', as in B, S and Ma (G's paraphrase, *giugne*, is unclear): although the internal, spiritual beauty known through the soul is qualitatively superior, and is in that sense prior to external, physical beauty, in temporal terms it is the latter that first excites the process of knowledge of beauty. Evidence for the alternative view may, though, be found at 44:1–2, where the poet speaks of 'the beauty that [he] first saw', i.e., the beauty of God that he knew before his life on earth (a Neoplatonic belief: see note to 15:2).

43

The rhyme-scheme of the quatrains, ABAB, is found only here in a complete sonnet, although it is occasionally used in partial sonnets: see p. xxi.

6, 'the phoenix': a legendary bird, reputed to die on its own funeral pyre and be reborn every 500 years.

8, 'another's hand is not enough ...': see 33:1–6.

12, 'two deaths': as frequently in M, those of the body and the soul.

12, 'my lord': almost certainly refers to Love.

44

1, 'the beauty that I first saw': before birth: see note to 42:14.

3, 'the image': of the beloved.

6, 'the thread': of life.

45

Written after the death either of an intimate friend or of M's brother Buonarroto (d. 1528), the only one of M's siblings to whom he appears to have been close.

4, 'our eternal lights': the sun and moon.

14-15, 'on that bank which one reaches ...': although interpretations differ in detail, M is undoubtedly here referring to heaven, which the soul can reach only through the death of the body; the body will then be restored to it at the last day (according to traditional Christian belief).

17, 'like someone who sees others going more speedily ...': see also Gu, C, B and Ma; this requires reconstructing the grammar thus: *'qual che vede altri più veloce andando ...'*; the inversion this implies in the normal word order (particularly the violent anticipation of *più*) is no stranger than that found elsewhere in M. These lines are obscure, but the interpretation given here seems to make better sense than 'like one who, going faster than all others ...' (so S, with D and G), since it is not clear why someone who goes faster than others should arrive later than they do.

46

For the occasion of the poem, see the introductory note to 45. M appended an explanatory prose passage: 'Lionardo. He [or she] was alone on earth in exalting the virtues with his great virtue; he did not have anyone who would work the bellows. Now in heaven he will have many companions, because entry there is given only to those to whom the virtues are pleasing; and so I hope that from up there he will complete my [hammer?] here below. At least he will have now in heaven someone to work the bellows; for he did not have any companion at the forge where the virtues are exalted.' 'Lionardo' may be the young son of Buonarroto, with whom M later had much to do. This is the first poem in which M makes sustained use of imagery from the visual arts, although he may have been directly influenced by Dante's *Paradiso* 2:127-32.

3, *tiello*: changed by G (following Gu) from *tienlo* of the original, for the sake of rhyme.

6, 'and all the more itself': in strict Christian terms an unorthodox sentiment, since God (here imaged as 'that divine hammer') was traditionally held to be totally immutable, unchanged even by his creative and providential activity.

10, 'is raised at the forge': the context of the use of the hammer here changes rather awkwardly from stonework to metalwork.

11, 'this one': it is not clear whether *questo* refers to a hammer (so Gu, C and G), as seems more likely, or to a blow (S).

12–14: the ambiguity inherent in line 11 obscures the meaning of the lines that follow.

47

See the introductory note to 45. The general tone of this poem and the specific reference to writings at lines 12–13 strongly suggest that the occasion of this poem was the death of a literary friend rather than that of M's brother.

2, 6, 7, *tolse*: the repetition of this word with the same meaning in each case is the most noticeable instance of M's occasional failure to vary the rhyme word. It should be noted that such failures tend to occur in incomplete poems, though see, e.g., 277:3 and 7, 292:3 and 6.

10–11: although the general sense of these lines seems clear, the grammar is not; the commonly understood meaning (adopted in the translation) requires understanding *l'alma* as *dell'alma*: M occasionally carried ellipsis to the point of omitting a grammatically required preposition: see note to 254:1.

14, 'he possesses heaven ...': or 'heaven possesses him ...' (so Gu and G): however, understanding 'he' as the subject draws a sharper contrast with death's expectations.

48

It has been suggested that this fine tercet reflects M's experience during the siege of Florence (1529–30), in whose defence against the pro-Medici forces he was deeply engaged. There is no hard evidence for this political interpretation, and the poem would seem rather to express M's characteristic view of life as a continual struggle.

49

1: this vigorous opening line will later be closely echoed in a description of Tommaso Cavalieri's beauty: 78:9.

3–4: on the relationship between Love and the image in the heart, see 38:9–11 and the note there; on the superiority of knowledge of the beauty interior to man, see 42 *passim*.

50

5, *Più e men*: it may be noted that Girardi's 1967 edition omits these words, presumably by an oversight.

51

It may be no accident that this poem, concerned with repentance in the face of death, is to be found on a sheet of drawings for the Medici tombs.

4, 'too long ... his end': so also G and Ma; S's 'delays too long at the end' seems unnecessarily prosaic.

17, 'mortal emotion': i.e., an emotion concerned only with what belongs to this mortal, transitory world.

22, 'I should not tire of my ways': *stanco* is left without a referent, but the implied object seems clearly to be the sinful ways of which M has been speaking (so also R, G, B and S).

24, 'I fear I do': so also Ma; or 'I do and fear ...' (so G). 'I fear to know' (as B and S) seems less likely, since it requires giving a curious meaning to *ch'il veggio*.

32, *nel mal ... vero*: a highly elliptic line, although its general sense seems clear: the evil use of free will is the source of its own loss; see 32:5.

52

Various, very different masters have been suggested for the faithful service spoken of here: republican Florence during the siege of 1529–30; the Medici after the fall of the republic; some beloved. There is no documentary evidence to favour any one of these.

5, 'phoenix': see the note to 43:6.

53

See introductory note to poem 52.

54

A mock love-poem, more ambitious and less rough in its jocularity than poem 20. In M's corpus it is exceeded in length only by poem 67. Like most of M's long poems, it is less than totally successful, even discounting the lacunae.

42, 'her': the switch from the second to the third person is disconcerting, and presumably indicates that M made no serious effort to revise the poem; it returns to direct address of the beloved at stanza 9 (line 66).

69–70, 'was I ... common crowd?': a clear mocking of the *dolce stil novo* tradition, but one which fits ill with the skittish and untutored character of the supposed lover.

56

This may be the first poem, or beginning of a projected poem, inspired by the young Roman nobleman, Tommaso Cavalieri (*c.* 1509/10–87). He was a man of outstanding physical beauty and great sensibility, who for M epitomized the Neoplatonic ideal of beauty of body and soul, and could therefore through love best lead to knowledge of divine beauty (see, e.g., Ficino, I.4 and II.9). The artist, who was probably introduced to Cavalieri in order to give him drawing lessons, was immediately captivated by him, as indicated by the early poems dedicated to Cavalieri, by the few extant early letters of M to him (see especially DCCCXCIX / Ra 191), and by references to Cavalieri in M's letters to others of the same period (notably in CMXXIII / Ra 194). The first years of their friendship were a period of high passion on M's part, and measured but deep affection on Cavalieri's (see, e.g., DCCCXCVIII). The two remained close friends until M's death. M paid Cavalieri the highly unusual compliment of doing several finished, 'presentation', drawings for him (see the note to 79:13), and a number of the figures in M's *Last Judgement* seem to owe their origin to sketches by Cavalieri. The latter's principal public enterprise was to help realize M's plans for the Campidoglio. M may have dedicated about forty poems to Cavalieri: see p. xxiv.

58

10, *incende*: changed by G (following Gu) from *infiamma* of the original, for the sake of rhyme.

11, 'see themselves in others': i.e., measure others by themselves.

59

M may have been influenced here by the discussion of the beneficial effects of mutual love in Ficino's *El libro dell'Amore*, I.4; in particular, the concluding line of the sonnet, with its surprising reference to the possibility of love's being broken by disdain (*sdegno*), may be explained by Ficino's reference there to love's inducing the lovers to strive for good 'so that they may not be held in contempt [*disprezzo*] by the beloved'. Although the Italian version of this work of Ficino was not published until 1544, it circulated widely in manuscript after Ficino, in 1474, made a translation of the Latin treatise *De amore* which (in a slightly shorter form) he had written five years earlier; the Latin version was first published in 1484.

7, Amor: it seems clear that it is personified love who is being spoken of here, even though Girardi's 1967 edition reverts to the *amor* of Gu and F.

12, e mille: changed by G (following Gu) from *e mill'altri* of the original, for the sake of metre.

13, a tal nodo ... a tanta fede: Girardi's 1967 edition has '*e tal nodo ... e tanta fede*', presumably through a printing error.

60

10, 'what you ... yourself': the soul or spiritual element.
10, 'do not be disdainful': an echo of 59:14.

61

10, angel: changed by G (following Gu) from *angelo* of the original, for the sake of metre.
10, 'alone': or 'unique' (C and S), or 'in his solitude' (G).
14, 'virtue': *virtute* can mean either power or moral virtue; perhaps both meanings are present here.

62

M appended two jocular remarks of similar tenor on drafts of this poem, one of which reads: 'At carnival time it seems permitted, for someone who is not going out masked, to do something mad.'
12, 'if fire ... to the heavens': in contemporary physics the upward movement of fire was explained by the fire's seeking to return (like all beings) to its natural location, which in this case was thought to be a sphere above the air surrounding the earth. The comparison of the soul's instinctual return to God to the natural movement upwards of fire was a common one: see, e.g., Dante, *Paradiso* I.109–20; Ficino, III.2 and IV.4.

63

1–3, 'So friendly ...': the following process is envisioned: stone gives rise to fire by a spark's being struck from it; the fire's intense heat reduces the stone (specifically marble) to dust, which is then made into lime and used in the construction of buildings. This imagery is rather a favourite in M's poetry.

5, 'It': i.e., the stone.

8, 'from hell': according to Catholic doctrine, souls who die repentant but still marked by the effects of their former sins must have the latter purged before they may enter heaven and see God. In M's time the realm in which this purification was achieved was often regarded as a section of hell.

64

2, 'the child ...': see note to 63:1–3.

66

M reworked this poem extensively, as he did many others: G's critical apparatus gives eighteen poems which underwent four or more major revisions: 66, 72, 76, 81, 106, 146, 157, 159, 174, 236, 246, 256, 259, 262, 272, 285, 289 and 296. Such revision did not by any means always result in poems of high quality; by contrast, many of M's finest poems appear to have been written quickly, with only minor reworking: see, e.g., poems 59, 83, 87, 133, 153 and 161.

5, 'I know ... to fight': a particularly striking example of M's freedom with word order: *qual* is anticipated from its natural place before *altra*. S goes against the common understanding of this line by linking *qual* with *militar*, and interpreting the latter as a soldier: 'Nor know I what soldier under another banner ...'.

9–11: these lines make it clear that the poem is addressed to Christ.

10, 'may you atone for my sin': literally, 'may my sin make itself just through you'. According to Christian doctrine, serious sin rendered its agent unjust in the eyes of God, a state which could only be rectified by the application to the sinner of the perfect merits of Christ: see the note to 280:7–8.

67

The longest of M's poems. Its two parts hang uneasily together: lines 1–48 are an idyllic account of peasant life; the remainder (the poem ends abruptly in the middle of stanza 15) is an allegorical description of various vices and virtues. The meaning of many details is obscure.

109, *vuol*: changed by G (following Gu) from *vuole* of the original, for the sake of metre.

68

Although this poem shares the same style and general theme as the latter part of poem 67, it is best regarded not as a single poem with 67 (so Gu) but as a separate poem (so F) of a broadly similar inspiration. Again, the meaning of many lines is open to dispute.

15, *'l ciel*: not, as in G, *l' ciel*.

34–5, 'she bears only ... her lord': 'only' (*sol*) may refer either to 'bosom' or to 'sign'; if the latter, then it is not clear what the sign may be; the former reading, as Ma suggests, makes the readily understandable point that breasts heavy with milk (for suckling her lord) are distinctive of this old woman.

41, 'their seven offspring': possibly a symbol of the so-called seven deadly or capital sins (the suggestion dates back to Michelangelo the Younger), i.e., those sins which were traditionally regarded as the most basic forms of evil, bringing death to the soul: pride, covetousness, lust, envy, gluttony, anger and sloth.

69

1, *né conviene*: changed by G (following Gu) from *né si conviene* of the original, for the sake of metre.

70

There is no solid evidence for S's suggestion that this poem may describe M's relationship to Tommaso Cavalieri. The thought of the poem is frequently obscure, but the general import seems to be that M is bewailing his subjection to the violent impulses of human passion (the recurrent image 'winds' is a traditional one for sensual passions). The poet oscillates between rejecting and accepting responsibility for his present situation. The obscurity of thought is no doubt due in part to the immense difficulties of the

sestina genre, which confines the poet throughout to the same six
end-words for the lines.

11, 'up there ... from the tree': clearly a reference to Adam and
Eve's sin of eating the forbidden fruit in the Garden of Eden; 'up
there' may indicate that M had in mind the Dantean image of the
Garden as located at the top of Mount Purgatory.

15, 'some unknown person': *non so qual* is variously interpreted
as personal (so B and Ma) and impersonal (G and S). The final
tercet suggests the former.

71

10, 'charity shown by others': or 'to show charity to others' (so
G).

12, *ben*: presumably on the basis of Cont's note, this word is
introduced by Girardi into his 1967 edition to correct metrical
defect.

12, 'the Poet': Dante, who vehemently criticizes Pistoia at *Inferno*
25:10-12.

72

The probable dating of this poem is deduced from the fact that
several drafts of it are found on the same sheet as the fragment of
a letter of January 1533 from M to Stefano di Tommaso. The
poem evolved markedly from its original version: see the intro-
ductory note to poem 66.

14, 'in my unworthy ... arms': the only direct expression of
physical yearning for Cavalieri (or any male) in the final version
of any of M's poetry, apart from the curious conceits of poem 94;
there may be indirect references at 88:3-4 and, though with less
likelihood, at 98:14 (see the note there).

75

The rhyme-scheme, ABA ABBA, suggests that M may have
intended to work up these lines to a full sonnet, partly by the
addition of a line to what is presently an opening tercet; on M's
usual rhyme-scheme in his sonnets, see p. xxxi.

76

One of the most heavily reworked of M's poems: see the intro-
ductory note to poem 66.

78

4, 'cut off from the truth': may refer either to the senses or more generally to the person concerned.

9, 'Your beauty is no mortal thing': an application to Cavalieri of what is said about Love in general at 49:1.

14, 'the fault were yours': there is a switch here from the singular to the plural (*abbiate*), which has never been satisfactorily explained.

79

9, 'he who speaks for me': the unidentified bearer of this poetic letter from M in Florence to Cavalieri in Rome. After their initial period of acquaintanceship in Rome in 1532–3, M spent the following year in Florence before he moved permanently to Rome in September 1534.

13, 'pictures of the basest kind': we know that M gave Cavalieri a number of drawings (see, e.g., V, p. 420, and *Ca* DCCCXCVIII–DCCCXCIX, CMXXXII / Ra 191), almost certainly with the object of helping Cavalieri to master the art of drawing. It seems much more likely that, in using the strong adjective *turpissime* here, M was being heavily self-deprecatory (as he was inclined to be about his art, as well as his poetry) than that he was referring disparagingly to the pagan subjects and/or sexual connotations of the drawings of the *Fall of Phaethon*, *Ganymede*, and *Tityus*; see S for a different interpretation.

14, 'people': this is the obvious sense of *persone*, and it is so understood by S and Ma. Although the logical difficulties that this causes have led most interpreters to regard *persone* as symbolic of writings, such an interpretation appears to have no linguistic justification. It seems better, on the whole, to observe the linguistic constraints as faithfully as possible, and to understand the plural as a reference in the polite plural form to Cavalieri himself, who offers his personal friendship in return for the works M has given.

80

8, 'the intellect on God': God as infinite eludes adequate comprehension by the human mind.

81

One of the most fully reworked of M's poems: G notes twelve

major stages of revision. It was originally directed to a woman, and subsequently (possibly in 1533) to a man, probably to Cavalieri. As often with M, the amount of effort expended bears little relationship to the final quality of the poetry: see the introductory note to poem 66.

82

5, 'separated from you': G's highly unusual understanding of *da te mosso*, 'attracted by you', seems most unlikely.

13, 'dear': like the English 'dear', *cara* bears the connotations both of being loved and of being costly.

83

3, 'my soul': a possessive adjective has to be supplied here for *l'anima*: G understands 'your [Cavalieri's] soul' (as does Ma, tentatively). However, since lines 9–14 clearly signify that human beauty in general, and Cavalieri's in particular, are the means whereby those such as M who gaze on this beauty may be drawn to God, 'my soul' seems more likely (so also B and S).

9–13, 'nothing more resembles ... nor have we any other sign ...': the strength of these statements is notable.

13, 'you': if, as seems likely, *v[i]* here means 'you', then we have one of the occasional instances in M of a disconcerting switch from the singular to the plural (see, e.g., 78:14, discussed above); that it is still Cavalieri who is being addressed is suggested by both the general logic of the poem and the echoing in line 13 of the *fede* pledged at line 8. It may well be, though, that it is 'there', the other common meaning of *vi*, which is to be understood; in this case, M would be referring not to Cavalieri (of whom he speaks at lines 1–8) but to human beauty in general (with which lines 9–13a are concerned).

84

10, 'in itself unmixed ... kind': it is not the rain (which is itself undifferentiated) but the seeds themselves that cause diversity in plant life.

85

This *capitolo* was composed in response to one of similar length

by Francesco Berni, a burlesque poet (see the introductory note
to poem 5). Berni's poem was sent to a common friend in Rome,
the painter-cleric Sebastiano del Piombo (1485–1547), but was
clearly intended for M. M responded in kind, with a poem pur-
porting to be from del Piombo, although M is the fictitious bearer
(lines 43–4); one MS of the poem is headed: 'Reply of Buonarroti
in the name of Fra Bastiano'. The text of Berni's poem is given in
full by G; on a much-quoted line from it, see p. xxi.

4–6, 'the greatest Doctor . . .': Pope Clement VII, Giulo de' Medici;
the periphrasis puns on *medico* (doctor).

7–9, 'He who . . .': Cardinal Ippolito de' Medici, a cousin of the
pope, termed 'the lesser Doctor' at line 11. In his poem Berni had
declared his faithful service to this cardinal.

10–12, 'him who holds . . .': Cardinal Ippolito's secretary, the
humanist writer Francesco Maria Molza.

13–15, '. . . would deny Christ . . .': a biting indictment of the
religious indifference of many in ecclesiastical positions.

19–21, 'The Meat . . .': Monsignor Pietro Carnesecchi, whose
name lent itself to a double pun, on *carne* (meat) and *secco* (dry);
the lines now have a bitter ring which was no part of the original
intent: Carnesecchi was much later (in 1567) beheaded on charges
of heresy, and his body burned.

28–30, 'These will be harmed . . .': M is parodying the notion that
poetry, like all art, is immortal: Berni's comic poetry, often rough
and plebeian in tone, has no right to such a claim, just as it is
totally unsuited to such epithets as 'divine' (line 27) and 'beautiful'
(line 32). Varchi in the first of his *Lezzioni* describes Berni as 'that
most ingenious poet of nonsense and amusement' (p. 52).

32–6, 'Votive offerings . . .': in his poem Berni had played on the
common reference to M as divine.

54, 'lose my cowl': in 1531 del Piombo had become a member of
a religious order, on taking up the post he had been offered at the
papal court, Keeper of the Seal (*piombo*, lead).

86

It is uncertain whether M's father died in 1531 or 1534. M's
reference to ninety years at lines 40–42 does not settle the matter
(we know that his father was born in 1444), since M may have
rounded out the figure for rhetorical purposes. Although as a
lament the poem is seldom moving and conveys little about M's
father, it reveals much about the poet himself.

13–15, 'My memory ...': a highly interesting indication of M's belief in the superiority of sculpture.

16–17, 'my brother ... unripe': see the introductory note to poem 45. Not even by modern standards can Buonarroto (1477–1528) in fact be considered as having died at a particularly young age, although M, in view of his father's age and his own seniority to his dead brother by two years, may be forgiven the hyperbole.

21, 'that place ... safest from the senses': the mind.

27, 'how powerfully ...': clear evidence that M regarded himself as exceptionally sensitive.

31–2, ... *profondo, / non fussi* ...: the meaning of these lines is clearer if the punctuation of older editions is retained (Gu, F, R, C), with a comma at the end of line 31.

39, 'the more ... over us': an obscure line; the translation turns on the belief that when M writes *'l falso persuaso* he is using an impersonal noun for a person or agent, as he occasionally does: see also 139:8, 162:15 (*bis*).

40, 'Ninety times': see introductory note to this poem.

40, 'bathe ... its bright torch': the curious imagery here may result from a play on *face* (torch) and *faccia* (face).

48, 'something I cannot write ...': a revealing indication of M's sense of the fragility of life and of the mutability of the will.

66, 'the earthly slime': in general M often oscillated between a positive and negative view of the human body, but he never spoke kindly of his own.

87

13, 'spouse': an image often used in Christian writings for the Church in general and for the individual soul in particular.

88

13, 'unless you prevent it': or 'unless you give it [my joy in life] back to me' (so G).

89

14, 'except what': *tanto* here has the force of *soltanto*: see also 246:2.

90

13–14, 'I restore light ... cure every poison': M's comparison of himself to Christ is striking. Although the comparison is unmistakable, M in fact handles the Gospel material with some freedom: Christ is occasionally portrayed as having used spittle to cure blindness (*Mark* 8:23 and *John* 9:6–7) and dumbness (*Mark* 7:33), but never to cure poisoning.

91

In a letter to del Riccio of 1542, M added this comment to his poem: 'Old things, fit for the fire, not to be seen by anyone' (CMXCIX / Ra 224).

92

5–6, 'his work ... who saddens': the reference is to Love.

94

The 'lowly worm' so admired and envied in this poem is the silkworm.

14, 'two winters': literally, 'two snows': *nevi* is G's understanding of the puzzling *neie* of the original (following a suggestion by F).

95

11, *Ecco*: this reading, for *echo* of the original, is to be preferred to G's *eco*: see note to 6:11. The reference here is to Echo as a mythological character, a nymph who was condemned by the goddess Juno to repeat only what others said (as a punishment for her chattering which prevented the goddess from discovering Zeus during his infidelities: see Ovid, *Metamorphoses*, 3:359ff.).

96

7, 'daring': *baldi* has the sense of both 'bold' and 'happy'.

97

3–4: with G, the translation understands lines 3 and 4 as linked, although there is much to be said for regarding them as independently carrying forward the series begun in line 1, as do Gu and F, who put a comma at the end of line 3; Cont (followed by Ma) urges a return to the older reading, although his reasoning does not seem compelling.

5–6: Cont again counsels strongly a return to the older reading of these lines as independent, with a comma at the end of line 5: see note to lines 3–4. Here, however, the case seems weaker, since line 6 appears to explain the *zoppa* with which line 5 ends (a point apparently taken by Ma, who here follows G's punctuation).

9–11: the *se* of line 12 seems also to govern the preceding tercet. The logic appears to be that the art of creating beauty surpasses nature because it comes from heaven; its heavenly origin enables it to outdo nature, even though the latter does perform well, and creates its own limited beauty. The application of line 11 to the artist and not to nature, an interpretation found in older commentaries, is excluded by the unmistakable use of the same phrase with regard to nature at 106:9–10.

9, 'the art of beauty': literally, 'the beautiful art': the context clearly suggests that the art of creating beauty is being referred to.

11, 'even though ... everywhere': or 'however well nature may strive everywhere' (so Cont). See also above, note to lines 9–11.

98

Certainty regarding the addressee is assured by the comment of Benedetto Varchi, in the first of his *Lezzioni*, that the poem was 'dedicated to M. Tommaso Cavalieri, a young Roman of the highest nobility' (p. 47). M later expressed his thanks to Varchi several times, without any demurral on the point (see, e.g., Ca MLXXVI / Ra 279).

7, *l'ore*: changed by G (following Gu) from *l'hor* of the original, for the sake of metre.

11, 'enter there': i.e., enter M's heart.

14, 'armed cavalier': clearly a pun on Cavalieri's name. Some (e.g., Clements [p. 145] and Hibbard [p. 231]) would also see this as a sexual pun, a view at best marginally strengthened by *nudo* in line 13, since this word can be used very generically in Italian, and is so understood in the translation; for a similar use, see 175:8.

99

M had a relationship with a young man, Febo di Poggio, in the year or years preceding his permanent move to Rome in 1534. Poems 99–100, with their references to Phoebus (*Febo*) and hill (*poggio*), seem certainly to speak of him; whether they lament simply the ending of the relationship or the death of Febo is not clear. What is evident from the little that remains of their correspondence is that their parting was not a happy one; it may even have occasioned an attempt at blackmail on the part of the younger man: see *Ca* CMXLI–CMXLII / Ra 198.

2, 'Phoebus': Apollo, the ideal of young, manly beauty, and a synonym for the sun.

2, 'Phoebus ... whole hill': see introductory note above.

100

See the notes to poem 99.

5, 'Happy bird': the reference is unclear; it may be either to the eagle, credited with the ability to gaze at the sun (see 80:3), or to the phoenix (see, e.g., 43:6 and note).

8, 'that height from which I fall ...': literally, 'that hill ...'; again the meaning is obscure; there may be an indirect reference to the fall of Phaethon, who hurled to his ruin from the sky after foolishly losing control of the solar chariot of his father, Phoebus (the subject of one of M's presentation drawings to Cavalieri: see the note to 79:13).

101

The first of a group of four poems in G's numbering dedicated to the subject of night, only the last of which can with any confidence be assigned a dedication to Cavalieri. Girardi has recently (1991 [pp. 111–12]) assigned a date to these poems close to that of the quatrain in reply to Strozzi (poem 247, *q.v.*), i.e., *c.* 1545. This sequence evinces a characteristic found frequently in M's poetry: reflections on the same subject (most frequently on love) come to radically different conclusions regarding its worth; this feature of M's poetry is heavily emphasized by Ma in his Introduction.

1, 'Phoebus': the sun.

1–4: it seems that the point being made is that, despite what common speech would seem to imply, night denotes not a positive entity but an absence: the lack of sunlight.

4, 'only': Cont's suggestion that *sol* stands for *solo* (only) and not *sole* (sun) allows a clear meaning to emerge from this line, which otherwise remains opaque.

9, 'Yet ... really is something': i.e., if one assumes the opposite of the view put forward at lines 1–4: see note above.

11, 'the latter ... creates it': according to the embryology of the time, only the male seed had an active part in conception.

13, 'so fragile': literally, 'in such great jealousy'; in the translation this phrase is understood to mean 'so aware of how easily it may be broken'; see also Cont.

102

1, *O notte, o dolce tempo* ...: a sonorous beginning whose quietly reflective tone is successfully carried through to the end.

2, 'all work ... peace': similarly Gu and Cont, although the meaning of this line remains unclear; it is difficult to see how G could justify his understanding of *assalta* as 'you invest'.

6, *ché ... appalta*: this is Gu's reading, to which G returns in his 1967 edition, possibly following the suggestion of Cont; the MSS reading, adopted by Girardi without change in his 1960 edition, is: *che l'umid' ombra e ogni quiet' appalta*.

7–8, 'and in dreams ...': it was commonly believed that during sleep the soul was partially released from the restrictions imposed by the body, and was thus able to some degree in dreams to come in contact with the purely spiritual realm of heaven.

103

13–14, 'Nights are more sacred ...': there may be a touch of humour in this otherwise rather bizarre conclusion.

104

The final tercet (particularly the use of the respectful plural form of address at line 14, *a voi*) suggests that the poem may have been addressed to Cavalieri.

105

4, 'him who ...': God.

4, 'assails': there seems no good reason to soften this dramatic word to something more readily intelligible like 'invests' (so G and S).

4, 'similar to himself': this phrase may qualify 'soul' (so also S, B and Ma) or 'love' (so Gu, R and G). Line 5, and M's assertion elsewhere of the soul's similarity to God (see, e.g., 42:12), make the former more likely, but the latter cannot be discounted,

especially in the light of poem 243:12–14 (on which see the note).
5, 'equal to himself': presumably this refers only to the soul's
being equal to God in being immortal.
8, 'beauty's universal form': in Neoplatonic philosophy, beauty is
conceived as existing without limitation (perfectly, 'universally')
in God; Ficino refers to God's 'countenance' as 'universal beauty'
(V. 4 and 5).

106

One of M's most heavily revised poems: see the introductory note
to poem 66. We have M's own testimony that this poem was
composed for Cavalieri. Writing to thank Benedetto Varchi (via a
friend) on behalf of Cavalieri on the occasion of the publication
of his highly commendatory lecture on M's poetry, in the course
of which Varchi had paid fulsome tribute to the physical and
moral qualities of Cavalieri (whom he had met in Rome [p. 47]),
M sent this poem with the following comment: '[Cavalieri] has
given me a sonnet I wrote for him … begging me to send it to
[Varchi]' (*Ca* MCXLIII / Ra 343).
9, 'This is what happens': i.e., they pass away.
13, 'veil': a common Petrarchan and Neoplatonic image for the
human body; the soul, by contrast, is immortal.

108

5, 'the phoenix': see note to 43:6.

109

This poem was sent to del Riccio in the summer of 1544 with a
note that apparently refers to those who had helped M during a
major illness earlier that summer. Despite the dating of that note,
G follows F in believing that the poem belonged originally to the
period in which the first Cavalieri poems were written. There does
not seem any good reason, however, for suggesting a dedication
to Cavalieri himself (as do B and S).
10, 'evil': the context suggests that *trista* does not here simply
have its primary meaning 'sad'; M quite frequently uses *tristo* in
its secondary sense of 'evil': see, e.g., 33:5, 85:15, and especially
the change at 285:4 from *falsa e ria* of earlier drafts to the Dantean
trista e pia of the final version (see *Inferno* 5:117).

12, 'most benefits him ... favour with them': similarly Gu. The line is obscure: G hazards 'most praises those (material) things that least merit them', while B suggests 'most praises those people who least merit it'; S's interpretation seems unsatisfactory: 'rewards most the one who wants to have [its praises] least'. The translation adopted here seems to allow line 13 to follow most naturally.

110

There seems no reason to doubt the veracity of the account appended to this poem by Michelangelo the Younger: 'Bernardo [Buontalenti] said that Michelangelo halfway up his stairwell had drawn in black and white the figure of death as a skeleton bearing a rough coffin on its shoulder, on which [these lines] were written' (see G, p. 294).

111

The first poem in Girardi's sequence to have been inspired by Vittoria Colonna (1490–1547). A member of one of Rome's most illustrious noble families, she married the Marchese di Pescara in 1509. The affection and fidelity of the young woman appear not to have been reciprocated by her soldier husband, who died in the service of the emperor in 1525, leaving his wife childless. Colonna was a woman of great culture and deep religious devotion, and a considerable poetess: her first poetry expresses her grief at her husband's death, while her later work is concerned entirely with religious subjects. She was closely associated with the movement for reform within the Roman Catholic Church, and was suspected of Protestant leanings, although it appears that no formal process against her was ever instigated. M was introduced to her around 1536; she became for him a trusted friend who attracted him by her moral rectitude and cultured religious devotion. M certainly dedicated a number of poems to her, perhaps as many as forty: see p. xxiv.

1, *S'egli è*: G supplies these words (on the basis of a parallel with 117 and 242) to make good a lacuna in the MSS.

9, 'the eye that does not see': i.e., the physical eye, which does not see divine things.

112

The first poem in Girardi's sequence to be assigned a dedication to 'the beautiful and cruel lady'. Almost forty of M's poems have traditionally been assigned a dedication to a woman described, from the content of the poems, as *la donna bella e crudele*; for the sake of information, those dedications are recorded in this translation (see p. xxiv). However, there is no documentary evidence of M's having been passionately in love with any woman in the way described in these poems, a relationship which, in any case, M's homosexual orientation would have made extremely unlikely. It has recently been proposed, notably by Liebert (pp. 326–8) and Cambon (pp. 66–111, *passim*), that some at least of these poems refer to darker aspects of M's relationship with Vittoria Colonna; on present evidence, this suggestion must remain highly speculative and seems unlikely to gain widespread support. The very modest quality of most of the poems in this group would confirm that it is best understood simply as a series of poetic exercises, not directed to any beloved, but capturing, often in clever images and pithy expressions, what are in essence fairly conventional views of unhappy and unrequited love. It is surely no accident that M wished to include all of the poems in this group in his intended publication (with the possible exception of poem 175: see note), and indeed appears to have composed many precisely for it.

11, 'where beauty exists alone': in the mind of God, in a pure and unlimited way.

12, 'the true image': the image of his beloved, who lives in the physical world, here envisioned as the true or real world.

115

The thought of this poem seems hybrid: while the phrase *cogli atti suo divin* (line 3) seems to suggest a connection with Colonna, the opening *mélange* would indicate a different context.

117

1–3, 'something beautiful ... to God': so also Gu, C and B; the reading 'a desire for something beautiful may carry the soul [or 'us'] from the world to God' (so G and S) requires supplying an object for the verb and a preposition before *alcuna cosa bella*. While neither of these is impossible, granted M's elliptic style, the former reading is linguistically more simple and seems sem-antically more logical.

13, 'who resembles ... came forth': so also S; it is certainly strange to talk of 'the eyes of God', but this seems the obvious meaning, and one not to be rejected in a poet who often coins unusual images, not least for God (see, e.g., poem 46). To avoid the difficulty, Gu, G, B and Ma adopt a quite radical strategy: 'who in her eyes reflects the eyes through which my soul manifests itself'. See also next note.

14, 'the first love': i.e., the love of the first good, God. This thought flows naturally from the interpretation of line 13 given in this translation.

118

7, 'my last, and first ...': i.e., last on earth and first in heaven.

10, 'from dying ... cruel death': only M's physical death will prevent the death of his soul.

120

8, 'even if': *e se* here has the force of the Latin *etsi*.

121

11, 'star': here a synonym for heaven. The line is scarcely to be taken literally, as an endorsement of the Platonic belief in the return of each soul to a star after the death of the body: see note to 126:1.

14, 'in peace or torment': in heaven or hell, in accordance with the soul's moral state at death: see the note to 140:3.

122

5, 'like a salamander': a mythical animal, lizard-like in form, supposed to live in, or be able to endure, fire.

11, 'a higher power than we ...': presumably Love immediately, and God ultimately.

15, 'not the will ... who kills me': his death is not willed by his beloved, although she is in fact killing him.

123

5, 'He who ...': i.e., Love.

126

1, 'If it is true ...': an expression of whimsy, rather than a serious hypothesis, although M may have been aware that belief in the transmigration of souls had been put forward by Plato: see, e.g., the myth of Er at the end of *The Republic*.

127

With 128, this poem takes a positive view of the fear of death, which has been treated negatively in 125.

128

1–3: if human beings were to cease fearing death, they would lose the greatest antidote to love.
17, 'he alone': i.e., death.

129

5, 'Which of these two reasons': that the proximity of the less beautiful enhances her beauty, or that her greater beauty brings pleasure to others.

130

A companion piece to poem 131 found on the same sheet, which can be dated to 1542. Below poem 130 M wrote: 'Messer Luigi – You, who have the spirit of poetry – please would you shorten and revise one of these madrigals, whichever seems to you the [less] lamentable, as I have to give it to a friend of ours' (*Ca* CMXCVIII / Ra 223). The last phrase may indicate that these two pieces were to be sent to Cavalieri, although their content scarcely suggests that they were inspired by him (this despite the fact that, as S points out, the gender of the addressee is not specified in the poems).
10, 'any threat of harm': to his soul after death.

131

See the introductory note to poem 130.

132

A companion piece to poem 133, which is the finer poem. Under poem 132 is the brief note: 'With my best wishes to messer Donato [Giannotti], reviser [or 'mender'] of badly done things.'

136

In preparing the poem for publication, M sent it to del Riccio with two variant lines for 12–13, and gave the directive: 'Take the less lamentable in the judgement of messer Donato [Giannotti].'

137

A companion to poem 138.
1, 'If you find joy': it seems more natural (with Gu and S) to regard the joy spoken of here as belonging to Love, who causes troubles, rather than to those afflicted by those troubles (so D, G and Ma).

139

1, 'covering': the harsh word *spoglia* for the lady's body contrasts sharply with the ascription to her of beauty and physical delicacy.
8, 'a sinner': as occasionally elsewhere, M uses an impersonal word (here, *peccato*) for a person: see also 86:39, 162:15.

140

3, 'whether heaven damns or saves': in accordance with the soul's moral state at death (M is here assuming the context of the Christian church, since grace is also necessary for heaven). According to traditional Christian belief, the definitive, universal judgement of mankind takes place at the end of time, when souls will be reunited to their bodies. This judgement has been commonly called the Last Judgement, to distinguish it from the judgement of each individual soul which is envisioned as occurring immediately after death. M's fresco on the east wall of the Sistine Chapel has remained one of the most powerful images of the former in Western culture.

142

The negative view of love expressed in the final lines makes it almost impossible to subscribe to S's view that this poem is 'probably for Vittoria Colonna, whom M credited with reviving his capacity for love in old age'. It seems to be much more readily grouped with those many poems of the decade 1536–46 in which M regrets the resurgence of love.

143

To del Riccio M wrote: 'Thank you for the melons and wine; I'm repaying you with a scribble.'

3, 'enclose me': M recurrently views the short time left to an old person before death as an enclosed space, in which the fire of love may burn intensely and thus (according to the different perspectives adopted by the poet) either consume or purify the person. See also poems 63:1–3 (and the note there) and 170: 5–14.

7, 'you are not satisfied': although not named, the addressee is clearly personified love.

144

8, 'though dead, I may live …': as frequently elsewhere, the contrast is between death in this world and life in the next.

145

When he sent this poem to del Riccio, M commented: 'This is for the soft cheeses; the next one will be for the olives, if it's worth that much.'

7, 'The better would turn out the worse': echoes 143:13.

146

See the introductory note to poem 66.

3, 'if you do not give …': G strangely makes *non* qualify *del tuo* to give the reading: 'if you give what is not yours'.

12, 'make her another time …': G and S appear to understand this as a request that Love change the lady during her (and M's) life. However, despite the overt seriousness of the poem, its underlying tone is light, and M seems better understood as playfully assuming a belief in reincarnation, as he does several times elsewhere: see, e.g., poems 52:1–2, 126:1, 284:4–6.

147

This may be the poem referred to in *Ca* CMLXIII / Ra 215: see G's long note. Although this poem (with slightly different wording) was originally put to music by Arcadelt as two separate madrigals (lines 1–8 and 9–19 respectively), and was so reproduced by Gu, the content of the poem strongly indicates that M intended it form a unity, and it was in fact given a single number by del Riccio for M's intended publication. Lines 1–8 would on their own be unique in both length and rhyme-scheme among M's madrigals; and lines 9–19 are readily understood as a response to the two questions which form lines 1–8. The fact that Arcadelt's version, with his musical setting, was published in 1539 strongly suggests that the poem was composed and in circulation several years before then. M showed himself anxious to express his thanks to Arcadelt: see *Ca* CMLXIV–CMLXV / *Ra* 216–17. A political interpretation of lines 9–19, once favoured (see Gu), is now rightly discounted.

9, *fra voi*: words supplied by G to make good a lacuna in the original.

9, 'powerful gods': undoubtedly a puzzling address. M may here be portraying Love as addressing his fellow gods, or as making an exhortation to human beings. The latter seems more likely: the words may be regarded as a tacit reminder of the dignity of man, who ought to view his life from the perspective of moral endeavour and eternal life, a reminder that is particularly apt when the lover has just confessed to the indignity of an unreciprocated, indeed apparently to the lady unwelcome, obsession. The addressee of lines 12ff. is, in any case, clearly the suffering lover.

11–12, 'through a thousand . . . you are dead': so also Gu (followed by D and C), whose punctuation (identical in F) is given here; G (followed by B, S and Ma) inserts a comma after *morti*, and would link *di mille 'ngiurie e torti* directly to the revenge spoken of at line 14, to give the reading 'you will be able to take revenge for the thousand wrongs and injuries . . .'. Either interpretation seems possible, although the proximity of the phrase quoted to mention of the poet's death at line 11 would seem to favour the former.

148

In G's sequence, this is the first of three poems in which the poet protests to his lady (very probably Vittoria Colonna) that he is unable to bear the degree of kindness she shows him. The brusque metaphor of M's postscript to del Riccio following poem 148 encapsulates the thought of the three poems: 'There is no point in giving a palace to someone who wants only half a loaf.' Although there is no documentary evidence for the order adopted by G, the clarity and strength of poem 150 suggest that the two madrigals were sketches that issued in that fine sonnet.

7–9, 'no wise man ... spur him on': so also Ma, although the meaning of these lines is highly disputed, and one's interpretation depends on how one reads *se non sé innalza e sprona*: S (following G) interprets them thus, 'No wise man ever wished (if he could rise no higher) for any joy that he's not able to bear', while B (following Gu and C) understands similarly, 'if he would not rise excessively'. The translation of the central phrase adopted here seems to give the three lines a tighter structure and a more readily comprehensible meaning.

14, 'in a measure he does not look for': similarly Gu; or, more simply and literally (as G, B, S and Ma): 'which he does not look for'. Against the latter is the fact that the poet is not protesting *total* surprise at his lady's kind attention, but asking for a lesser degree of kindness from her; M's customarily elliptic style would seem to justify the more nuanced interpretation.

149

The thought of this poem is obscure, since M makes a puzzling distinction between what 'his soul' is capable of and what 'he' can do (which is in fact much less) in the central lines, 5–10. His main point seems to be that his strictly spiritual element (the soul), when in the presence of his extraordinarily kind and noble beloved, rises to such heights that his normal powers of comprehension are left bewildered: see also poem 154:11–13 and the note there.

6, 'what': although M most often uses *chi* in its normal sense of 'who', he occasionally employs it impersonally: see note to 34:11. Since the word is used here within a comparison that would seem to be unduly restricted by a personal referent (despite S), the impersonal seems better (so also C, G and B).

10–11, 'she must learn ... appear ungrateful before her': understood literally, lines 10b–11 do not make sense: 'and here it is necessary that I [or she] learn that what I can leads me ungrateful before her'. Gu, G, B and S solve the problem by understanding the subject of *impari* as 'I', and by giving *ingrato* the at least highly unusual meaning 'unworthy'. It seems to do less violence to the text to understand *impari* as 'she learns'; to accord *ingrato* its normal meaning of 'ungrateful'; and (with D and Ma) to extend the meaning of *a lei mi mena* ('leads me to her') to signify 'leads me before her with the appearance of [one who is ungrateful]'.

150

8, 'this would ... but life itself': so also D and B; Gu, G and S, however, take the phrase *più che 'l pianger* to be part not of the object of *toglia*, but of its subject, along with *mercé* of line 5, to give the reading: 'it [your grace] seems to take [away] my life more than my tears do.' One's interpretation depends on how heavily one thinks M is pressing the analogy; that adopted here assumes a lighter touch: strictly, *pianger* is not the equivalent of good news, and to highlight it, as does the interpretation of G and S, weakens the main thrust of the poem, which is to emphasize the potentially fatal effect of the lady's kindness.

151

Justly, one of M's most famous poems, which, like the following two, looks to the visual arts for imagery to illuminate M's situation when confronted with the moral and spiritual nobility of Vittoria Colonna. The dedication to her is deduced from the tone and subject of the poems; the absence of any reference to her in Varchi's extensive discussion of this poem in the first of his *Lezzioni* would seem to stem from a lack of detailed acquaintance with M's circumstances.

7, 'that I may not live hereafter': i.e., eternally in heaven, with God.

8, 'my art': the analogy is carried more easily in Italian, since *arte* has a wider range of meanings including skill, ability gained through practice.

10: the comma at the end of this line (already in Gu and F) is added in Girardi's 1967 edition, perhaps at the suggestion of Cont.

152

9–10, 'can so remove from my outer being': only through the influence of Colonna will M's outer being, physical and sensual, dominate him less, and thus allow the good works within his soul to emerge.

153

11, 'such narrow spaces': the eyes. It is a tribute to M's poetic versatility that he exploits a similar thought to comic effect at 54:73–80.

154

9–10, 'to ascend ... mortal body': i.e., to have direct knowledge of God even during life on earth: see also, e.g., 39:11, 248:1–4.

11–13, 'Yet I do recognize ... escape its death': on an earlier distinction in M's poetry between 'I' and 'my soul', see poem 149 and the introductory note to that poem. Lines 11–13 here seem to suggest that spiritual communion with God gained through Vittoria Colonna, even though it assures M's soul of salvation, can be so radically distinct from ordinary thought as to leave no impress on it.

155

4, 'what it means to live between': so also G and B. Although grammatically the more natural sense of *qual mezzo sia* would be 'what the mean may be' (between sweetness and bitterness), and is so understood by Gu, C, S and Ma, this interpretation would seem to be excluded by the final lines.

156

Beneath this poem M wrote: 'To be revised by day'.

157

On the revision of this poem, see the introductory note to poem 66. When sending it to del Riccio, M commented: 'This is for the trout; the sonnet I told you about will be for the pepper, which isn't worth as much; but I can't write.' Despite the alienness to the modern mind of the psychology adopted in this poem, the main point M is making seems readily understandable. A short account of how psychological processes were understood in terms of spirits can be found in Ficino, VI.9, where the author remarks: 'wherever the continuous attention of the soul is carried, there also fly the spirits'. M may, however, have been looking back to the thirteenth-century *dolce stil novo*, a poetic school which made much use of this mode of envisioning the emotions.

158

5, 'The fruit': i.e., of love.

5, 'the rind': M's body, as he approaches death in old age.

159

See the introductory note to poem 66. Beneath the poem is the copy of a letter M wrote to Vittoria Colonna, expressing similar sentiments (*Ca* CMLXXXIII / Ra 201).

160

6, 'infinite mercy': these words need to be understood precisely: the lady could not continue to be infinitely merciful to her lover if she received significant recompense from him in the form of faithful service.

10–11, 'seem to be': so also Gu, C and G; some such phrase appears to be required by the logic of the text, as it does in an earlier passage where the lover's ingratitude is also spoken of: see 149:10–11, and the note there.

161

This poem can be securely dated to 1538–41: it is found on the same sheet as the beginning of a draft of a letter which, in its final form, was sent sometime in 1538–41 with poem 162 (see below); and the present madrigal is similar in content to that poem. This dating is confirmed by the handwriting of the autograph version.

14, 'my soul while still with me': a clear instance of M's distinguishing between his soul and himself: see introductory note to poem 149.

162

Found on the same sheet as a letter to Vittoria Colonna, *c.* 1538–41 (*Ca* CMLXVII / Ra 202), concerning a crucifixion scene that M had drawn for her.

1, 'Sometimes ... my left': the right food was symbolic of virtue, the left of vice.

6, 'which ... disappears': however, Gu, R, G and S would refer the phrase to the person just spoken of, to read: 'who gets lost on every path and misses his goal'.

15, 'the humble sinner ... he who is perfectly good': impersonal nouns for persons: see the note to 139:8.

163

7, 'full of all salvation': the translation understands *salute* in its religious sense, but the word has many meanings: safety, health, greeting. The religious overtones are suggested by the preceding lines, and by a certain similarity in the phrase to the opening descriptive phrase for the Blessed Virgin in the commonest prayer to her, the Hail Mary: 'full of grace', *gratia plena* (which echoes *Luke* 1:28). Such borrowing of religious terms would not have been regarded as blasphemous in the poetic love tradition with which M was familiar.

11, '**Lights never seen before**': this translates literally a line whose meaning remains uncertain. Taken purely at their face value, the words suggest that M has seen Colonna only once. To avoid this difficulty, G paraphrases: 'O lights which have no equal!'; this seems the most likely interpretation, since it stays close to the literal meaning and makes good sense. To emphasize that M had very probably seen Colonna many times before he penned these words, many interpreters from Gu onwards have given to the words a sense which they would scarcely bear in any other context: 'Lights never seen enough!' Lines 11–13 in any case would seem to indicate that the context for this poem is the years 1541–4, when the marchesa lived in Viterbo to be near Cardinal Pole and his circle, and M consequently saw her at least comparatively rarely.

13, '**for to see ... forgetting them**': literally 'for rarely seeing is next to forgetting'; again, a difficult line. It is given clarity and force, however, if one understands (with most commentators) that *veder* implicitly has the same object in line 13 as it has explicitly in line 12, i.e., *le*, the eyes of the beloved. If this is the case, then the line suggests that, if M sees the eyes of his lady only rarely, he may well forget the spiritual benefit he derived from them.

164

3, '**both the arts**': sculpture and painting.

165

10, '**which are confined ...**': i.e., Colonna's eyes are directed exclusively to heaven (so also D and S); this interpretation of *circonscritti* seems much more plausible than that favoured by G and B, 'which are closed ...', a reading which would at best fit awkwardly with the accusation of familiarity levelled at M in this poem.

12, 'other ... time': as they stand, the words *né più vi vidi c'una volta sola* cause a difficulty similar to that discussed at 163:11. They are understood literally by Gu and S, but seem to call for an interpretation suggested by C, and taken up by G and B: M has never seen Colonna other than as she looked the first time he saw her, i.e., as one who evoked his wonder and respect.

166

9, *mortal*: changed by G (following Gu) from *mortale* of the original, for the sake of metre.
11, *sol*: changed by G (following Gu) from *solo* of the original, for the sake of metre.

167

M's laconic postscript to del Riccio reads: 'For last night's duck.'
1, 'from that very place in me': the heart, as indicated at line 6.

169

M commented to del Riccio: 'This really is a scribble.'

170

6, *s'il*: the autograph reads *sil*, and Cont would understand *sì [che] 'l*, 'so that' (and not 'just as').

171

Under this poem M wrote to del Riccio: 'Please would you send me back the last madrigal which you don't understand, so that I may revise it, because that importunate beggar for drafts – that is Urbino – was in such a hurry he didn't let me look it over' (*Ca* MLVII / Ra 250). On Urbino, see the introductory note to poem 300.
8, 'that customary place': the memory.

172

Under this poem M wrote: 'I am not putting this down as a scribble, but as a dream.' It has plausibly been suggested that the imaginary protagonist of this poem is a model distractingly preening herself as she sits for the artist.

12, 'by contrast': the contrast with M's ugliness is implied rather than stated.

173

Referring to the colour of the paper on which this poem was written, M's punning postscript reads: 'One speaks of divine things on a sky-blue background (*in campo azzurro*).'

174

See the introductory note to poem 66.

175

G believes that the documentary evidence is sufficiently strong to make it likely that this poem was intended for publication, although it is not normally so regarded: see G, p. 360.

11, 'what': so also S; *chi* can certainly bear this meaning in M's poetry: see note to 34:11. Gu, C and G, however, understand 'who'. The impersonal interpretation is strongly favoured by the fact that M goes on to make it clear that only flight will save him.

177

This and the following poem were written for the poet Gandolfo Porrino on the death of Fausta Mancini Attavanti (who appears to have been his beloved); these poems were intended as both a tribute and a polite refusal on the part of the artist to accede to Porrino's request that he do a portrait of the young woman. See also the introductory note to the following poem.

4, 'left-handed': *mancina*, a graceless pun on the dead woman's name; see lines 3-4 of the following poem.

178

See note to poem 177. The rhymes in this sonnet echo those of the first of two sonnets sent by Porrino to M requesting a portrait.

3-4, 'the common people ...': see the note to 177:4.

12-13, 'formed afresh by God': i.e., in heaven.

13, 'to fulfil your noble desire': a verb needs to be supplied here: with S and Ma, the translation assumes that what is being referred to is simply Porrino's desire for a portrait; Gu would refer the fulfilment to the future life. D, C and G would understand a more active role for the heavenly figure, that of raising Porrino's desire beyond anything mortal, and read: 'to elevate your noble desire'.

179

This is the first of a series of fifty poems, consisting of 48 quatrains, a madrigal (poem 192) and a sonnet (193), sent to Luigi del Riccio in the course of the year following the death of his beloved young relative (a first cousin once removed) Cecchino [Francesco] Bracci in January 1544. The death of the youth, aged fifteen, occasioned a large number of poetic testimonies (del Riccio recorded twelve), a fact that may reflect not only regret at the passing of a young person of singular beauty and good character, but also the political frustrations, epitomized in that death, of the community of Florentine exiles to which his family belonged. M's poems are in part a way of making up to del Riccio for his refusal fully to comply with his request that he sculpt Cecchino's tomb: this was indeed designed by M, but executed by M's untalented if loyal assistant Urbino: see *Ca* MXXVI / Ra 239 (cited below, poem 206) and *Ca* MXLVI / Ra 259.

184

1, 'the Arms family': there is a pun here, as in several other poems, on Cecchino's family name, Bracci (*braccio* [plural, *bracci*] = arm).
4, *far*: changed by G (following Gu) from *fare* of the original, for the sake of metre.

185

1, 'I': the speaker in this poem is Cecchino's body, distinguished from his soul at line 3.
4, 'scarcely notices ... change of state': the premise here is the Neoplatonic belief that the soul pre-exists the body; the speaker asserts that his soul's union with his body had lasted for such a short time that his soul had scarcely noticed that the union had occurred.

186

M paraphrased this poem in the following note to del Riccio: 'Our dead friend speaks, saying, "If Heaven took every beauty from all other men on earth to make me alone beautiful, as it did, and if by divine decree on the Day of Judgment I had to return as I was when alive, it follows from this that the beauty, which Heaven gave me, cannot be restored to those from whom it was taken, but that I must be eternally more beautiful than others, and they ugly." But this is the reverse of the conceit you suggested to me yesterday – one is fanciful and the other true' (Ca MXIX / Ra 235).

4, 'if he must ...': the reference is to the Christian belief that the soul will be reunited with its body at the end of time, when the Last Judgement takes place.

188

4, 'more beautiful than ever': see note to 186:4. Enhanced bodily beauty will derive from the increased beauty of the soul (in those who die at peace with God), which will have been made perfect through full union with God in knowledge and love.

190

M commented to del Riccio: 'If you do not want any more of these, do not send me anything else' (i.e., any other gift of food or drink).

191

3, 'by the fear that I cause': apparently a reference to dreams.

192

When sending this poem to del Riccio, M added the postscript: 'I should be ashamed, being so much in your company, not some-times to speak in Latin, albeit incorrectly. Donato's sonnet seems to me as fine as anything written in our time. But, having poor taste, I am no more able to judge of cloth newly-spun, although of the Romagna, than of worn brocades, which make even a tailor's dummy appear fine. Write to him, tell him this, give him this, and commend me to him' (Ca MXVIII / Ra 234). Donato Giannotti was a leading Florentine exile, and occasional poet, who helped del Riccio prepare M's poetry for the publication that never eventuated. The opening words of M's postscript pre-sumably refer to a comment made by Giannotti on line 7 (on which see the note below) in an earlier draft of M's poem; there is further evidence in Giannotti's *Dialogi* (p. 65) that M's knowledge of Latin was rudimentary. Most of the postscript concerns a poem on Cecchino's death sent by Giannotti to del Riccio, with the request that he show it to M for his judgement; despite the apparently deferential tone of his response, M shows some spirit in defending his own poem and criticizing Giannotti's.

7, 'quite blamelessly': the (ungrammatical) Latin phrase *sine peccata* – literally 'without sin(s)' – hangs in the air: the translation (with S, B and Ma) understands it to refer to the subject of the sentence within which it occurs; Gu and C, quite improbably, regard it as a description of heaven, where one cannot sin.

193

M sent a corrective to the original version of this poem: 'Messer Luigi, the last four lines of the above octet of the sonnet that I sent you yesterday are contradictory, so I am asking that you return it to me, or that you insert these in their place, to make it less clumsy, or that you revise it for me.' There follow the four lines of the present edition, except that line 6 begins with *del* instead of *col*.

8, 'not indeed from you': so also Gu, D, C and G; others (e.g., S and B) would interpret *già* as softening rather than strengthening the preceding *non*, to give the reading: 'not so much from you'; in favour of the former interpretation is the fact that M frequently uses *già* to heighten rather than qualify the word to which it refers (see, e.g., 187:4, 240:6, 298:2); and in the next poem (again not an isolated instance) Cecchino is explicitly said to be alive in del Riccio. M's point in the present contrast seems to be that it is only in someone as close to Cecchino as del Riccio that the young man remains present.

12, 'one lover ... the other': this would not have been, in terms of the philosophy of M's time, the banality it may well now appear; such a process of transformation was accorded a physiological base: see, e.g., Ficino, VII.8.

13, 'a model': strictly, *essa* refers to *forma*, mentioned at line 9; the justification for 'model' is that *forma* signifies the soul as animating a body, and what M is stating here is that it is only a soul which is embodied (in short, a bodily form) that can guide and inspire an artist to create a likeness.

194

M's postscript reads: 'I did not want to send this to you, because it is a really clumsy thing, but the trout and truffles [you sent] would leave heaven no choice. My best wishes.'

195

M added the clarification: 'A person who sees the dead Cecchino speaks to him, and Cecchino replies.'
1, 'two hours': of agony, presumably a periphrasis for a short illness.

196

M added the interesting comment: 'This fulfils the promise of fifteen scribbles; I am not obliged [to write] any more of them for you, if another does not come from paradise, where he is.' This seems to indicate that M had promised del Riccio fifteen commemorative poems or epitaphs, and that he would write no more unless he received heavenly inspiration. M's later comments on the poems he did write would indicate that he was moved to extend the sequence out of a desire to console an old friend and thank him for his small gifts of food and drink, while the poems themselves might well suggest that the poet valued the opportunity to reflect on death, a subject that frequently engaged his interest.

197

M's comment to del Riccio has given rise to much speculation: 'Take the two lines given below, which are a moral lesson [*cosa morale*]; I'm sending you this to make up the series of fifteen scribbles.' The two lines are:

> fan fede a quel ch'i' fu' grazia nel letto
> che abbracc[i]ava e 'n che l'anima vive.
> (bear witness to him for whom I was a grace in bed
> what it was he embraced and what it is that the soul lives in.)

These two additional lines were clearly meant as alternatives to lines 3-4 of the quatrain. Quite apart from the problem of how it might accord with what M said in his comment on 196 regarding making up the promised fifteen 'scribbles', this postscript raises the question of whether M was suggesting that del Riccio's relationship with Cecchino was homosexual. Such would be the immediate import that the comment has for the modern mind, and perhaps also for a contemporary of M. It has to be borne in mind, though, that the sharing of beds without any sexual implication was much more common in Renaissance times than in our own. Clements, perhaps unjustly, would see the highly wrought language in which M had earlier written to del Riccio regarding Cecchino (*Ca* CMLXIII / Ra 215) as indicating, on M's own part, an affection for the young man that went 'beyond the bounds of discretion' (Clements, 1963: p. 97).

198

M added: 'For the salted mushrooms, since you do not want anything else.'

199

M's lapidary comment reads: 'This clumsy [thing], said a thousand times, for the fennel.'

200

Smith (1963: pp. 362–3) offers this poem as one of several which make the Cecchino sequence worthy of serious attention.

201

M commented: 'It is the trout who say this, not I; however, if the lines do not please you, do not marinate [the trout] any more without pepper.'
4, 'I was born ...': i.e., born into true, eternal life, where death plays no part.

202

The poem appears to be a pure conceit, since there is no record of a portrait of Cecchino, other than that sculpted on his tomb.
4, 'where I could not': i.e., Florence, from which Cecchino's family was in exile.

204

3, 'more than when he had an abundance of me': the translation understands the ungrammatical and puzzling phrase *più c'averne copia* along the same lines as Gu, C, S and Ma; G and B would interpret more strongly: 'more than when he had me entirely with him'.

206

When he sent the poem to del Riccio, M added the comment: 'I'm making you a return for the melons with a draft, but not the design as yet; but I'll certainly do it, as I can design a better one. Commend me to Baccio and tell him that if I had those concoctions here which he gave me there with you, I should be another Gratian. And thank him on my behalf' (*Ca* MXXVI / Ra 239). Del Riccio had sent M two melons and a bottle of wine, with a request for a design that M had promised for a bust of Cecchino, since the artist had disapproved of one submitted to del Riccio. Baccio Rontini was M's physician when he was nursed through a serious illness in del Riccio's apartments; the reference to Gratian is obscure.

3. 'If what ... with me': i.e., if my soul has been condemned to eternal death in hell. According to the common philosophy of the time, the rational soul was directly infused by God into the human embryo when this had reached a sufficiently advanced stage; nature could not create the distinctively human faculty of reason, being confined to supplying for it the physical and animal substratum, 'the mortal part' (see line 4).

207

M's postscript reads: 'For the turtledove [*tortola*]; it is up to Urbino to repay you for the fish, which he has gobbled up.' On Urbino, see the introductory note to poem 179, and the note to 300:10.

208

To del Riccio, M wrote: 'Revise as you see fit.'

209

4, 'may ... exemplar': nature was envisioned as performing its work in accordance with the perfect exemplars in God's mind of all the different genera, here that of the human being.

210

2, 'what': an impersonal meaning for *chi* seems required by lines 3–4 (similarly G): see the note to 34:11. Gu, B and S would understand the word simply as 'who'.

211

M's postscript reads: 'Clumsy things! The spring is dry; one must wait until it rains, and you are in too much of a hurry.'

212

2, 'the Arm': see note to 184:1.
4, 'it was its right alone ...': so also Ma: this interpretation seems to give the most natural meaning to *toccava*, and the best logical sense to the quatrain as a whole; most interpreters, however, take the last line to mean 'since otherwise it [death] was being left to kill only those less lovely'.

213

1, 'that Arm': see the note to 184:1.

214

M wrote to del Riccio: 'The tomb speaks to whoever reads these lines. Clumsy things; but since you want me to do a thousand of them, there are bound to be all kinds.'

215

4, 'immortalize in stone': through commissioning a beautiful tomb: see the introductory note to poem 179.

216

This poem is preceded by the note: 'Above the tomb.'
2, 'form and life': in the composite of body and soul, the soul in its entirety (as vegetable, animal and rational) was regarded as the source of all the qualities other than sheer physicality (supplied by matter, which is in itself formless); the conceit of lines 2–4 is that as the body is made beautiful directly by the soul, so is the tomb indirectly, since a beautiful tomb would be constructed only for a beautiful human being.

217

1, 'the phoenix': see note to 43:6.

2, 'more fully appreciated': so also C and S; *di più stima* is understood by G and B to mean 'more beautiful': this requires an odd meaning for the words, and one which makes the thought flow less easily.

218

M's brief postscript reads: 'For the fig-bread.'

4, 'to carry off a winter flower': Cecchino died in midwinter (8 January 1544).

219

This poem is preceded by the directive, 'Below the head, which may speak [these words]', and followed by the very different, practical comment: 'Hope to see you next St Martin's Day, if it does not rain.'

3, 'because I alone ...': these words seem to refer, in a hyperbolic tribute, to Cecchino's time on earth: heaven is cut off from the earth, because now, after Cecchino's death, there is no one on earth of such goodness as to be able to commune with God in paradise.

220

4, 'it enjoys': i.e., heaven enjoys (so also Gu and G); grammatically, the subject may be Cecchino's soul (so B), but this would make the contrast between Rome and heaven less marked.

222

1, 'Arm': see the note to 184:1.

2, 'yields': so also Gu and S; this better accords with the literal meaning of *cede*, and with the 'gathering' spoken of at line 1, than does 'falls' (as G, B and Ma interpret).

223

Poems 220–22 are on the same sheet. After this quatrain M added the comment: 'Since poetry tonight is becalmed, I am sending you four crude ring-cakes [*berlingozzi*] for the miser's three honey-cakes [*berriquocoli*]. My best wishes to you. Your Michelangelo at Macel de''; for the final word of the street in which M lived, Macel de' Corvi ('Slaughterhouse of the Crows'), the poet substituted a drawing of a crow. The 'honey-cakes' may refer either to del Riccio's gifts of food to M, or to other poems on Cecchino's death by a less prolific writer than M, possibly Giannotti.

4, 'many dead': i.e., spiritually dead, through their sins: cp. poem 219.

224

1, ... *gli occhi, e 'l corpo e l'alma*: punctuated as in Gu; G's punctuation here is confusing, with the comma placed not after *occhi* but after *corpo*; F and Ma do not have either comma.

4, 'for a life ... many years': i.e., for the life of heaven, often denied to those to whom a long life on earth offers many occasions for sin.

227

2, 'the great day': the day of the Last Judgement: see note to 140:3.

228

M's postscript reads: 'For the fun of it, not to make up the number', although this is in fact the final extant poem regarding Cecchino (on a possible missing quatrain, see Clements, pp. 140 and 150, n. 2).

230

An earlier version of this poem was directed to a man; G suggests that that version may have been inspired by Cavalieri, and the change of addressee occasioned by M's preparation of the poem for publication.

6–7, 'a noble heavenly figure': see note to 209:4.

231

Between this poem and a variant for the last line, M wrote to del Riccio: 'For Lent; your Michelangelo commends himself to you.'

232

10–11, 'my hope's being weak ...': i.e., M's hope of receiving eternal life after death.

233

Under the poem, M wrote to del Riccio: 'For one of the mullet-roe [or 'tunny-roe'] relishes.'

1–4, 'open ... closed ...': the basic image, a relatively frequent one in M's poetry, is of the greater intensity of fire in an enclosed space, with old age, bounded by death, being envisaged as such a space, in which the fire of love burns: see, e.g., 143:3 (and the note to that line) and 170:5–8.

235

We have M's testimony that this and the following poem were composed for Vittoria Colonna: M included them in a letter to an old friend in Florence (Father Fattucci) several years after the marchesa's death, with the comment: 'I'm sending you one or two of the verses I used to write for the Marchesa di Pescara, who was devoted to me [mi voleva grandissimo bene] and I no less to her. Death deprived me of a very great friend' (Ca MCXLVII / Ra 347). G believes that the present poem was intended for publication, despite its absence from most modern reconstructions of M's projected anthology.

1, 'A man in a woman': the words read strangely, not to say offensively, today, although they were clearly intended as a compliment. In M's time, despite significant changes in Renaissance society, education (especially higher education) remained largely the prerogative of men; male dominance was particularly evident with regard to religious leadership (the immediate context here), since in the Catholic Church holy orders were restricted to male celibates. Colonna was widely admired as a woman of exceptional culture and religious sensibility. M probably has in mind here principally Colonna's poetry, which we know he treasured; he would not be parted from his copy of two sets of her poems which she had sent to him (Ca MCLX–MCLXI / Ra 360–1).

11–12, 'through water and fire': i.e., in R's phrase, 'the tears of repentance and the flames of a pure love'; there may well be an implicit comparison with the purgation undergone by souls after death.

236

On the revision of this poem, see the introductory note to poem 66; on its dedication, see the introductory note to poem 235. The general meaning of the present poem seems clear enough, even though details are disputed. The thought evolves relatively clearly if, as the translation assumes, the principal subject of the second quatrain is the same as that of the first, i.e., the human mind: this is man's divine part both in the range of its operations and in its direct origin from God: see the note to 206:3.

1, 'man's divine part': see the introductory note.

2–3, 'that double power': a highly elliptic reference to the combined powers of mind and hand.

4, 'it ... gives': similarly Gu, C and B; others (D, G and S) believe that a new subject, the sculptor, is implicitly being introduced here.

4, 'and this is not ...': M wishes to emphasize the role of the mind, and to scout the idea that sculpting is merely the labour of an artisan.

5, 'It': i.e., the divine part: so also Gu; most commentators (e.g., D, C, G, B and S) regard the subject as generic: 'it is no different with regard to ...'

6, 'before': G seems to be alone in thinking that *anz[i]* is to be understood as 'in a shorter time than ...'.

8, 'the divine part ...': the subject of *pruova e rivede* is disputed: D and S take it to be the artist; G and B construe lines 7–8 very differently, and would read (as B phrases it): 'the beautiful, wise and shrewd mind [of the artist] reworks his concepts and harmoniously orders what he would depict'.

14, 'if it is to ...': the translation retains the ambiguity of the Italian: the subject of *gastiga e 'nsegna* may be either *mercé* (so Gu, R, D, C and B) or *penitenzia* (so S); the former seems much more likely.

237

2, 'the first art': sculpture.

7, 'the beauty which first existed': although a modern reader's instinct might well be to assume that it is the beauty of the work of art that is remembered, most commentators are agreed that what is being spoken of is the soul's remembrance of God's perfect beauty from its life before bodily existence.

238

3, 'the unique money': almost certainly a reference to virtue.

4, 'nature spends down here': this probably means 'spends in good works' (so D, C, G and S), although it may signify 'spends wastefully' (so B and Ma), i.e., virtue is not in fact realized on earth.

239

An earlier autograph version carries a note by M, 'Sent', possibly indicating that he sent the poem in that form to Colonna.

8, 'in their task': of destruction.

240

5, 'for her, who is its creation': all souls are directly created by God; here the beloved, as divine also in her goodness, has a particular claim on God's protection.

9, 'to her more noble part': literally, 'on her right side': the right was regarded as superior to the left, and often understood symbolically – here of the soul's superiority to the body (see also 162:1–2). The poet goes on, however, to contrast the soul adversely with the 'rock' or statue, since the soul will depart from this world at the death of the body.

12, 'Nature alone': the thought is obscure here, but the poet seems to be implying that nature alone is required to seek vengeance on death, since the work of man, the sculpture, will remain.

241

To del Riccio M commented: 'Since you want some scribbles, I cannot send you other than what I have. Too bad for you; your Michelangelo commends himself to you.'

11, 'fear': engendered by the thought of death.

242

M wrote beneath the poem: 'From [or 'as'] sculptors [*Da scultori*]'.

12, 'features': it seems better, with S, to understand *membra* as referring to facial features rather than to the bodily members as a whole.

243

1, *idol*: changed by G (following Gu) from *idolo* of the original, for the sake of metre.

3, 'these two objects': i.e., the lady's image and the lover's heart.

7, 'arguments': *scorte*: literally, 'escorts' or 'guides'. Despite the almost jaunty tone of lines 7–8, the tercets put forward a serious defence of love.

10–11, 'dwells in my love': there may here be an appropriation of Christian ideas: see Christ's words to his disciples at the Last Supper, as reported in *John* 15:1–12.

12–14: the basic meaning of these lines seems clear: love for one's fellow human beings is a preparation for the love of God, to be attained perfectly after death – a theme central to both Christianity and Neoplatonism. What is not clear is how precisely the imagery (and logic) of these lines is meant to function, since there is no evident reason why love's being a magnet will make the soul return to God. What M may have in mind is that 'the love enkindled', having its source in personified Love, who is to be associated with God (and perhaps even to be identified with him), draws 'the ardour' – which is to be understood as natural to the soul (so also G) – to itself and hence to God. Support for this reading may be found in the fact that M commonly (though not exclusively) uses *ardore*, *ardere* and *ardente* for the love of a human being or human beauty; the transient nature of the object of such ardour is sometimes given prominence, as, e.g., at 166:7, 168:4, 260:11, 272:1–2, 274:2, 276:9; for the less common use of these words with respect to love for God, see 257:2 and 296:10.

244

4, 'ungracious ... grace': the translation attempts to catch the word-play, unforced in the Italian, of *fa ... grazia la disgrazia mia*.

13, 'pilgrim soul': see note to 16:1.

245

13–15: rather confusingly, G (in common with other editors) does not make clear that these last lines are part of the dialogue, the reply of the first speaker to the second; quotation marks have been added here.

246

This madrigal evolved from a few lines of a much longer *capitolo* with which, despite several reworkings, M was apparently never satisfied: see the introductory note to poem 66.

2, 'only': it seems clear that *tanto* here is to be understood as *soltanto*, and not (despite S) in its usual sense of 'greatly': see also 89:14.

17, 'the reward of martyrdom': as occasionally in M, a conventional love poem unexpectedly introduces a more serious, religious perspective.

247

The Florentine academician Giovanni di Carlo Strozzi penned a laudatory, if rather flat, quatrain in praise of M's statue of Night located in the Medici funerary chapel; M found it unwelcome, presumably irritated that such praise should come from one who was closely, if perhaps innocently, associated with the repressive regime of Duke Cosimo (on whom see the note to 249:4). M's distaste is particularly evident in the final line of his quatrain, which rejects the somewhat precious invitation in the corresponding line of Strozzi's poem to waken the merely sleeping figure of Night and make it speak. M's poem is datable from a conversation of early 1546 reported by Giannotti (pp. 44–5).

248

The first of two poems (see also 250) on Dante. M was regarded in his time as an expert on Dante: his close knowledge of, and admiration for, that poet's work is certainly evident both in his own poetry and in the dialogues on Dante's *Inferno* recorded by Giannotti; and M's *Last Judgement* was clearly influenced by Dante.

1, 'He came down from heaven': indirectly, perhaps M's highest praise of Dante, since the words echo clearly a phrase from the Latin creed expressing belief in Christ's divine origin: *descendit de caelis*.

2, 'the just and the merciful hell': respectively hell proper, where unrepentant sinners are eternally punished, and that part of hell where sinners who repented before death are purged of the effects of sin and prepare for heaven; see also the note to 63:8. Lines 2–

3 refer to the three parts of Dante's journey in *The Divine Comedy*, through Hell and Purgatory to Heaven.

6, 'nest': this image for Florence may be borrowed from *Inferno* 15:78.

7, *l' premio*: Cont plausibly suggests that the *l* of the MSS should be understood as *l[i]* (= *gli*); G has *'l*.

10, 'works': a literal translation of *opre*, which may be intended to evoke Dante's moral greatness as well as his literary stature.

249

Del Riccio testified to the political import of this poem, by writing above the autograph version: 'By messer Michelangelo Buonarroti, who in the lady signifies Florence.'

4, 'one man alone': Duke Cosimo de' Medici, whose long, in many ways benevolent, but undoubtedly tyrannous, regime had begun in 1537 (and was to last for more than thirty years). In his last years M appears to have softened his attitude to the duke, who several times expressed his wish that M return to Florence. There seems no good reason to doubt that what finally prevented M from agreeing to return was his belief that his work in redesigning and overseeing the construction of St Peter's Basilica in Rome for successive popes was willed by God: see *Ca* MCCLX / Ra 436.

12, 'in which great abundance ...': this point had already been made, at 245:7–12, in a non-political context; it is difficult, particularly in view of this parallel, to see how G could justify his interpretation of lines 12–13, that what restricts great desire is the fear of losing the good possessed.

250

See the introductory note to poem 248. To Giannotti M wrote beneath the poem: 'Messer Donato, you ask me for what I do not have.'

4, 'rise ... to speak of his least merit': the elliptic text leaves the reader to supply an infinitive after *salire*. Although G, B and S understand 'to imitate', it seems best to return to an older tradition (see Gu, R and C) which would see a precise contrast between lines 3 and 4, i.e., between *words*, of reproval (3) and of praise (4).

251

This and the following poem show M at his least appealing as a person: so sensitive to a real or presumed slight from an old and devoted friend, Luigi del Riccio, that he is prepared to regret the very health which he owes to del Riccio's generous care in offering him the hospitality of his own apartments in the Palazzo Strozzi when he was seriously ill. It is uncertain whether the poems date from after the first such occasion, in the summer of 1544, or the second, in the winter of 1545–6. The nature of the slight is not specified in either poem, but may be connected with an incident spoken of in a letter M sent to del Riccio early in 1546 (*Ca* MLVI / Ra 244), where M complains bitterly that del Riccio had published something of M's without permission (a poem or, perhaps more likely, a print based on a design by M).

12, 'Offence': *sdegno* carries a range of meanings; here some word such as 'offence' seems more appropriate than the more usual 'anger' or 'disdain'.

14, *mille piacer ... tormento*: a quotation from Petrarch, *Rime*, 231:4.

252

See the introductory note to poem 251. Del Riccio responded to this madrigal with another, using similar rhymes.

9, 'spurs us to look': with S (and, implicitly, Gu), the translation takes the subject of *sprona* to be the sun, and not (as C, G and Ma) the eye. The former seems to fit better with the parallel drawn, since M's desire to be grateful was made lame by a source outside himself.

253

On the earlier MS of this poem M wrote: 'Poem born at night while I am in bed – to be revised tomorrow evening.' On the later MS he commented: 'It would be as sweet as the apples [*pome*] of Adam, but I have no apples [or 'honey'? – *mele*] in my body.'

254

Under the poem M wrote to del Riccio: 'The old love has put out a shoot [*rampollo*] or rather a sprout [*tallo*].'

1, 'of the lady': with S, the translation takes *Donn[a]* to be a particularly striking example of M's frequent habit of elision; in this case a preposition and an article are omitted, with *Donna* standing for '*Della donna*' ('*Della donna ... le chiave*'). While omission of the preposition is rare in M, it is not unknown: see 47:11, where *di* is omitted before *l'alma*; indeed if the reading of 260:10 adopted in this translation is correct, then that line offers another instance of the omission of a preposition before *donna*: see the note, *ad loc*. The alternative in the present instance, though adopted by most commentators (see Gu, R, C, G, B and Ma), requires accepting that M changes from direct address in lines 1–5 to indirect speech in the rest of the poem, which is difficult to believe; the switch of address in poem 54 should not be offered as a parallel (see the note to 54:42), since that poem is unfinished and gives no evidence of having been revised, while the present one was intended for publication, and was certainly revised.

9, 'she forbids ...': so also R and S; the subject of *vieta* and *tira* may, however, be 'Love' (so Gu, C, G and B). In favour of the former is the fact that the main point of the poem is to emphasize the role of the lady, of whom, in fact, lines 11–13 go on immediately to speak, as if in explanation of lines 9–10.

255

Many commentators (e.g., Girardi in his edition of 1967 and B) follow F in assigning to this poem a dedication to Vittoria Colonna; however, the reference to youth (*giovanezza*) in its final line seems more than adequate justification for G's earlier caution that F's attribution had been made 'with too much confidence'.

256

One of the most heavily reworked of M's poems: see the introductory note to poem 66.

15, 'familiarity': for another instance of *uso* as 'familiarity', also in the context of use of the eyes, see 165:2 and 8.

257

10, *cor*: changed by G (following Gu) from *core* of the original, for the sake of metre.

258

5, 'pilgrim soul': see note to 16:1.
11, 'splendour': the manifestation in finite beauty of the infinite God; in paraphrasing *splendore* as 'bodily beauty', G is at best potentially misleading: while it is true that it is the fact that Colonna's goodness and love are embodied that make them manifest (in contrast to God's), the emphasis is always on her *spiritual* qualities.
15, 'the heart ... not see': a very different sentiment is voiced at 268:5–6.

259

One of the most substantially revised of M's poems: see the introductory note to poem 66. In two earlier versions of this poem there appear the words *signor mie* ('my lord': see G, pp. 422–5, summarized by B); this may well indicate that the poem was inspired by Cavalieri, whom he addressed several times with this title in his poetry.
1, 'my burning desire': this phrase seems clearly to refer to love of a human being, a point for which confirmation may be found in M's frequent use of *ardente* and cognate words when the object of love is human: see the note to 243:12–14.
10, *la beltà c'ogni*: G (in common with most editors, including F, but not Gu) puts a comma after *beltà*. This is regrettable, since it requires understanding M to be saying that it is false to place hope in *any* beauty, whereas the text is ambiguous: it could (and, in the opinion of the translator, should) be understood as repudiating the placing of hope precisely in that beauty which is subject to change, i.e., physical beauty.

260

G is quite right to reject, on the basis of lines 9–11, a dedication to Colonna (which F proposed); but he forces the evidence when he roundly declares that these lines indicate that the poem is 'certainly dedicated to Cavalieri'.
7, 'this': i.e., vain passion.
10, 'it is too unlike a woman': so also G (and similarly Gu and C); although 'a woman is too unlike it' (so, in essence, S) is grammatically possible, it seems preferable to understand love as the continuing subject. To make 'a woman' the subject involves

several difficulties: it requires assuming that there is an implied complement for *dissimil*; it breaks the direct contrast throughout the rest of the poem between love and merely sensual ardour; and, by introducing a third subject, it makes 'former' and 'latter' of line 12 read awkwardly. Although it tells against the translation adopted here that a preposition must be understood before *donna*, this is not an insurmountable objection: see the note to 254:1. Love for women was unflatteringly compared to love for men in the Neoplatonist tradition; when Ficino characterized the two loves as common (*vulgare*) and heavenly (*celeste*) respectively (VI.14), he went out of his way to stress that the superiority of the latter stems from its aim, which is intellectual and educative (as compared with a love motivated by the desire for copulation and procreation), and to condemn copulation between males.

261

1, 'Though long delay ...': in having one's love responded to.

262

A very heavily revised poem: G lists six versions; see the introductory note to poem 66.
9, 'what': so also Gu, C, G, B and S; the context makes this more plausible than 'who' (as Ma); see also the note to 34:11.

263

3–4, 'Terce ... Nones ... Vespers': three of the Church's so-called Hours (religious services); the three named take place respectively in the morning, afternoon and early evening.
4, 'night': this relatively unusual meeting for *sera* is required by the preceding words.
5, 'my age and ... fortune in love': literally, 'my birth and my fortune', *mie parto e mie fortuna*. The significance of *parto* is disputed: while 'destiny' (so G) is attractive, it makes 'fortune' somewhat redundant; 'age' seems to fit well with what the poet goes on to say of *parto*, that it toys with death. The words 'in love' (suggested by G's paraphrase) have been added to 'fortune' in the translation to avoid any confusion with material wealth.
10, 'the other life': eternal life after death.
16, 'there remains ... in his memory': so also Gu, R, C, B, S and Ma; the line is understood very differently by G: 'if the memory

of past faults speaks only to our ears and not also to our hearts
...'. G's interpretation has the advantage that it gives *orecchio* its
natural meaning, but requires understanding a contrast between
the ear and the heart for which there is no evidence in the text.

264

4, 'as a special privilege': so also Gu, R and C; S understands
con previlegio as 'exclusively' (cf. also G: 'col marchio del suo
privilegio'): in the sixteenth century, the phrase *con privilegio*
appeared on title-pages of books to indicate exclusive publishing
rights.
4, 'your soul': a possessive adjective must be supplied for *l'alma*:
since lines 7–14 speak of the poem's recipient, 'your' seems much
more likely (so G, B and Ma) than 'my' (so Gu and S).
9, 'like a cross ...': the displaying of a cross, symbol of Christ's
death, was traditionally thought to make demons flee.

265

The poem turns on the idea that beauty which is realized on earth
is a reflection of a perfect, heavenly model.
11–13, 'But though ...': these lines express an idea that is not
integrated into the thought of the poem: lines 14–16 would flow
naturally after line 10.
13, 'holy writings': a clear indication that the dedicatee is Colonna:
her poetry was mainly religious in inspiration: see note to 235:1.

266

5, 'the place': Colonna's face.
11, 'buried': under the ashes of the 'great fire' which is now almost
spent.

267

A highly ironic, yet moving, autobiographical sketch. With poem
85, this is one of M's only two successful long poems; it is notable
that both poems treat their subjects humorously and are written
in the same poetic genre. Lines 1–6 introduce the two main themes:
M's body, and his physical surroundings. Lines 7–15 concentrate
on the latter, lines 16–45 on the former. It is only in the final lines,
46–55, where M turns to consider his cultural achievements, that

bitterness overwhelms the comic tone. Several of the details of the poem are obscure, although this scarcely affects the power of the overall impression. G notes that he makes good the many elisions characteristic of the copyist of the MS.

4, 'my dark tomb': M's house. It seems in fact to have been of modest size, rather than genuinely cramped as this and the following line would suggest. M may have had in mind the contrast between his house and the surrounding 'rich palaces' (line 30), or between it and the ample dwellings to which many highly successful artists of the later Renaissance became accustomed.

5, 'Arachne ...': an oblique reference to the cobwebs with which M's house must have abounded: Arachne, a Lydian woman who presumptuously challenged the goddess Athena to a competition in weaving, was changed by the goddess into a spider after she committed suicide when her challenge failed: see Ovid, *Metamorphoses* VI, 5–145.

13, 'Cats' corpses ...': the general sense is clear, though not the details.

15, *non vien a vicitarmi*: this is the reading of Girardi's 1967 edition (possibly on the basis of Cont's suggestion), while the 1960 edition had *non vïen a mutarmi*: clearly *vicitarmi* makes readier sense, and is in any case closer to the MS *sucitarmi* (changed by del Riccio); and with the longer word the metrical diaeresis earlier in the line ceases to be appropriate.

18, 'a good meal': literally, 'bread and cheese' (*'l pan e 'l formaggio*), apparently signifying solid sustenance.

21, 'my breath itself ...': M's soul, then, has even less chance of escaping by that route.

22, 'I am ... ruptured ...': M may simply have meant this line to have a cumulative effect indicating the ravages wrought by old age, but it is possible that *crepato* refers to M's hernia condition.

25, 'I find ... in melancholy': the line reads literally, 'my happiness is melancholy'; one of M's most open acknowledgements of his depressive nature. See also *Ca* DCCIV / *Ra* 170.

27–9: S draws attention to an intriguingly close parallel with lines 16–17 in Berni's poem, *Sonnetto sopra la mula d'Alcionio*.

28, 'the feast of the Ugly Old Woman': for the sake of English readers who may be unfamiliar with Italian customs, the translation here takes a liberty with the text, which speaks simply of 'the feast of the Magi': this feast is, of course, that of the Epiphany (*l'Epifania*), when the Magi were shown the Christ child (according to the account of *Matthew* 2:9–12). In Italy during the night of this feast (6 January) gifts were traditionally put out for children, unless they were thought not to deserve gifts, in which case they were left ashes and coal; both kinds of 'present' were supposedly left by an old woman who came down the chimney. The old woman took on the name of the feast in its popular form, *la Befana*; she became proverbial for an old hag, the point to which M is alluding here.

34, 'a hornet in a jug': almost certainly a reference to tinnitus, mentioned also at line 44; M suffered from this condition at least from his early forties: see *Ca* CCLXXXVI / *Ra* 119.

36, 'three pills of pitch …': this has been variously interpreted; perhaps the most likely candidate is kidney stones, from which M suffered.

46-8, 'My scribblings …': his love poetry. There is a significant contrast between the light wit of line 46 and the heavy exaggeration of lines 47–8: in the former, M describes his love poetry in traditionally effete terms which do not in fact aptly apply to his own poetry, from which Muses and flowery grottoes are notably absent.

49, 'rag-dolls': in the light of lines 52–4, the reference here is presumably to M's visual art in general, rather than simply to his sculpture.

52, 'The esteemed art': sculpture: see, e.g., 237:2.

270

2, 'things I do not have': literally, 'things which I am not', or 'things that do not exist'.

272

One of the most heavily revised of M's poems: see the introductory note to poem 66. This is a curiously hybrid poem: the love spoken of at lines 1–2 is evidently sensual, quite unlike that referred to in the following two lines, which seem equally clearly to evoke Vittoria Colonna; more generally, in the octave the poet appears to wish to be taken once more by Love, whom he then repudiates in the sextet.

13, 'more merciful arrows': those of God.

273

5, 'other place': *altrove* clearly refers to people. M elsewhere uses the image of place in a personal sense: see, e.g., 266:5.

7–8, 'the sickness ...': almost certainly a reference to the effect of original sin inherited by all human beings from Adam and Eve, although M may also have in mind the Neoplatonic idea that the soul is weakened by being in a body. In the overtones of dispersion present in this ascription of enfeeblement to the human race (*disperso / ha l'intelletto ...*), M may be suggesting that in his sinful state the human being is so drawn by the superficial attractions of the variety of things in this world as to be unable to concentrate his mind and so find God (often referred to in the Christian tradition as the *unum necessarium*, the one thing necessary, after *Luke* 10:42): cp. the prayer for singleness of mind with which poem 286 begins. According to the Neoplatonic tradition, one of the effects of the soul's fall into the body is that it pays excessive attention to the infinite multiplicity of corporeal things: see, e.g., Ficino VII, 14.

9, 'open': unless we think M guilty of tautology, *capace* cannot be understood in its most literal sense; a general word such as 'open' (similarly B, *pronto*, 'ready') seems better than the more evidently pious *disposto*, 'disposed' (Gu, Piccoli, C and G) or the more intellectual 'capable' (S).

10, 'if one can so put it': strictly, the infinite God cannot be grasped by the finite human mind.

274

4, 'as I was before': either a reference to former earthly love (so Gu and Ma), or, as seems more likely, to the love of God enjoyed by the soul before its time in the body (so C, G and S).

9, 'Love': here identified with God (or with Christ, the God-man), as is apparent from the *Signor* of line 13. Even in M's late, almost exclusively religious, poetry this is an unusual identification, though cf. 291:5.

275

4, 'heap of stones': so also G and B; this is a more likely meaning of *lapedicina* than 'little stone' (so Piccoli and S).

276

A remarkable testimony to M's attraction to human beauty in both male and female; this should temper the undoubtedly just ascription to him of a homosexual orientation.

2, 'Any object that …': line 5 makes clear that by 'object' M has in mind only human beings; this is a notable indication of what is apparent from M's art and poetry as a whole, that his concern was almost exclusively with human beauty.

6, 'envy': literally, 'jealousy', but M seems to have in mind the contrast between his own state in old age and human beauty in its full vigour, rather than any rivalry for the affection of another human being; *gelosia* is also used in a broad sense at 101:13 (see note there).

12, 'passes beyond': i.e., beyond merely mortal beauty.

13, 'god': this understanding of *die* (as a form of *dio*), common to recent commentators (see G, B, S and Ma), seems more likely than the more oblique 'day' (from *dì* or *dia*) of older interpretations (Gu, D, R and C), where day is understood as a synonym for eternal life; for *Die* as 'God', see poem 231: 11.

14, 'covering': *spoglia*: the contrast between this harsh and contemptuous reference to the body in the final word and the eulogy of human beauty earlier in the poem is striking.

277

1550 saw the publication of what turned out to be an epoch-making work in art history, Vasari's *Le vite de' più eccellenti pittori scultori e architettori*; the author sent M a copy, and in the present poem M offers his compliments and thanks. In his book, Vasari, who was proud of his tutelage under M (p. 365) and frequently mentioned his friendship with him (a friendship that deepened with the years, although it never apparently became genuinely intimate, on M's part at least), praised M as the culmination of the entire evolution of art. Despite the present poem, it seems that M felt Vasari's treatment of him in his book to be seriously lacking: Condivi's short biography, which was published in 1553, has all the appearance of being an indirect attempt by M to set the record straight. The point was not lost on Vasari, who, in the light of that biography, modified and amplified his own life of Michelangelo in the second edition of his work, published in 1568. It has been suggested, perhaps over flatteringly, that in this poem M displayed shrewdness with regard to Vasari's particular talents, and some prescience, by declaring that in turning from art to writing Vasari had set his hand to a more noble task.

1, 'with your stylus': this instrument is undoubtedly meant to signify drawing, as 'colours' does painting.

14, 'despite nature': so also Gu (who reads *essa*), B and Ma, although *esse* would normally be a plural form; R and G take it to be so, and understand the word to refer directly to *memorie* (line 12) and indirectly to the fleetingness of memories: despite its grammatical attractiveness, this interpretation does not take sufficient account of the immediately preceding *voi*.

279

This is the most significant expression in M's later years of the passion for human beauty that had inspired him through most of his life, a passion that is, however, explicitly or implicitly rejected in much of his late, narrowly exclusivist Christian poetry. In this poem M's inspiration is religiously sanctioned by the effect of the beauty of the human face (lines 2–4), and above all by the divine origin of noble human beings, who, M believes, are patterned after the exemplars of them that exist in the divine mind (lines 5–8). See also the introductory note to poem 284.

280

1–3: for a similar sense of oppressive, hidden sin see 291:1–4.

3, 'it': i.e., the grave sin.

7–8, 'subject to your law': presumably the law of atonement, in the light of lines 5–6. According to traditional Christian belief, all human beings must offer to God infinite recompense for the sin against the infinite majesty of God which Adam committed, a sin in which all human beings are implicated through their descent from him. Such recompense can in fact be made only by the God-man Christ: he is both infinitely good and a member of the offending human race, though not himself tainted by Adam's sin, since he was divinely conceived in the womb of the Virgin Mary through the direct agency of God's Holy Spirit. The inherited 'original sin' also leaves each human being with a tendency to sin which he or she cannot fully resist without the grace of Christ. These doctrines were given full official status in the Catholic Church by the Council of Trent, in its decrees on original sin and justification (1546–7).

282

This tercet lacks a main verb, and the sense is consequently unclear. The present translation would link it to the kind of sentiments expressed in poems 283 and 285.

283

This seems to be the first sketch of a sextet for a projected sonnet, even though lines 2 and 5 do not rhyme. Although poetically faulty, these few lines strongly reinforce the impression of disillusionment with art in several of M's late poems (but see also the introductory note to the next poem).

1, *car*: changed by G (following Gu) from *caro* of the original, for the sake of metre.

6, 'in what, then, . . .': so also G, although any interpretation must be conjectural.

284

The attitude to art in this poem is in harmony with the more positive tone of poems 276–7, 279 and, to a lesser extent, 300; but it runs counter to the negativity of most others of this period, notably 283 and, above all, 285.

1, 'If in your name': there is no way of determining whether the addressee is God or a human being, although the former seems much more likely (so also Piccoli, C and S).

285

See the introductory note to poem 66. This is justly regarded as one of M's finest poems, despite its heavily negative evaluation of his artistic endeavours. Although the poem was sent by M to Vasari in September 1554 (with a highly ironic comment against himself: *Ca* MCXCVII / Ra 390), there is no reason to believe that it was inspired by, or dedicated to, him. The poem was heavily revised between its inception in 1552 and the final version sent to Vasari, who replied with a sonnet using the same rhymes.

1–4: the steady beat in the single movement of the opening line contrasts effectively with the broken rhythms of the following line-and-a-half, which in turn give way to the smoother flow of 3b–4.

1, 'My life's journey': *mia*, as the concluding word of line 1, emphasizes the personal quality of the poem, while lines 3–4, beginning with *al comun*, set M's individual life within the context of the destiny of the whole human race.

5, 'fond': *affettüosa* is a particularly difficult word to translate; it indicates a harmful dominance of the emotions.

8, 'that which ...': this line may refer generically to a tendency in all human beings to make some finite thing their supreme good instead of God (as M had done with art), or it may be speaking specifically of love, viewed as the commonest human *idol e monarca*.

10, 'a double death': the temporal death of the body and the eternal death of the soul, both clearly referred to at line 11.

14, 'which on the cross ...': M implicitly conveys the encircling movement of the embrace spoken of in this line by delaying to the end the object of the verb with which the line opens.

288

M sent this sonnet in March 1555 to an old friend, Monsignor Beccadelli (on whom see the introductory note to poem 300), perhaps in reply to one sent earlier that month; we know that the archbishop quickly responded with a sonnet using similar rhymes (G, p. 455). Shortly after sending the poem to one old friend M sent a copy to another, Father Fattucci: see the introductory note to the next poem.

8, 'selfish love': literally, 'own love', *propio amor*; in looking for an English equivalent, it seems better to avoid the term 'self-love', since the Catholic tradition did not condemn love of self as such, but only an excess of such love, to the exclusion of God and one's neighbour. It may be, though, that M is careless of orthodoxy at this point; certainly poems such as 289 indicate a perilously high degree of self-disgust.

12, 'Make me hate ...': perhaps the strongest repudiation in M's late poetry of the beauty in which he had earlier found such inspiration, human and divine.

289

See the introductory note to poem 66. A copy of this and poem 288, with a strongly self-deprecatory comment, were sent via Vasari to an old friend, Giovan Francesco Fattucci, chaplain at Florence Cathedral, in May 1555: see *Ca* MCCVI / Ra 399. This

poem is the most direct expression of the importance M attached
to the virtue of faith, a central and contentious subject in Reform-
ation debates. Although the sentiment here is strongly fideistic,
it does not exceed the bounds of the Catholic orthodoxy then
prevailing: there is no excess repudiation of merit based on faith
here, or indeed in any of M's poems, even the most pessimistic of
his later years.

3, 'pardon of you, who are supremely to be desired': literally,
'pardon of the supreme desire'.

8, 'the grace whole and entire': although *né ... n'ho grazia intiera
e piena* is ambiguous, and may signify that M thought that he had
no faith whatever, it seems more likely that he is professing an
inadequate degree of that virtue.

13, *don*: changed by G (following Gu) from *dono* of the original,
for the sake of metre.

14, 'another key': it is clear that M is referring to faith, the subject
of lines 1–11: faith is the key which corresponds, in the subjective
realm, to that of the redemption effected by Christ's death in the
objective realm (spoken of at lines 12–13). Both 'keys' are required
for salvation, faith being the basic element of grace, which is
the participation by the individual in the infinite merits of the
redemption.

290

1, 'burden': *salma* signifies literally a corpse (and is so understood
here by S), and symbolically a burden; the symbolic sense seems
preferable, as referring to M's sins (so also Gu, C, G and B).

8, 'sinful': although *trist[a]* is here accorded its primary meaning
('sad') by C and S, the context seems to suggest the secondary
sense adopted in the translation: see note to 109:10.

10, 'pure': here the symbolic meaning of *gastigato* (literally,
'chastised') is undoubtedly required.

11, 'your severe arm': as S suggests, M may well have had in mind
the figure of Christ in his own *Last Judgement*, whose upraised
arm spells doom for many.

293

3, 'both deaths': see note to 285:10.

9, *car*: changed by G (following Gu) from *caro* of the original, for
the sake of metre.

10–11, 'for my soul ...': highly elliptic lines. The principal diffi-
culty is that the main part of the final clause, *perché l'alma sia*,
lacks a past participle necessary for its grammatical and semantic
completion. What seems to be happening is that, in the words of
line 10 just quoted, M is speaking of a second creation of the soul
through the grace of Christ after the death inflicted on the soul by
sin (see 280:7–8 and note there), to be contrasted with the soul's
first creation (referred to at line 11), when it was made out of
nothing at the beginning of its existence. The poet would, there-
fore, have us supply some such word as *ricreata* after *sia*, to give
the sense proposed in the translation. To the elliptic contrast
between the original creation of the soul (line 11) and its recreation
or redemption (line 10b) there may be a parallel in the abrupt
words of 298:5: there M, addressing Christ but speaking of
mankind, writes: *creato, il redemisti* ... The image of the redemp-
tion precisely as a second creation has strong foundations in the
New Testament: see especially 2 *Corinthians* 5:17, *Galatians* 6:15,
Ephesians 2:10 and 4:24.

13, '**halve for me**': an image already sketched with reference to
Vittoria Colonna's distant, heavenly nobility: see poem 156.

294

12, '**given to understand**': *comprenda* (like the English
'comprehend') carries the double sense of 'contains' and 'under-
stands'.

295

5, *Il mondo è cieco*: there seems little doubt that this common
enough phrase is modelled on Dante's *Purgatorio* 16:66, since the
rest of the quatrain reflects the views put forward by Virgil later
in that canto.

7, '**the light**': of grace, presumably (so G and Ma): cf. line 12 and
87:11.

9, '**when will that happen** ... ?': 'when will death come?' or 'when
will the soul be illumined by saving grace?' The former seems
more likely in view of lines 12–14.

11, '**mortal**': i.e., subject to damnation (spiritual death), contrary
to the soul's intrinsic orientation to immortal life.

296

A poem on whose revision M spent much labour: see the introductory note to poem 66.

4, 'or that it hastens . . .': both text and meaning here are disputed. The principal editions read *e là* (so Gu, F and G), but others prefer *o là* (so B, S and Ma). Ma's suggestion that the phrase *non fa che morte* governs line 4 as well as line 3b gives good sense to these lines, and lies behind the present translation. G's interpretation appears to force the text, since it requires understanding *morte* as 'the thought of death', and *e* as 'which', to give the reading: 'this does not mean that the thought of death abandons me, which recurs less frequently to him who is less troubled by it'. Other interpretations likewise require diverging from the normal meaning of common words: Gu and B understand *e* as 'which' and 'because' respectively, while S (possibly following D's interpretation) takes *o* to mean 'though'.

6, 'if it is . . .': religiously, perhaps M's single most pessimistic line.

297

4, 'I do not . . .': so also S; others (e.g., G, B and Ma) would make the subject *il mal voler*, understanding that the evil will finds no rein within itself.

298

8, 'servant of the servants': there seems no hint of irony here, although this phrase is a close echo of a common papal title, *servus servorum Dei*.

12, 'It took . . .': a subject has to be supplied for *Tolse*. It seems that M is reverting to the subject of lines 9b–10, *il ciel* (so also C), a periphrasis for God, rather than abruptly introducing God directly as a new subject, 'He took . . .' (so G and S).

299

The poem can be dated from the draft of a letter of 1555 on the verso of the autograph. The evidence for identifying the donor of the gifts with Vasari is somewhat tenuous: the latter mentions in his *Vite* that he once sent to M a gift of the high-quality candles M liked (p. 423), and candles is one of the gifts mentioned in the poem's opening line. See also the note to line 14.

4, 'I am ... St Michael': i.e., M cannot adequately reciprocate: St Michael was often portrayed carrying the scales of justice. The rest of the poem is a somewhat laboured attempt to specify the inadequacy.

13, 'in terms of merit': it seems necessary to give *per merto* this precise sense: M is not saying simply that the gift of himself would count as nothing (as lines 12–13 are commonly understood), but that even were he to give his whole self this would not be of any merit comparable to that embodied in the donor's action: for where the latter's act of giving was unsolicited, M would merely be repaying a debt, something that is required.

14, 'for it is ...': behind this apparently rather charming conclusion may lurk M's recurrent dislike of being in anyone's debt, often implied or stated in his letters and poems: it is displayed to least pleasant effect in poems 251–2 (*q.v.*), and indeed was rather grumpily in evidence when V's gift of candles arrived (see introductory note above).

300

A measured, though warm and moving, expression of M's inability to accept an invitation to visit from M's long-standing friend monsignor Ludovico Beccadelli, a religiously liberal prelate who had in effect just been banished from Rome by the conservative administration of Pope Paul IV to the archbishopric of Ragusa in distant Dalmatia (see also poem 288). The poem dates from between February 1556, when Beccadelli's invitation was sent (in the form of a sonnet), and March 1557, by which date the archbishop had already been in possession of M's reply for some time. The quietly positive view of the world in the octave contrasts with the tone of most of M's late poetry: see note to poem 284.

4, 'enjoying one another on earth': in his invitation sonnet (see G, p. 471), Beccadelli had looked forward to being with M forever in heaven.

10, 'Urbino': M's loyal assistant and servant for over a quarter of a century, who died in December 1555; M had hoped that Urbino would be a comfort and support in his old age (see *Ca* MCCXIX / Ra 410); see also the note to F41.

14, 'to lodge': perhaps a gently ironic suggestion of a reversal of roles after death.

301

8, 'show yourself': spiritually, in prayer; this is also, presumably, the subject of lines 3–4.

302

5, car: changed by G (following Gu) from *caro* of the original, for the sake of metre.

Notes to the Appendix

FI

A quotation from Petrarch's *Trionfo della morte*, 2:34.

F4

A quotation from Petrarch's *Rime*, 269:1.

FII

A quotation from Dante's *Inferno*, 13:142.

FI3

A quotation, slightly altered, of Petrarch's *Rime*, 271:1–4.

FI4

The first and fourth lines are the opening words of Petrarch's *Rime*, 129.

F22

A quotation of the opening line of Petrarch's *Vallis Clausa*, his Latin elegy to the place where he spent many of his middle years; it is found on a sheet (variously dated) with a drawing of a urinating putto. Beneath M's transcription are the words: 'Please do not make me draw this evening, because Perino is not there.' Perino may be Gherardo Perini: see note to poem 18:6.

F24

The first line is a quotation from Dante's *Purgatorio*, 9:34, with *Dedal* substituted for *Achille*.

F25

The sheet on which these words are written has been cut in half.

F27

The sheet on which these words are written has been cut in half.

F30

Debile (line 2) is conjectural.

F31

A quotation of the octave of Petrarch's *Rime*, 236, with several small modifications. M's *spronare* at line 5 (instead of Petrarch's *frenare*, 'to rein in') does not make good sense.

F34–9

These are quotations from poems by M; the poems themselves are now lost, and our only evidence for them are these citations by Varchi in the first of his *Lezzioni* (see the introductory note to poem 151); Varchi is presumably quoting from complete poems. The loss of such a significant number of poems is a further indication that many other poems by M may well have disappeared.

F38

'his way of acting conquered my fortune': or 'my fortune conquered his way of acting'.

F40

A quotation from Dante's *Paradiso*, 29:91, inscribed on the upright beam of the cross in a *Pietà* drawn by M for Vittoria Colonna.

F41

A quotation from Petrarch's *Rime*, 206:45, written by M at the head of a letter from him to the widow of Urbino (*Ca* MCCXLVI / Ra 431), assuring her of his continued love for her dead husband and of his concern for her and her family; see the note to poem 300:10.

SUGGESTIONS FOR FURTHER READING

No single book can hope to do justice to the many-sided genius of Michelangelo. All of the following works are fundamental, in ways I have tried to suggest in the thumbnail sketch after each. For obvious reasons, Michelangelo's art has been more fully explored than his poetry; it is perhaps surprising, though, that the latter still lacks a full-length, basic study that can be warmly recommended.

Bull, G., *Michelangelo: A Biography* (London: Viking, 1995). Fills an obvious gap: there has hitherto been no modern biography of Michelangelo in English.

Cambon, G., *Michelangelo's Poetry: Fury of Form* (Princeton: Princeton University Press, 1985). Stimulating on individual problems, but assumes some knowledge of the poetry and is not easy to read.

Clements, R. J., ed. and trans., *Michelangelo: A Self-Portrait. Texts and Sources* (New York: Prentice Hall, 1963). Basic documentation under various thematic heads.

— *The Poetry of Michelangelo* (New York: New York University Press, 1965). Remains the best lengthy introduction to the poetry, and is a mine of information, but quotes the poetry only in translation and from a disconcerting variety of sources.

Condivi, A., 'Life of Michelangelo Buonarroti', in Michelangelo, *Life, Letters, and Poetry*, trans. by G. Bull (Oxford: Oxford University Press, 1987), pp. 1–73. Translation of a fundamental contemporary document, first published in 1553; based on conversations with Michelangelo.

Hibbard, H., *Michelangelo* (Harmondsworth: Penguin, 2nd edn, 1985). Principally concerned with Michelangelo's art, studied in its evolution; lucidly written, and aware of the importance of Michelangelo's poetry.

Ramsden, E. H., ed. and trans., *The Letters of Michelangelo*, 2 vols (London: Peter Owen, 1963). A pioneering work in its time; vigorous translation, with elegant and interesting introductions and appendices; still fundamental for English readers.

Salmi, M., ed., *The Complete Work of Michelangelo*, 2 vols (London: Macdonald, 1966). A collaborative volume by excellent scholars, originally published in Italian to mark the fourth centenary of Michelangelo's death; covers all aspects of Michelangelo's work, and is generously illustrated.

Saslow, J., *The Poetry of Michelangelo: An Annotated Translation* (New Haven: Yale University Press, 1991). Has many very useful features, including a lengthy introduction and ample notes, but caution must be used in consulting the translation.

Smith, A. J., 'Matter into grace: Michelangelo the love poet', in *The Metaphysics of Love: Studies in Renaissance Poetry from Dante to Milton* (Cambridge: Cambridge University Press, 1985), pp. 150–76. A sympathetic and highly sensitive study; the best short introduction to the poetry in English.

Tolnay, C. de, *The Art and Thought of Michelangelo* (New York: Pantheon, 1964). Translation of a brief, magisterial overview, first published in German in 1949, by the doyen of post-war experts on Michelangelo's art.

Vasari, G. 'Life of Michelangelo Buonarroti', in *Lives of the Artists*, vol. 1, trans. by G. Bull (Harmondsworth: Penguin, 1987), pp. 325–442. A fundamental contemporary account of Michelangelo's life, often from a perspective significantly different from Condivi's *Life*; Bull's translation, easily accessible in every sense, is a slightly abridged version of Vasari's second, revised edition of 1568.

BIBLIOGRAPHY OF WORKS CITED

Editions

Rime di Michelagnolo Buonarroti, ed. by Michelangelo il Giovane (Florence: I Giunti, 1623).

Le rime di Michelangelo Buonarroti, ed. by C. Guasti (Florence: Le Monnier, 1863).

Die Dichtungen des Michelagniolo Buonarroti, ed. by C. Frey (Berlin: Grote, 1897).

Michelangiolo Buonarroti, *Rime*, ed. by E. N. Girardi (Bari: Laterza, 1960).

Michelangiolo Buonarroti, *Rime*, ed. by E. N. Girardi (Bari: Laterza, 1967). [Contains some revisions to the 1960 edition; no critical apparatus]

Rime e lettere di Michelangelo, ed. by P. Mastrocola (Turin: UTET, 1992).

Commentaries

Michelangelo poeta: Scelta di rime, comm. by F. Rizzi (Milan: Treves, 1924).

Michelangelo Buonarroti, *Rime*, comm. by V. Piccoli (Turin: Unione Tipografica, 1930).

Michelangelo Buonarroti, *Rime*, comm. by A. Dobelli (Milan: Signorelli, 1931).

Michelangelo Buonarroti, *Rime*, comm. by G. R. Ceriello (Milan: Rizzoli, 1954).

Michelangelo Buonarroti, *Rime*, comm. by E. Barelli (Milan: Rizzoli, 1975).

The Poetry of Michelangelo: An Annotated Translation [with facing text], J. M. Saslow (New Haven: Yale University Press, 1991).

Rime e lettere di Michelangelo, comm. by P. Mastrocola (Turin: UTET, 1992).

English Translations

The Sonnets of Michael Angelo Buonarroti and Tommaso Campanella, trans. by J. A. Symonds (London: Smith, Elder, 1878).

The Complete Poems of Michelangelo, trans. by J. Tusiani (New York: Noonday, 1960).

The Sonnets of Michelangelo, trans. by E. Jennings (London: The Folio Society, 1961).

Complete Poems and Selected Letters of Michelangelo, trans. by C. Gilbert (Princeton: Princeton University Press, 3rd edn, 1980).

The Poetry of Michelangelo: An Annotated Translation, trans. by J. M. Saslow (New Haven: Yale University Press, 1991).

The Complete Poetry of Michelangelo, trans. by S. Alexander (Athens: Ohio University Press, 1991).

Other Works

Bardeschi Ciulich, L., *Costanza ed evoluzione nella scrittura di Michelangelo* (Florence: Cantini, 1989).

Berni, F., *Rime*, ed. by G. Bàrberi Squarotti (Turin: Einaudi, 1969).

Cambon, G., See 'Suggestions for Further Reading' (p. 341).

Clements, R. J., See 'Suggestions for Further Reading' (p. 341).

Colonna, V., *Rime*, ed. by A. Bullock (Bari: Laterza, 1982).

Condivi, A., See 'Suggestions for Further Reading' (p. 341).

Contini, G., Review of Girardi's edition, *Lingua Nostra* 21 (1960), pp. 68–72.

Dante, *The Divine Comedy*, 3 vols, trans. by C. S. Singleton (Princeton: Princeton University Press, 1970–5).

Ficino, M., *Commentary on Plato's Symposium on Love*, trans. by S. Jayne (Dallas: Spring, 1985).

Giannotti, D., *Dialogi di Donato Giannotti de' giorni che Dante consumò nel cercare l'Inferno e 'l Purgatorio*, ed. by D. Redig de Campos (Florence: Sansoni, 1939).

Girardi, E. N., 'La notte di Michelangiolo', in *Letteratura come bellezza: Studi sulla letteratura italiana del Rinascimento* (Rome: Bulzoni, 1991), pp. 109–18.

Hibbard, H., See 'Suggestions for Further Reading' (p. 341).

Il carteggio di Michelangelo, 5 vols, posthumous edition of G. Poggi, ed. by P. Barocchi and R. Ristori (Florence: Sansoni [vols 1–3] and SPES [vols 4–5], 1965–83).

Liebert, R. S., *Michelangelo: A Psychoanalytic Study of His Life and*

Images (New Haven: Yale University Press, 1983).

Lorenzo de' Medici, *Selected Poems and Prose*, trans. by J. Thiem *et al.* (Pennsylvania: Pennsylvania State University Press, 1991).

Ovid, *Metamorphoses*, 2 vols, ed. and trans. by F. J. Miller (London: Heinemann, 2nd edn, 1921).

Petrarch, *Petrarch's Lyric Poems: The* Rime sparse *and Other Lyrics*, ed. and trans. by R. M. Durling (Cambridge, Mass.: Harvard University Press, 1976).

— *Rime, Trionfi e poesie latine*, ed. and trans. by F. Neri *et al.* (Milan: Ricciardi, 1951).

Plato, *The Republic*, trans. by H. D. P. Lee (Harmondsworth: Penguin, 1955).

Poliziano, A., *Rime*, ed. by D. Delcorno Branca (Florence: L'Accademia della Crusca, 1986).

Quaglio, A. E., Review of Girardi's edition, *Lettere Italiane* 14 (1962), pp. 115–18.

Smith, A. J., 'For the death of Cecchino Bracci', *Modern Language Review* 58 (1963), pp. 355–63.

— *The Metaphysics of Love:* see 'Suggestions for Further Reading' (p. 342).

Summers, D., *Michelangelo and the Language of Art* (Princeton: Princeton University Press, 1981).

Varchi, B., *Due lezzioni, nella prima delle quali si dichiara un sonetto di M. Michelagnolo Buonarroti* (Florence: L. Torrentino, 1549).

Vasari, G., See 'Suggestions for Further Reading' (p. 342).

INDEX OF FIRST LINES

ACKNOWLEDGEMENTS

I should like to thank G. Laterza e Figli for permission to use Girardi's edition as the basis of this work. I owe many debts to the University of Sussex, where I am privileged to teach: its interdisciplinary programme has allowed me to discuss ideas on Michelangelo with a broad range of students, and it gave me a term's study leave to pursue research and writing on this book. My particular thanks go also to two friends and colleagues elsewhere: to Robin Kirkpatrick of the University of Cambridge, who first broached this project with me, and to Corinna Salvadori Lonergan of Trinity College, Dublin, who read the typescript in its entirety and offered many valuable comments. The staff of various libraries have offered courteous and efficient help, notably those of the University of Cambridge and the Laurentian Library in Florence; Angela Dillon Bussi of the latter has been the essence of kindness. The Casa Buonarroti in Florence has been a working haven on several trips; Pina Ragionieri, the Director, and her assistants Elena Lombardi and Elisabetta Archi, have been unfailingly generous and helpful. I am grateful to Hilary Laurie of Everyman for her enthusiastic interest and for her helpful guidance on editorial matters, and to her colleague Andrea Henry for her sympathetic overseeing of the process of transforming a typescript into the printed word. My principal debt is to my wife, who shares my love for Michelangelo's poetry and has helped forward this work in a wide variety of ways, not least by her self-sacrifice in enabling me to find time to bring it to a conclusion. My children more than deserve the dedication to them of such fruits as my labour has produced.